Say It Loud

Also by Catherine Ellis and Stephen Drury Smith:
Say it Plain: A Century of Great African American Speeches

Say It Loud

Great Speeches on Civil Rights and
African American Identity

Edited by Catherine Ellis and Stephen Drury Smith

THE NEW PRESS

NEW YORK
LONDON

Requests for permission to reproduce selections from this book should be mailed to:
Permissions Department, The New Press, 38 Greene Street, New York, NY 10013.

Published in the United States by The New Press, New York, 2010
Distributed by Perseus Distribution

LIBRARY OF CONGRESS CATALOGING-IN-PUBLICATION DATA

Say it loud: great speeches on civil rights and African American identity /
edited by Catherine Ellis and Stephen Drury Smith.
p.   cm.
Includes bibliographical references.
ISBN 978-1-59558-113-6 (hc.)
1. African Americans—Civil rights—History—20th century—Sources.
2. African Americans—Civil rights—History—21st century—Sources.
3. Civil rights movements—United States—History—20th century—Sources.
4. Civil rights movements—United States—History—21st century—Sources.
5. African Americans—Race identity—History—Sources.
6. African Americans—Ethnic identity—History—Sources.
7. Speeches, addresses, etc., American—African American authors.
8. United States—Race relations—History—20th century—Sources.
9. United States—Race relations—History—21st century—Sources.
10. African American orators—Biography.   I. Ellis, Catherine, 1964–
II. Smith, Stephen, 1960–

E185.615.S255 2010
73'.0496073—dc22
2010010895

The New Press was established in 1990 as a not-for-profit alternative
to the large, commercial publishing houses currently dominating the
book publishing industry. The New Press operates in the public interest
rather than for private gain, and is committed to publishing, in innovative
ways, works of educational, cultural, and community value that are often
deemed insufficiently profitable.

www.thenewpress.com

Composition by dix!

Printed in the United States of America

2 4 6 8 10 9 7 5 3 1

This book is dedicated to
Jackie Ellis and Oleg Svetlichny,
John Ellis and Elaine Hirschl Ellis,
Janet Evans Smith and Robert Drury Smith

CONTENTS

PREFACE

This is the second anthology of great speeches by African Americans meant for the eye and ear. Our first book/CD project, *Say It Plain*, chronicled an array of black leaders across the twentieth century exhorting the nation to make good on its promise of democracy. This collection opens in the middle years of the modern civil rights movement. It captures speeches by an eclectic mix of African American orators arguing about how best to pursue freedom and equality in a nation still deeply marked by racial inequities.

Say It Loud is titled after the classic 1969 James Brown anthem "Say It Loud, I'm Black and I'm Proud." This anthology is meant to illuminate the evolution of ideas and debates pulsing through the black freedom struggle from the 1960s to the present and the way these arguments are suffused with basic questions about what it means to be black in America.

As with our first book, these words were meant to be heard. You can listen to excerpts of all but one speech on the CD that comes with this book. Each address was recorded at a live event, such as a rally, funeral, or graduation ceremony. Sometimes the speech was directed strictly at African Americans and at other times to a broader racial mix. In any case, these impassioned, eloquent words continue to affect the ideas of a nation and the direction of history.

The one speech missing from the excerpt CD is Ossie Davis's eulogy for Malcolm X. To our knowledge, there is no recording of the original speech made in Harlem in 1965, which Davis wrote out the night before the funeral. (Davis later recorded the eulogy for Spike Lee's film, *Malcolm X.*) Even so, we were eager to include Davis's moving address in this collection.

We also wish to note that there were a number of historic and exciting speeches that we wanted to include in this collection but could not. In some cases, the cost of publication rights was beyond the reach of this nonprofit project. Also, there are the limits of space. *Say It Loud* is not a complete catalog but a representative sampling of the rich, sophisticated, and often contentious dialogue about civil rights and African American identity in the past fifty years.

A Note About Transcripts

The transcripts for this book were drawn from audio and video recordings. In some cases, we were able to start with existing transcripts in the public domain and check them against recordings. At other times, we produced the transcripts ourselves, with the help of dedicated colleagues. Each transcript here has been checked against the recordings by at least two sets of ears. Occasionally, words in some of the recordings are hard to hear. We've used our best judgment to make the most faithful transcripts we can.

—Catherine Ellis and Stephen Drury Smith

ACKNOWLEDGMENTS

We are deeply grateful to the people who helped with this book/CD and documentary project. Chief among them is our editor at The New Press, Marc Favreau, a patient and enthusiastic guy. Our editor at American Radio Works (ARW), Catherine Winter, lent her tremendous skills to this book and our writing.

We thank other talented members of the ARW team who helped in transcribing speeches, gathering permissions, and producing the companion radio documentary and Web site. They include Ellen Guettler, Suzanne Pekow, Frankie Barnhill, Ochen Kaylan, Tricia Kostichka, and Emily Torgrimson. At American Public Media, Sarah Lutman and Judy McAlpine generously supported this project. Rachel Reinche and Mitzi Gramling provided essential legal help.

Thanks go to the librarians and archivists who helped us unearth important speeches. They include Kenneth J. Chandler, archivist of the National Archives of Black Women's History; Joellen El Bashir, curator of Manuscripts, and Tewodros (Teddy) Abebe, assistant archivist, at the Moorland-Spingarn Research Center at Howard University; Chuck Howell, curator at the Library of American Broadcasting; and Brian De Shazor and the staff at Pacifica Radio Archives. Thanks, also, to documentary producer Shola Lynch.

We are indebted to the speakers, or their heirs, who granted us permission to include their words in this book. This collection is theirs.

Finally, a shout-out to our children, Henry, Ben, Nina, and Kobe. You are always, always in our hearts.

Say It Loud

1.

MALCOLM X (1925–1965)

"The Ballot or the Bullet"

King Solomon Baptist Church, Detroit, Michigan—April 12, 1964

Malcolm X was one of the most dynamic, dramatic, and influential figures of the civil rights era. He was an apostle of black nationalism, self-respect, and uncompromising resistance to white oppression. Malcolm X was a polarizing figure who both energized and divided African Americans, while frightening and alienating many whites. He was an unrelenting truth teller who declared that the mainstream civil rights movement was naïve in hoping to secure freedom through integration and nonviolence. The blazing heat of Malcolm X's rhetoric sometimes overshadowed the complexity of his message, especially for those who found him threatening in the first place. Malcolm X was assassinated at age thirty-nine, but his political and cultural influence grew far greater in the years after his death than when he was alive.

Malcolm X is now popularly seen as one of the two great martyrs of the twentieth-century black freedom struggle, the other being his ostensible rival the Rev. Martin Luther King Jr. But in the spring of 1964, when Malcolm X gave his "Ballot or the Bullet" speech, he was regarded by a majority of white Americans as a menacing character. Malcolm X never directly called for violent revolution, but he warned that African Americans would use "any means necessary"—especially armed self-defense—once they realized just how pervasive and hopelessly entrenched white racism had become.[1]

He was born Malcolm Little in 1925 in Omaha, Nebraska. His father, Earl, was a Baptist preacher and follower of the black nationalist Marcus Garvey. Earl Little's political activism provoked threats from the Ku Klux Klan. After the family moved to Lansing, Michigan, white terrorists burned the Littles' home. A defiant Earl Little shot at the arsonists as they got away. In 1931, Malcolm's father was found dead. His family suspected he'd been murdered by white vigilantes. Malcolm's mother, Louise, battled mental illness and struggled to care for her eight children during the Great Depression. She was committed to a state mental institution when Malcolm was twelve. He and the other young children were scattered among foster families. After completing the eighth grade, Malcolm Little dropped out when a teacher told him that his dream of becoming a lawyer was unrealistic for a "nigger."[2]

As a teenager, Malcolm Little made his way to New York, where he took the street name Detroit Red and became a pimp and petty criminal. In 1946, he was sent to prison for burglary. He read voraciously while serving time and converted to the Black Muslim faith. He joined the Nation of Islam (NOI) and changed his name to Malcolm X, eliminating that part of his identity he called a white-imposed slave name.

Malcolm X was released in 1952 after six years in prison. With his charisma and eloquence, Malcolm rose rapidly in the Nation of Islam. He became the chief spokesman and field recruiter for NOI leader Elijah Muhammad. As historian Peniel Joseph describes it, NOI's unorthodox interpretation of Islam was mixed with a doctrine of black personal responsibility and economic self-sufficiency, along with "theological fundamentalism, anti-white mythology, and total racial separation as the means to black redemption."[3] Wearing impeccable suits, maintaining an air of fierce dignity, and adhering to a strict code of moral propriety, Malcolm X was a living demonstration of how the NOI could save a wayward people from racial submission and personal self-destruction.

The Nation dismissed the conventional civil rights movement—with its protest marches and demands for equal rights legislation—as impotent and misguided. As Malcolm X declared in this speech, the only effective solution to racial inequality was black economic and social separatism.

As Malcolm X's national prominence grew, so did a rift between him and Elijah Muhammad. Malcolm X far overshadowed his mentor in the public sphere. He also grew disillusioned by Elijah Muhammad's scandalous personal behavior; the Messenger fathered several children through affairs with his secretaries. The conflict deepened when Muhammad suspended Malcolm X for saying that President John F. Kennedy's assassination represented "the chickens coming home to roost" because of the war in Vietnam.[4] Finally, in March 1964, Malcolm X left the Nation of Islam and charted his own course of militant black nationalism.

On April 12, 1964, one month after splitting with the NOI, Malcolm X gave his "Ballot or the Bullet" speech at King Solomon Baptist Church in Detroit (he'd given the address nine days earlier in Cleveland, but the Detroit version is regarded by some scholars as definitive).[5] It was the fullest declaration of his black nationalist philosophy. Mainstream black ministers in Detroit tried to block Malcolm X from using the church, saying "separatist ideas can do nothing but set back the colored man's cause." But the church hall had already been rented out for the event.[6]

"The Ballot or the Bullet" became one of Malcolm X's most recognizable phrases, and the speech was one of his greatest orations. Two thousand people—including some of his opponents—turned out to hear him speak in Detroit. President Lyndon Johnson was running for reelection in 1964, and Malcolm X declared it "the year of the ballot or the bullet." He outlined a new, global sensibility in the fight for racial justice: "We intend to expand [the freedom struggle] from the level of civil rights to the level of human rights."

Malcolm was now free of the NOI's ban on members participating in the mainstream civil rights movement. He encouraged black militants to get involved in voter registration drives and other forms of community organizing to redefine and expand the movement.[7]

The day after his Detroit speech, Malcolm X embarked on an overseas tour that included a life-changing pilgrimage to the Muslim holy city of Mecca. Known as the hajj, the pilgrimage must be carried out at least once in a lifetime by every able-bodied Muslim who can afford to do so. The racial diversity he experienced in the Middle East, especially among Muslims, led him to discard his strict notions of black separatism for a wider, more inclusive movement against white supremacy and colonialism. In the summer of 1964, Malcolm X announced a new effort, the Organization of Afro-American Unity (OAAU).

In the last months of his life, Malcolm X's conflict with the Nation of

Islam grew increasingly bitter. Elijah Muhammad and the NOI had a long history of using violence and intimidation against members who strayed. In February 1965, Malcolm X's home was firebombed. He publicly blamed the Nation of Islam and predicted he would be killed. Malcolm X was shot to death on February 21, 1965, as he prepared to speak at an OAAU rally at the Audubon Ballroom in New York. Three black men, all members of the NOI, were convicted and sent to prison for the murder.

In an editorial after his death, the *New York Times* described Malcolm X as "an extraordinary and twisted man, turning many true gifts to evil purpose."[8] Actor and activist Ossie Davis eulogized him as "our own black shining prince."[9] In death, he became a seminal figure to an increasingly militant generation of young African Americans, a beacon for activists in the 1960s Black Power and Black Arts movements.

In assessing Malcolm X's impact, theologian James Cone wrote: "More than anyone else he revolutionized the black mind, transforming docile Negroes and self-effacing colored people into proud blacks and self-confident African-Americans."[10] By the end of the twentieth century, Malcolm X was recognized in mainstream culture as a hero of the civil rights era. The militant radical whose image once provoked fear and hatred among many white Americans was celebrated in mainstream movie theaters, on Black History Month posters in elementary school classrooms, and on a 1999 postage stamp issued by the United States government.

MR. MODERATOR, Reverend Cleage, brothers and sisters and friends, and I see some enemies. [laughter/applause] In fact, I think we'd be fooling ourselves if we had an audience this large and didn't realize that there were some enemies present.

This afternoon we want to talk about the ballot or the bullet. The ballot or the bullet explains itself. But before we get into it, since this is the year of the ballot or the bullet, I would like to clarify some things that refer to me personally, concerning my own personal position.

I'm still a Muslim. That is, my religion is still Islam. [applause] My religion is still Islam. I still credit Mr. Muhammad for what I know and what I am. He's the one who opened my eyes. [applause] At present I am the minister of the newly founded Muslim Mosque Incorporated, which has its offices in the Theresa Hotel right in the heart of Harlem, that's the Black Belt in New York City. And we realize that Adam Clayton Powell is a Christian minister, he has Abyssinian Baptist Church, but at the same time he's more famous for his political struggling. And Dr. King is a Christian minister from Atlanta, Georgia, or in Atlanta, Georgia, but he's become more famous for being involved in the civil rights struggle. There's another in New York, Reverend Galamison. I don't know if you've heard of him out here. He's a Christian minister from Brooklyn, but has become famous for his fight against the segregated school system in Brooklyn. Reverend Cleage, right here, is a Christian minister here in Detroit, he's head of the Freedom Now Party. All of these are Christian ministers. [applause] All of these are Christian ministers, but they don't come to us as Christian ministers, they come to us as fighters in some other category.

I am a Muslim minister. The same as they are Christian ministers, I'm a Muslim minister. And I don't believe in fighting today on any one front, but on all fronts. [applause] In fact, I'm a Black Nationalist freedom fighter. [applause] Islam is my religion but I believe my religion is my personal business. [applause] It governs my personal life, my personal morals. And my religious philosophy is personal between me and the God in whom I believe, just as the religious philosophy of these others is between them and the God in whom they believe. And this is best this way. Were we to come out here discussing religion, we'd have too many differences from the out start and we could never get together.

So today, though Islam is my religious philosophy, my political, economic, and social philosophy is Black Nationalism. You and I—[applause] As I say, if we bring up religion, we'll have differences, we'll have arguments, and we'll never be able to get together. But if we keep our religion at home, keep our religion in the closet, keep our religion between ourselves and our God, but when we come out here we have a fight that's common to all of us against an enemy who is common to all of us. [applause]

The political philosophy of Black Nationalism only means that the black man should control the politics and the politicians in his own community. The time when white people can come in our community and get us to vote for them so that they can be our political leaders and tell us what to do and what not to do is long gone. [applause]

By the same token, the time when that same white man, knowing that your eyes are too far open, can send another Negro in the community, and get you and me to support him, so that he can use him to lead us astray, those days are long gone too. [applause]

The political philosophy of Black Nationalism only means that if you and

I are going to live in a black community—and that's where we're going to live, 'cause as soon as you move into one of their . . . soon as you move out of the black community into their community, it's mixed for a period of time, but they're gone and you're right there all by yourself again. [applause]

We must, we must understand the politics of our community, and we must know what politics is supposed to produce. We must know what part politics play in our lives. And until we become politically mature, we will always be misled, led astray, or deceived or maneuvered into supporting someone politically who doesn't have the good of our community at heart. So the political philosophy of Black Nationalism only means that we will have to carry on a program, a political program, of reeducation—to open our people's eyes, make us become more politically conscious, politically mature. And then, we will—whenever we are ready to cast our ballot, that ballot will be cast for a man of the community, who has the good of the community at heart. [applause]

The economic philosophy of Black Nationalism only means that we should own and operate and control the economy of our community. You would never have found—you can't open up a black store in a white community. White man won't even patronize you. And he's not wrong. He got sense enough to look out for himself. It's you who don't have sense enough to look out for yourself. [applause]

The white man, the white man is too intelligent to let someone else come and gain control of the economy of his community. But you will let anybody come in and control the economy of your community, control the housing, control the education, control the jobs, control the businesses, under the pretext that you want to integrate. Nah, you're out of your mind. [applause]

The political . . . the economic philosophy of Black Nationalism only means that we have to become involved in a program of reeducation, to educate our people into the importance of knowing that when you spend your dollar out of the community in which you live, the community in which you spend your money becomes richer and richer, the community out of which you take your money becomes poorer and poorer. And because these Negroes, who have been misled, misguided, are breaking their necks to take their money and spend it with the Man, the Man is becoming richer and richer, and you're becoming poorer and poorer. And then what happens? The community in which you live becomes a slum. It becomes a ghetto. The conditions become run-down. And then you have the audacity to complain about poor housing in a run-down community, while you're running down yourselves when you take your dollar out. [applause]

And you and I are in a double trap, because not only do we lose by taking our money someplace else and spending it, when we try and spend it in our own community, we're trapped because we haven't had sense enough to set up stores and control the businesses of our community. The man who is controlling the stores in our community is a man who doesn't look like we do. He's a man who doesn't even live in the community. So you and I, even when we try and spend our money on the block where we live or the area where we live, we're spending it with a man who, when the sun goes down, takes that basket full of money to another part of the town. [applause]

So we're trapped, trapped, double-trapped, triple-trapped. Any way we go, we find that we're trapped. And every kind of solution that someone comes up with is just another trap. But the political and economic philosophy of Black Nationalism . . . the economic philosophy of Black Nationalism shows our people the importance of setting up these little stores and developing them and expanding them into larger operations. Woolworth didn't start out big like they are today; they started out with a dime store, and expanded, and expanded, and expanded until today they are all over the country and all over the world, and they getting some of everybody's money.

Now this is what you and I—General Motors, the same way, it didn't start out like it is. It started out just a little rat-race type operation. And it expanded and it expanded until today it's where it is right now. And you and I have to make a start. And the best place to start is right in the community where we live. [applause]

So our people not only have to be reeducated to the importance of supporting black business, but the black man himself has to be made aware of the importance of going into business. And once you and I go into business, we own and operate at least the businesses in our community. What we will be doing is developing a situation wherein we will actually be able to create employment for the people in the community. And once you can create some employment in the community where you live, it will eliminate the necessity of you and me having to act ignorantly and disgracefully, boycotting and picketing some cracker someplace else trying to beg him for a job. [applause]

Anytime you have to rely upon your enemy for a job, you're in bad shape. [applause] When you—and he is your enemy. You wouldn't be in this country if some enemy hadn't kidnapped you and brought you here. [applause] On the other hand, some of you think you came here on the *Mayflower*. [laughter]

So as you can see, brothers and sisters, today—this afternoon it is not our intention to discuss religion. We're going to forget religion. If we bring up religion we'll be in an argument. And the best way to keep away from arguments and differences, as I said earlier, put your religion at home, in the closet, keep it between you and your God. Because if it hasn't done anything more for you than it has, you need to forget it anyway. [laughter and applause]

Whether you are a Christian or a Muslim or a Nationalist, we all have the same problem. They don't hang you because you're a Baptist; they hang you 'cause you're black. [applause] They don't attack me because I'm a Muslim. They attack me 'cause I'm black. They attacked all of us for the same reason. All of us catch hell from the same enemy. We're all in the same bag, in the same boat.

We suffer political oppression, economic exploitation, and social degradation. All of 'em from the same enemy. The government has failed us. You can't deny that. Any time you're living in the twentieth century, 1964, and you walking around here singing "We Shall Overcome," the government has failed you. [applause] This is part of what's wrong with you, you do too much singing. [laughter] Today it's time to stop singing and start swinging. [laughter and applause]

You can't sing up on freedom. But you can swing up on some freedom. [cheering] Cassius Clay can sing. But singing didn't help him to become the heavyweight champion of the world. Swinging helped him. [applause]

So this government has failed us. The government itself has failed us. And the white liberals who have been posing as our friends have failed us. And once we see that all of these other sources to which we've turned have failed, we stop turning to them and turn to ourselves. We need a self-help program, a do-it-yourself philosophy, a do-it-right-now philosophy, a it's-already-too-late philosophy. This is what you and I need to get with. And the only time—the only way we're going to solve our problem is with a self-help program. Before we can get a self-help program started, we have to have a self-help philosophy. Black nationalism is a self-help philosophy.

What's so good about it—you can stay right in the church where you are and still take Black Nationalism as your philosophy. You can stay in any kind of civic organization that you belong to and still take Black Nationalism as your philosophy. You can be an atheist and still take Black Nationalism as your philosophy. This is a philosophy that eliminates the necessity for division and argument, 'cause if you're black, you should be thinking black. And if you're black and you not thinking black at this late date, well, I'm sorry for you. [applause]

Once you change your philosophy, you change your thought pattern. Once you change your thought pattern, you change your attitude. Once you change your attitude, it changes your behavior pattern. And then you go on into some action. As long as you got a sit-down philosophy, you'll have a sit-down thought pattern. And as long as you think that old sit-down thought, you'll be in some kind of sit-down action. They'll have you sitting in everywhere. [laughter]

It's not so good to refer to what you're going to do as a sit-in. That right there castrates you. Right there it brings you down. What goes with it? What—think of the image of someone sitting. An old woman can sit. An old man can sit. A chump can sit, a coward can sit, anything can sit. Well, you and I been sitting long enough, and it's time for us today to start doing some standing and some fighting to back that up. [applause]

When we look at other parts of this Earth upon which we live, we find that black, brown, red, and yellow people in Africa and Asia are getting their independence. They're not getting it by singing, "We Shall Overcome." No, they're getting it through nationalism. It is nationalism that brought about the independence of the people in Asia. Every nation in Asia gained its independence through the philosophy of nationalism. Every nation on the African continent that has gotten its independence brought it about through the philosophy of nationalism. And it will take Black Nationalism to bring about the freedom of twenty-two million Afro-Americans, here in this country, where we have suffered colonialism for the past four hundred years. [applause]

America is just as much a colonial power as England ever was. America is just as much a colonial power as France ever was. In fact, America is more so a colonial power than they, because she is a hypocritical colonial power behind it. [applause] What is twentieth . . . what, what do you call second-class citizenship? Why, that's colonization. Second-class citizenship is nothing but twentieth-century slavery. How you gonna to tell me you're a second-class citizen? They don't have second-class citizenship in any other government on this Earth. They just have slaves and people who are free!

Well, this country is a hypocrite! They try and make you think they set you free by calling you a second-class citizen. No, you're nothing but a twentieth-century slave. [applause]

Just as it took nationalism to remove colonialism from Asia and Africa, it'll take Black Nationalism today to remove colonialism from the backs and the minds of twenty-two million Afro-Americans here in this country. And 1964 looks like it might be the year of the ballot or the bullet. [applause]

Why does it look like it might be the year of the ballot or the bullet? Because Negroes have listened to the trickery and the lies and the false promises of the white man now for too long, and they're fed up. They've become disenchanted. They've become disillusioned. They've become dissatisfied. And all of this has built up frustrations in the black community that makes the black community throughout America today more explosive than all of the atomic bombs the Russians can ever invent. Whenever you got a racial powder keg sitting in your lap, you're in more trouble than if you had an atomic powder keg sitting in your lap. When a racial powder keg goes off, it doesn't care who it knocks out the way. Understand this, it's dangerous.

And in 1964, this seems to be the year, because what can the white man use, now, to fool us? After he put down that March on Washington—and you see all through that now, he tricked you, had you marching down to Washington. Had you marching back and forth between the feet of a dead man named Lincoln and another dead man named George Washington, singing "We Shall Overcome." [applause]

He made a chump out of you. He made a fool out of you. He made you think you were going somewhere, and you end up going nowhere but between Lincoln and Washington. [laughter]

So today our people are disillusioned. They've become disenchanted. They've become dissatisfied. And in their frustrations, they want action. And in 1964, you'll see this young black man, this new generation, asking for the ballot or the bullet. That old Uncle Tom action is outdated. The young generation don't want to hear anything about "the odds are against us." What do we care about odds? [applause]

When this country here was first being founded, there were thirteen colonies. The whites were colonized. They were fed up with this taxation without representation. So some of them stood up and said, "Liberty or death!" I went to a white school over here in Mason, Michigan. The white man made the mistake of letting me read his history books. [laughter] He made the mistake of teaching me that Patrick Henry was a patriot, and George

Washington—wasn't nothing nonviolent about ol' Pat or George Washington. "Liberty or death" is was what brought about the freedom of whites in
this country from the English. [applause]

They didn't care about the odds. Why, they faced the wrath of the entire
British Empire. And in those days, they used to say that the British Empire
was so vast and so powerful that the sun would never set on it. This is how
big it was, yet these thirteen little scrawny states, tired of taxation without
representation, tired of being exploited and oppressed and degraded, told
that big British Empire, "Liberty or death." And here you have twenty-two
million Afro-Americans, black people today, catching more hell than Patrick
Henry ever saw. [applause]

And I'm here to tell you, in case you don't know it, that you got a new
generation of black people in this country who don't care anything whatsoever about odds. They don't want to hear you ol' Uncle Tom, handkerchief
heads talking about the odds. No! [laughter and applause] This is a new
generation. If they're going to draft these young black men and send them
over to Korea or to South Vietnam to face eight hundred million Chinese . . .
[laughter and applause] If you're not afraid of those odds, you shouldn't be
afraid of these odds. [applause]

Why is America—why does this loom to be such an explosive political
year? Because this is the year of politics. This is the year when all of the
white politicians are going to come into the Negro community. You never
see them until election time. You can't find them until election time. [ap-
plause] They're going to come in with false promises. And as they make
these false promises, they're going to feed our frustrations, and this will only
serve to make matters worse. I'm no politician. I'm not even a student of
politics. I'm not a Republican, nor a Democrat, nor an American—and got
sense enough to know it. [applause]

I'm one of the twenty-two million black victims of the Democrats. One
of the twenty-two million black victims of the Republicans and one of the
twenty-two million black victims of Americanism. [applause] And when I
speak, I don't speak as a Democrat or a Republican, nor an American. I
speak as a victim of America's so-called democracy. You and I have never
seen democracy—all we've seen is hypocrisy. [applause]

When we open our eyes today and look around America, we see America
not through the eyes of someone who has enjoyed the fruits of Americanism. We see America through the eyes of someone who has been the victim
of Americanism. We don't see any American dream. We've experienced only

the American nightmare. We haven't benefited from America's democracy. We've only suffered from America's hypocrisy. And the generation that's coming up now can see it. And are not afraid to say it. If you go to jail, so what? If you're black, you were born in jail. [applause]

If you black, you were born in jail, in the North as well as the South. Stop talking about the South. As long as you south of the Canadian border, you South. [laughter and applause] Don't call Governor Wallace a Dixie governor; Romney is a Dixie governor. [applause]

Twenty-two million black victims of Americanism are waking up, and they are gaining a new political consciousness, becoming politically mature. And as they become, develop this political maturity, they're able to see the recent trends in these political elections. They see that the whites are so evenly divided that every time they vote, the race is so close they have to go back and count the votes all over again. Which means that any bloc, any minority that has a bloc of votes that stick together is in a strategic position. Either way you go, that's who gets it. You're in a position to determine who'll go to the White House and who'll stay in the doghouse. [laughter]

You're the one who has that power. You can keep Johnson in Washington D.C., or you can send him back to his Texas cotton patch. [applause] You're the one who sent Kennedy to Washington. You're the one who put the present Democratic administration in Washington, D.C. The whites were evenly divided. It was the fact that you threw eighty percent of your votes behind the Democrats that put the Democrats in the White House.

When you see this, you can see that the Negro vote is the key factor. And despite the fact that you are in a position to be the determining factor, what do you get out of it? The Democrats have been in Washington, D.C., only because of the Negro vote. They've been down there four years. And they're—all other legislation they wanted to bring up, they've brought it up, and gotten it out of the way, and now they bring up you. And now they bring up you! You put them first and they put you last. Because you're a chump! [applause] A political chump.

In Washington, D.C., in the House of Representatives there are 257 who are Democrats. Only 177 are Republican. In the Senate there are 67 Democrats. Only 33 are Republicans. The party that you backed controls two-thirds of the House of Representatives and the Senate, and still they can't keep their promise to you. 'Cause you're a chump. [applause]

Any time you throw your weight behind a political party that controls two-thirds of the government, and that party can't keep the promise that it made to you during election time, and you're dumb enough to walk around continuing to identify yourself with that party, you're not only a chump but you're a traitor to your race. [applause]

What kind of alibi do they come up with? They try and pass the buck to the Dixiecrats. Now, back during the days when you were blind, deaf, and dumb, ignorant, politically immature, naturally you went along with that. But today, as your eyes come open and you develop political maturity, you're able to see and think for yourself, and you can see that a Dixiecrat is nothing but a Democrat—in disguise. [applause]

You look at the structure of the government that controls this country, is controlled by sixteen senatorial committees and twenty congressional committees. Of the sixteen senatorial committees that run the government, ten of them are in the hands of Southern segregationists. Of the twenty congressional committees that run the government, twelve of them are in the hands of Southern segregationists. And they're going to tell you and me that the South lost the war? [laughter and applause]

You, today, are in the hands of a government of segregationists. Racists, white supremacists, who belong to the Democratic party but disguise themselves as Dixiecrats. A Dixiecrat is nothing but a Democrat. Whoever runs the Democrats is also the father of the Dixiecrats. And the father of all of them is sitting in the White House. [applause] I say, and I'll say it again, you got a president who's nothing but a Southern segregationist from the state of Texas. They'll lynch you in Texas as quick as they'll lynch you in Mississippi. Only in Texas they lynch you with a Texas accent, in Mississippi they lynch you with a Mississippi accent. [cheering]

The first thing the cracker does when he comes in power, he takes all the Negro leaders and invites them for coffee. To show that he's all right. And those Uncle Toms can't pass up the coffee. [laughter/applause] They come away from the coffee table telling you and me that this man is all right. [laughter] 'Cause he's from the South, and since he's from the South he can deal with the South. Look at the logic that they're using. What about Eastland? He's from the South. Why not make him the president? If Johnson is a good man 'cause he's from Texas, and being from Texas will enable him to deal with the South, Eastland can deal with the South better than Johnson! [laughter and applause]

Oh, I say you been misled. You been had. You been took. [laughter and applause] I was in Washington a couple of weeks ago while the senators were filibustering, and I noticed in the back of the Senate a huge map, and on this map it showed the distribution of Negroes in America. And surprisingly, the same senators that were involved in the filibuster were from the states where there were the most Negroes. Why were they filibustering the civil rights legislation? Because the civil rights legislation is supposed to guarantee voting rights to Negroes from those states. And those senators from those states know that if the Negroes in those states can vote, those senators are down the drain. [applause] The representatives of those states go down the drain.

And in the Constitution of this country, it has a stipulation wherein whenever the rights, the voting rights of people in a certain district are violated, then the representative who's from that particular district, according to the Constitution, is supposed to be expelled from the Congress. Now, if this particular aspect of the Constitution was enforced, why, you wouldn't have a cracker in Washington, D.C.! [applause]

But what would happen? When you expel the Dixiecrat, you're expelling the Democrat. When you destroy the power of the Dixiecrat, you are destroying the power of the Democratic Party. So how in the world can the Democratic Party in the South actually side with you, in sincerity, when all of its power is based in the South?

These Northern Democrats are in cahoots with the Southern Democrats. [applause] They're playing a giant con game, a political con game. You know how it goes. One of 'em comes to you and makes believe he's for you. And he's in cahoots with the other one that's not for you. Why? Because neither one of 'em is for you. But they got to make you go with one of 'em or the other.

So this is a con game, and this is what they've been doing with you and me all of these years. First thing, Johnson got off the plane when he become president, he ask, "Where's Dickey?" You know who Dickey is? Dickey is old Southern cracker Richard Russell. Lookie here! Yes, Lyndon B. Johnson's best friend is the one who is ahead, who's heading the forces that are filibustering civil rights legislation. You tell me how in the hell is he going to be Johnson's best friend? [applause] How can Johnson be his friend and your friend too? No, that man is too tricky. Especially if his friend is still ol' Dickey. [laughter and applause]

Whenever the Negroes keep the Democrats in power, they're keeping the Dixiecrats in power. This is true! A vote for a Democrat is nothing but a vote for a Dixiecrat. I know you don't like me saying that. I'm not the kind of person who come here to say what you like. I'm going to tell you the truth whether you like it or not. [applause]

Up here in the North you have the same thing. The Democratic Party don't—they don't do it that way. They got a thing they call gerrymandering. They maneuver you out of power. Even though you can vote, they fix it so you're voting for nobody. They got you going and coming. In the South, they're outright political wolves; in the North they're political foxes. A fox and a wolf are both canine, both belong to the dog family. [laughter and applause] Now, you take your choice. You going to choose a Northern dog or a Southern dog? Because either dog you choose, I guarantee you, you'll still be in the doghouse.

This is why I say it's the ballot or the bullet. It's liberty or it's death. It's freedom for everybody or freedom for nobody. [applause] America today finds herself in a unique situation. Historically, revolutions are bloody—oh yes they are. They have never had a bloodless revolution. Or a nonviolent revolution. That don't happen even in Hollywood. [laughter] You don't have a revolution in which you love your enemy. And you don't have a revolution in which you are begging the system of exploitation to integrate you into it. Revolutions overturn systems. Revolutions destroy systems.

A revolution is bloody, but America is in a unique position. She's the only country in history in the position actually to become involved in a bloodless revolution. The Russian Revolution was bloody, Chinese Revolution was bloody, French Revolution was bloody, Cuban Revolution was bloody. And there was nothing more bloody than the American Revolution. But today, this country can become involved in a revolution that won't take bloodshed. All she's got to do is give the black man in this country everything that's due him, everything. [applause]

I hope that the white man can see this. 'Cause if you don't see it, you're finished. If you don't see it, you're going to become involved in some action in which you don't have a chance. We don't care anything about your atomic bomb; it's useless, because other countries have atomic bombs. When two or three different countries have atomic bombs, nobody can use them. So it means that the white man today is without a weapon. If you want some action, you've got to come on down to Earth, and there's more black people on Earth than there are white people. [applause]

I only got a couple more minutes. The white man can never win another war on the ground. His days of war, victory, his days of battleground victory are over. Can I prove it? Yes. Take all the action that's going on on this Earth right now that he's involved in. Tell me where he's winning—nowhere. Why, some rice farmers, some rice farmers! Some rice eaters ran him out of Korea—yes, they ran him out of Korea. Rice eaters, with nothing but gym shoes and a rifle and a bowl of rice, took him and his tanks and his napalm and all that other action he's supposed to have and ran him across the Yalu. Why? Because the day that he can win on the ground has passed.

Up in French Indochina, those little peasants, rice growers, took on the might of the French army and ran all the Frenchmen—you remember Dien Bien Phu! The same thing happened in Algeria, in Africa. They didn't have anything but a rifle. The French had all these highly mechanized instruments of warfare. But they put some guerrilla action on. And a white man can't fight guerrilla warfare. Guerrilla action takes heart, takes nerve, and he doesn't have that. [cheering] He's brave when he's got tanks. He's brave when he's got planes. He's brave when he's got bombs. He's brave when he's got a whole lot of company along with him. But you take that little man from Africa and Asia, turn him loose in the woods with a blade. A blade. [cheering] That's all he needs. All he needs is a blade. And when the sun comes down, goes down, and it's dark, it's even-Steven. [cheering]

So it's the ballot or the bullet. Today, our people can see that we're faced with a government conspiracy. This government has failed us. The senators who are filibustering concerning your and my rights, that's the government. Don't say it's Southern senators, this is the government. This is a government filibuster. It's not a segregationist filibuster, it's a government filibuster. Any kind of activity that takes place on the floor of the Congress or the Senate, that's the government. Any kind of dillydallying, that's the government. Any kind of pussyfooting, that's the government. Any kind of act that's designed to delay or deprive you and me, right now, of getting full rights, that's the government that's responsible. And anytime you find the government involved in a conspiracy to violate the citizenship or the civil rights of a people in 1964, then you are wasting your time going to that government expecting redress. Instead you have to take that government to the world court and accuse it of genocide and all of the other crimes that it is guilty of today. [applause]

So those of us whose political and economic and social philosophy is Black Nationalism have become involved in the civil rights struggle. We have injected ourselves into the civil rights struggle. And we intend to expand it from the level of civil rights to the level of human rights. As long as you fight it on the level of civil rights, you're under Uncle Sam's jurisdiction. You're going to his court expecting him to correct the problem. He created the problem. He's the criminal! You don't take your case to the criminal. You take your criminal to court. [applause]

When the government of South Africa began to trample upon the human rights of the people of South Africa, they were taken to the UN. When the government of Portugal began to trample upon the rights of our brothers and sisters in Angola, it was taken before the UN. Why, even the white man took the Hungarian question to the UN. And just this week, Justice Goldberg was crying over three million Jews in Russia, about their human rights—charging Russia with violating the UN Charter because of its mistreatment of the human rights of Jews in Russia. Now you tell me how can the plight of everybody on this Earth reach the halls of the United Nations and you have twenty-two million Afro-Americans whose churches are being bombed, whose little girls are being murdered, whose leaders are being shot down in broad daylight? Now you tell me why the leaders of this struggle have never taken [recording impaired] their case to the UN?

So our next move is to take the entire civil rights struggle—problem—into the United Nations and let the world see that Uncle Sam is guilty of violating the human rights of twenty-two million Afro-Americans right down to the year of 1964—and still has the audacity or the nerve to stand up and represent himself as the leader of the free world? [cheering] Not only is he a crook, he's a hypocrite. Here he is standing up in front of other people, Uncle Sam, with the blood of your and my mothers and fathers on his hands. With the blood dripping down his jaws like a bloody-jawed wolf. And still got the nerve to point his finger at other countries. In 1964 you can't even get civil rights legislation, and this man has got the nerve to stand up and talk about South Africa or talk about Nazi Germany or talk about Portugal. No, no more days like those! [applause]

So I say in my conclusion, the only way we're going to solve it: we got to unite. We got to work together in unity and harmony. And Black Nationalism is the key. How we gonna overcome the tendency to be at each other's throats that always exists in our neighborhood? And the reason this tendency exists—the strategy of the white man has always been divide and conquer. He keeps us divided in order to conquer us. He tells you, I'm for separation and you're for integration; what you and I are for is freedom. [applause] Only, you think that integration will get you freedom; I think that separation will get me freedom. We both got the same objective, we just got different ways of getting at it. [applause]

So I studied this man, Billy Graham, who preaches white nationalism. That's what he preaches. [applause] I say, that's what he preaches. The whole church structure in this country is white nationalism. You go inside a white church—that's what they preaching, white nationalism. They got Jesus white, Mary white, God white, everybody white—that's white nationalism. [cheering]

So what he does, the way he circumvents the jealousy and envy that he ordinarily would incur among the heads of the church—whenever you go into an area where the church already is, you going to run into trouble. Because they got that thing, what you call it, syndicated . . . they got a syndicate just like the racketeers have. I'm going to say what's on my mind, because the preachers already proved to you that they got a syndicate. [applause] And when you're out in the rackets, whenever you're getting in another man's territory, you know, they gang up on you. And that's the same way with you. You run into the same thing. So how Billy Graham gets around that, instead of going into somebody else's territory, like he going to start a new church, he doesn't try and start a church, he just goes in preaching Christ. And he says anybody who believe in him, you go wherever you find him.

So this helps all the churches, and since it helps all the churches, they don't fight him. Well, we going to do the same thing, only our gospel is Black Nationalism. His gospel is white nationalism, our gospel is Black Nationalism. And the gospel of Black Nationalism, as I told you, means you should control your own, the politics of your community, the economy of your community, and all of the society in which you live should be under your control. And once you feel that this philosophy will solve your problem, go join any church where that's preached. Don't join any church where white nationalism is preached. Why, you can go to a Negro church and be exposed to white nationalism. 'Cause when you are on, when you walk in a Negro church and see a white Jesus and a white Mary and some white angels, that Negro church is preaching white nationalism. [applause]

But, when you go to a church and you see the pastor of that church with a philosophy and a program that's designed to bring black people together and elevate black people, join that church. Join that church. If you see where the NAACP is preaching and practicing that which is designed to make Black Nationalism materialize, join the NAACP. Join any kind of organization—civic, religious, fraternal, political, or otherwise—that's based on lifting the black man up and making him master of his own community. [applause]

2.

LORRAINE HANSBERRY
(1930–1965)

"The Black Revolution and the White Backlash"

Forum at Town Hall sponsored by the Association of Artists for Freedom,
New York City—June 15, 1964

In 1959, playwright Lorraine Hansberry made history as the first black woman to have a show produced on Broadway. The play was *A Raisin in the Sun*, a story about a black working-class family in Chicago trying to escape the ghetto. At the time, most people thought a play about African Americans would be a box-office flop. Instead, *Raisin* was a hit. It ran on Broadway for nineteen months, was made into a movie starring Sidney Poitier in 1961, and is now considered a classic of the American theater.

For writer James Baldwin, the most striking thing about the play was what it did for African Americans. "I had never in my life seen so many black people in the theater," he wrote. "And the reason was that never before, in the entire history of the American theater, had so much of the truth of black people's lives been seen on the stage. Black people had ignored the theater because the theater had always ignored them."[1] Hansberry's success helped open doors for scores of black writers and artists who followed, in both theater and the wider cultural mainstream.

Lorraine Hansberry was born in 1930. She grew up on the south side of Chicago, a place rigidly segregated by race. In 1937, Hansberry's parents challenged Chicago's restrictive housing covenants by moving into an all-white neighborhood. Whites fought back. A mob gathered around the house and someone threw a brick, barely missing young Lorraine's head. Years later, in a letter to the *New York Times*, Hansberry recalled her mother "patrolling the house all night with a loaded German luger," while her father was away fighting the battle in court.[2]

Working closely with the NAACP, Hansberry's father took the case all the way to the U.S. Supreme Court and eventually won. The ruling in *Hansberry v. Lee* helped to outlaw housing discrimination across the country. Still, the legal victory proved no match for Chicago's entrenched racism; blacks and whites remained apart.

Hansberry's parents, Carl and Nannie, were prominent members of their community and often hosted African American luminaries who came through town. The couple were die-hard Republicans, but it was two of their left-wing guests—W.E.B. Du Bois and Paul Robeson—who came to have a deep influence on their daughter's political views.[3]

When Hansberry moved to New York City in 1950, Robeson gave Hansberry her first "real" job as a writer for his new paper, *Freedom*. The publication had a strong socialist bent, and Hansberry declared optimistically to a friend that it would become "the journal of Negro liberation."[4] Du Bois also wrote articles for the paper and taught Hansberry African history at the Jefferson School of Social Science, a Marxist school shut down by the U.S. government at the height of the McCarthy era.[5] Du Bois and Robeson were dogged by anticommunist forces, but Hansberry—still relatively unknown—escaped the same persecution.

Hansberry's 1959 success with *Raisin* gave her a prominent voice in the struggle for black liberation. She delivered this speech at the Town Hall forum in 1964. The memory of her father's failure to shake segregation through legal means shaped her plea for action. Having tried "respectable" ways to battle injustice, she said, it was time to get radical.

The forum was sponsored by the Association of Artists for Freedom, a loose coalition of well-known black performers and writers that included Sidney Poitier, James Baldwin, and actress Ruby Dee. One of the founders, Ossie Davis, told the *New York Times*, "We meet from time to time to talk and argue . . . about what we as artists can do, how we can express the anguish for the moral situation we find in this country, but not as civil rights pleaders."[6]

The Town Hall forum was designed for white liberals and black activists to have an open conversation about tensions mounting between them in the civil rights movement. Charles Silberman, one of the white panelists, described the strain in a book he published in early 1964: "[W]hen the struggle for Negro rights moves into the streets, the majority of [white] liberals are reluctant to move along with it. They are all for the Negroes' objectives, they say, but they cannot go along with the means."[7] During the forum, Hansberry blasted this reluctance, declaring, "We have to find some way with these dialogues to show and to encourage the white liberal to stop being a liberal and become an American radical."

Writing in her journal two days later, Hansberry described the event as explosive: "Negroes are so angry and white people are so confused and sensitive to criticism."[8] The black panelists included writers Paule Marshall, John O. Killens, and LeRoi Jones, along with actors Ossie Davis and Rudy Dee. James Wechsler, a columnist for the *New York Post*, was another of the white panelists. He wrote that the Association of Artists for Freedom was "ambushing captive white liberals."[9] Meanwhile, Nat Hentoff argued in the *Village Voice* that the white panel members were "estranged from Negro reality." He said Wechsler "simply did not have the capacity to really listen to what was being said."[10]

During the Town Hall forum, Lorraine Hansberry was battling more than ideas—she was fighting cancer. Her body was beginning to wither, and she was on painkillers. Robert Nemiroff, her former husband, says she "rose from a sickbed," determined to participate in the forum and "set forth the need for a new militancy and a radically new relationship between Blacks and Whites in the freedom struggle."[11]

Privately, though, Hansberry worried she was becoming a coward. "Do I remain a revolutionary?" she wrote in her journal. "Intellectually— without a doubt. But am I prepared to give my body to the struggle or even my comforts? . . . Comfort has come to be its own corruption."[12] In July 1964, Hansberry wrote that when she regained her health she might travel to the South "to find out what kind of revolutionary I am."[13]

Hansberry never got the chance. She died on January 12, 1965, at the age of thirty-four.

HOW DO YOU TALK about three hundred years in four minutes? [sighs, laughter, applause] Was it ever so apparent we need this dialogue? [laughter, applause]

I wrote a letter to the *New York Times* recently, which didn't get printed, which is getting to be my rapport with the *New York Times*. They said that it was too personal. What it concerned itself with was, I was in a bit of a stew over the stall-in, because when the stall-in was first announced, I said, "Oh, My God, now everybody's gone crazy, you know, tying up traffic. What's the matter with them? You know. Who needs it?" And then I noticed the reaction, starting in Washington and coming on up to New York among what we are all here calling the white liberal circles, which was something like, you know, "You Negroes act right or you're going to ruin everything we're trying to do." [laughter] And that got me to thinking more seriously about the strategy and the tactic that the stall-in intended to accomplish.

And so I sat down and wrote a letter to the *New York Times* about the fact that I am of a generation of Negroes that comes after a whole lot of other generations and my father, for instance, who was, you know, a real "American"-type American: successful businessman, very civic-minded, and so forth; was the sort of American who put a great deal of money, a great deal of his really extraordinary talents, and a great deal of passion into everything that we say is the American way of going after goals. That is to say that he moved his family into a restricted area where no Negroes were supposed to live and then proceeded to fight the case in the courts all the way to the Supreme Court of the United States. And this cost a great deal of money. It involved the assistance of NAACP attorneys and so on, and this is the way of struggling that everyone says is the proper way to do, and it eventually resulted in a decision against restrictive covenants, which is very famous, *Hansberry v. Lee*. And that was very much applauded.

But the problem is that Negroes are just as segregated in the city of Chicago now as they were then [laughter], and my father died a disillusioned exile in another country. That is the reality that I'm faced with when I get up and I read that some Negroes my own age and younger say that we must now lie down in the streets, tie up traffic, stop ambulances, do whatever we can, take to the hills if necessary with some guns and fight back, you see. This is the difference.

And I wrote to the *Times* and said, "Can't you understand that this is the perspective from which we are now speaking? It isn't as if we got up today and said, you know, 'What can we do to irritate America?'" [laughter] It's because that since 1619, Negroes have tried every method of communication, of transformation of their situation, from petition to the vote, everything. We've tried it all. There isn't anything that hasn't been exhausted. Isn't it rather remarkable that we can talk about a people who were publishing newspapers while they were still in slavery in 1827, you see? We've been doing everything—writing editorials, Mr. Wechsler, for a long time. [applause]

And now the charge of impatience is simply unbearable. I would like to submit that the problem is that, yes, there is a problem about white liberals. I think there's something horrible that Norman Podhoretz, for instance, can sit down and write the kind of trash that he did at this hour. [applause] That is to say, that a distinguished American thinker can literally say that he is more disturbed at the sight of a mixed couple or that anti-Semitism from Negroes—and anti-Semitism from anybody is horrible and disgusting, and I don't care where it comes from—but anti-Semitism, somehow, from a Negro apparently upsets him more than it would from a German fascist, you see. This was the implication of what really gets to him. [applause] Well, you have to understand that when we are confronted with that, we wonder who we are talking to and how far we are going to go.

The problem is, we have to find some way with these dialogues to show and to encourage the white liberal to stop being a liberal and become an American radical. [applause] I think that then it wouldn't . . . when that becomes true, some of the really eloquent things that were said before about the basic fabric of our society—which after all, is the thing which must be changed [applause] to really solve the problem. The basic organization of American society is the thing that has Negroes in the situation that they are in, and never let us lose sight of it.

When we then talk with that understanding, it won't be so difficult for people like Mr. Wechsler, whose sincerity I wouldn't dream of challenging, when I say to him [laughter]—his sincerity is one thing; I don't have to agree with his position. But it wouldn't be so difficult for me to say, well, now, when someone uses the term "cold war liberal," that it is entirely different, you see, the way that you would assess the Vietnamese war and the way that I would, because I can't believe . . . [applause] I can't believe that anyone who is given what an American Negro is given—you know, our viewpoint—can believe that a government which has at its disposal a Federal Bureau of Investigation which cannot ever find the murderers of Negroes and by that method . . . [applause] and shows that it cares really very little about American citizens who are black, really are over somewhere fighting a war for a bunch of other colored people, you know, [laughter] several thousand miles—you just have a different viewpoint.

This is why we want the dialogue, to explain that to you, you see. It isn't a question of patriotism and loyalty. My brother fought for this country, my grandfather before that, and so on, and that's all a lot of nonsense when we criticize. The point is that we have a different viewpoint because, you know, we've been kicked in the face so often, and the vantage point of Negroes is entirely different, and these are some of the things we're trying to say. I don't want to go past my time. Thank you. [applause]

3.

OSSIE DAVIS
(1917–2005)

Eulogy for Malcolm X

Faith Temple Church of God in Christ,
New York City—February 27, 1965

Actor Ossie Davis and his wife, Ruby Dee, were so deeply involved in the freedom struggle of the 1950s and '60s that they have been called "the first couple of the civil rights movement."[1] They took part in countless fund-raisers and demonstrations. They were recruited to emcee the 1963 March on Washington. And they were friends with many of the movement's leaders, including Martin Luther King Jr. and Malcolm X. Davis was an accomplished writer as well as an actor, and he was called on to eulogize Malcolm X after he was assassinated. Davis decided to speak at the funeral for the controversial Malcom X in spite of the damage it might have caused his mainstream acting career. Davis's eulogy would be among the most memorable words he ever wrote.

Ossie Davis was born in the small town of Codgell, Georgia. His birth name was Raiford Chatman Davis, but a clerk at the local courthouse misheard his mother speak his initials, R.C., and marked him down as "Ossie." In an autobiography, Davis explained that the clerk was white, and in Jim Crow Georgia, his mother did not dare contradict him. The name stuck.[2]

Davis got his own lesson in the realities of discrimination when he was a small boy. Davis's father, Kince, helped build and maintain a short-line railroad owned by a local white land baron named Sessoms. The line carried timber and livestock on a twenty-three-mile stretch to a town in the next county. On several occasions, Ku Klux Klansmen warned Davis's father that the position of crew boss was white man's work. But Kince Davis had a pistol in his belt and the protection of his powerful employer. "The Klan never came," Davis recalled. "A black man with Daddy's skill was a rare and precious commodity to Sessoms and the other big men who ran things. They didn't mind giving him a white man's job as long as they didn't have to give him a white man's pay."[3] Seeking greater independence, Kince Davis later quit the job to start his own herbal medicine business. For the rest of the time Ossie lived with his parents, they struggled to get by.

Ossie Davis was the oldest of five children. His parents could not read, but they were enthusiastic storytellers. As a schoolboy, Davis consumed books with a ravenous hunger and dreamed of becoming a writer. He began acting in plays and operettas in high school. After graduating in 1934, Davis hitchhiked to Washington, D.C., to live with his aunts and attend Howard University. He came under the influence of professor Alain Locke, a writer and philosopher whose anthology *The New Negro* was a defining text of the black artistic and intellectual movement known as the Harlem Renaissance. Locke encouraged Davis to pursue formal training as an actor. Davis dropped out of Howard after his junior year and moved to Harlem, where he worked odd jobs and sometimes slept on park benches while learning the theater trade.

After serving in World War II, Davis landed the lead role in the 1946 Broadway play *Jeb*, about a disabled veteran in racist Louisiana. The play was a flop, but it established Davis as an actor to watch. It also introduced him to actress Ruby Dee; the couple married two years later. Davis and Dee appeared together in numerous theatrical, film, and television productions, including Lorraine Hansberry's groundbreaking play, *A Raisin in the Sun*, and several films by Spike Lee. Meanwhile, Davis wrote his own plays, including *Purlie Victorious*, which opened on Broadway in 1961 with Dee in a starring role. *Purlie* is a comedy about racial stereotypes centered on an itinerant black preacher who tries to start an integrated church. It was turned into a movie, and then returned to Broadway as a hit musical.

Davis also worked as a movie director, creating one of the first successful "blaxploitation" films of the 1970s, *Cotton Comes to Harlem*. Blaxploitation was a genre of streetwise urban movies aimed at African Americans. It generally featured black heroes outwitting white villains to a soul and funk soundtrack.

In 1995, Davis and Dee were awarded the National Medal of Arts. In 2004, they were jointly recognized at the Kennedy Center Honors for their artistic achievements, and for breaking open "many a door previously shut tight to African American artists."[4] In February 2005, Davis was acting in a film being shot in Miami when he died of natural causes in his hotel room. He was eighty-seven years old.

Davis and Dee met Malcolm X in the early 1960s. Dee's brother was one of Malcolm X's disciples and introduced them. They became friends. Most of Malcolm X's followers were the common folk of Harlem, and Malcolm, with his fundamentalist religious beliefs, as dictated by the Nation of Islam, disapproved of the theater. But historian Peniel Joseph says the Broadway actors became Malcolm X's gateway to New York's radical black intelligentsia. "Davis and Dee formed this core group of second-tier celebrities who served as sounding boards, secret fund-raisers, and trusted confidants for much of Malcolm's career," Joseph writes.[5] Meantime, they were also firm supporters of Martin Luther King Jr. Davis marched with King during civil rights demonstrations in the South.

Supporting Malcolm X involved professional risk for mainstream performers like Davis and Dee. "He was saying some pretty rough things, especially about whites," Davis told an interviewer. "Some of us, you know, had our jobs out in the white community—we really didn't want to get too close to Malcolm."[6] Still, Malcolm X was a frequent guest at the couple's home in the suburbs of New York City. "Malcolm . . . was refreshing excitement," Davis later explained in the magazine *Negro Digest*. "And you always left his presence with the sneaky suspicion that maybe, after all, you were a man!"[7] Malcolm X visited Davis in the last week of his life. He talked about his break with the Nation of Islam and the firestorm that ensued. "Malcolm at the end was a hunted and haunted man," Davis wrote. "Running for his life; his home firebombed."[8]

Malcolm X was shot to death on February 21, 1965, as he prepared for an indoor rally in New York. His pregnant wife and four children witnessed the killing. Three members of the Nation of Islam were convicted and sent to prison for the murder. When Davis and Dee heard the news of Malcolm X's assassination, they drove to Harlem and walked the streets through

the night, talking with the gathering crowds about the killing. "The situation was hostile and explosive," Davis wrote.⁹

Harlem was full of riot police and threats of violence. The mosque
where Malcolm had preached was firebombed. Given the risks, Malcolm's supporters had a hard time finding a venue for the funeral. They
finally secured the Faith Temple Church of God in Christ. Malcolm X's
lawyer, Percy Sutton, approached Davis to give the eulogy. Davis was the
choice of Malcolm X's widow, Betty Shabazz. Davis was surprised by the
request—he'd been Malcolm's friend but was not a Muslim. Sutton explained that Davis was widely respected and could help keep the peace.
"You're the least controversial person we can think of," Davis recalled
Sutton telling him. "The Muslims would accept you. The left wing will accept you. The right wing will accept you. The black folks will accept you.
The white folks will accept you. So you're it." Davis agreed.¹⁰

The funeral took place on Saturday morning, February 27, 1965. Looking out over the casket, Davis reminded the mourners of Malcolm X's
deep commitment to Harlem and its African American citizens. He recalled
the pride and determination that the powerful orator could stir within his
people. "Malcolm was our manhood, our living black manhood!" Davis declared. He concluded the eulogy with words that would be repeated often:
"We shall know him then for what he was and is—a prince, our own black
shining prince, who didn't hesitate to die, because he loved us so."¹¹

HERE, AT THIS FINAL HOUR, in this quiet place, Harlem has come to bid
farewell to one of its brightest hopes—extinguished now, and gone from us
forever.

For Harlem is where he worked and where he struggled and fought—his
home of homes, where his heart was; and where his people are—and it is,
therefore, most fitting that we meet once again—in Harlem—to share these
last moments with him.

For Harlem has ever been gracious to those who have loved her, have
fought for her, and have defended her honor even to the death. It is not
in the memory of man that this beleaguered, unfortunate, but nonetheless
proud community has found a braver, more gallant young champion than
this Afro-American who lies before us—unconquered still.

I say the word again, as he would want me to: Afro-American; Afro-
American Malcolm, who was a master, was most meticulous in his use of

words. Nobody knew better than he the power words have over minds of men. Malcolm had stopped being "Negro" years ago.

It had become too small, too puny, too weak a word for him. Malcolm was bigger than that. Malcolm had become an Afro-American, and he wanted—so desperately—that we, that all his people, would become Afro-Americans too.

There are those who will consider it their duty, as friends of the Negro people, to tell us to revile him, to flee, even from the presence of his memory, to save ourselves by writing him out of the history of our turbulent times.

Many will ask what Harlem finds to honor in this stormy, controversial, and bold young captain. And we will smile. Many will say, "Turn away"—away from this man, for he is not a man but a demon, a monster, a subverter, and an enemy of the black man. And we will smile. They will say that he is of hate—a fanatic, a racist who can only bring evil to the cause for which you struggle.

And we will answer and say unto them: Did you ever talk to Brother Malcolm? Did you ever touch him or have him smile at you? Did you ever really listen to him? Did he ever do a mean thing? Was he ever himself associated with violence or any public disturbance? For if you did, you would know him. And if you knew him, you would know why we must honor him: Malcolm was our manhood, our living, black manhood! This was his meaning to his people. And in honoring him, we honor the best in ourselves.

Last year, from Africa, he wrote these words to a friend: "My journey," he says, "is almost ended, and I have a much broader scope than when I started out, which I believe will add new life and dimension to our struggle for freedom and honor and dignity in the States. I am writing these things so that you will know for a fact the tremendous sympathy and support we have among the African states for our Human Rights Struggle. The main thing is that we keep a United Front wherein our most valuable time and energy will not be wasted fighting each other."

However we may have differed with him—or with each other about him and his value as a man—let his going from us serve only to bring us together now.

Consigning these mortal remains to earth, the common mother of all, secure in the knowledge that what we place in the ground is no more now a man, but a seed, which, after the winter of our discontent, will come forth again to meet us.

And we shall know him then for what he was and is—a prince, our own black shining prince, who didn't hesitate to die, because he loved us so.

4.

MARTIN LUTHER KING JR. (1929–1968)

"Where Do We Go from Here?"

Convention of the Southern Christian Leadership Conference, Atlanta, Georgia—August 16, 1967

Martin Luther King Jr. was the most powerful voice for nonviolent social change in the twentieth-century civil rights movement. But when he gave this speech in August 1967, it seemed his power was waning, his voice drowned out by urban riots and the militant rhetoric of young black activists. In July of 1967, violence tore at black neighborhoods in several American cities. In Newark, New Jersey, twenty-three people were killed and more than a thousand thrown in jail. An even larger riot engulfed Detroit a few weeks later. Black people in America's inner cities were fed up with poverty and police repression. To some of them, Martin Luther King's message of peaceful protest seemed increasingly irrelevant.

King used this annual address to the Southern Christian Leadership Conference (SCLC) to underscore his commitment to nonviolence. He said using violence to change society was not only morally wrong, it almost never worked. "At best," he said, recent riots had "produced a little additional antipoverty money allotted by frightened government officials and a few water sprinklers to cool the children of the ghettos. It is something like improving the food in the prison while the people remain securely incarcerated behind bars." What was needed, King said, was not a revolution, but "a strategy for change, a tactical program that will bring the Negro into the mainstream of American life as quickly as possible."

This was the tenth annual convention of the SCLC. The organization was formed in 1957 to coordinate the increasing number of civil rights protests in the South. King had been head of the SCLC from its start. Speaking to some five hundred delegates packed into his home church—Ebenezer Baptist Church in Atlanta—King summed up the immense victories they had achieved in their ten-year attack on Jim Crow. "Things are different now," King said. "In assault after assault, we caused the sagging walls of segregation to come tumbling down."

When King delivered this address, however, he was battling inner desperation. By 1967, King had come to a depressing realization: The civil rights victories he had helped win had done little to improve economic conditions for poor blacks. "We must face the fact," he told the crowd at Ebenezer, "that the Negro still lives in the basement of the Great Society," a reference to President Lyndon Johnson's sweeping antipoverty programs launched in 1964.

Three years after that launch, King was speaking frequently about a "new phase" of the civil rights movement. It would focus on economic justice for poor people. "We aren't merely struggling to integrate a lunch counter now," he told an audience in Los Angeles, "we're struggling to get some money to be able to buy a hamburger or a steak when we get to the counter."[1] The fight against poverty, King said, would cost billions more dollars than past campaigns for civil rights.

The U.S. poverty rate was near an all-time low in 1967—roughly 12 percent—but for African Americans it was more than double that. Blacks still endured much higher rates of unemployment, illiteracy, and malnourishment than whites. King began calling for "a radical redistribution of economic and political power."[2]

King's right-wing critics had long labeled him a communist. King knew his demand for the redistribution of wealth would draw their fire. The FBI used King's alleged communist leanings as a pretext for spying on him and his associates. King addressed these critics in his SCLC speech, explaining that he was not a communist. The inspiration for his ideas came not from Marx or Lenin, he said, but from the Gospel of Jesus Christ. Scholar and activist Vincent Harding was one of King's longtime confidants. Harding described King as "one of these 'crazy' members of the Christian community who really took Jesus seriously and believed that the way you get closest to the divine is by getting closer and closer to the most outcast members of the society." Harding continued, "That's a hard path, but once you have chosen it you know that there's no easy alternative."[3]

King announced at the SCLC conference that a bold program was needed to help the nation's poor. He said he would meet soon with his associates to plan a new campaign involving massive civil disobedience. Privately, King remained gloomy. If the SCLC's new attack on poverty and racism failed, he told a reporter, "I would say to the nation, 'I've done my best.' "[4] He knew of nothing else to try.

Four months after giving this speech, on December 4, 1967, King held a press conference in Atlanta announcing plans for what he hoped would be the longest-running protest in the history of the nation's capital. King called it the Poor People's Campaign. He intended to dramatize the suffering of the nation's poor by bringing thousands of them to Washington, D.C. Poor people would live together on the National Mall—the long strip of land between the U.S. Capitol and the Lincoln Memorial—and engage in widespread civil disobedience. King wanted to force Lyndon Johnson and the federal government to deal with poverty.

King never saw the protest take place. He was assassinated in Memphis, Tennessee, on April 4, 1968, three weeks before the campaign was set to begin. In reaction to King's death, more than a hundred American cities exploded in violence. Most of the destruction was confined to urban, black neighborhoods.

King's death was grieved even by the militant African Americans who had dismissed his message as increasingly irrelevant. Angela Davis wrote that she was shocked by the news of King's death, and then hit by guilt. "We had severely criticized Martin Luther King for his rigid stance on nonviolence," she wrote. "Some of us, unfortunately, had assumed that his religion, his philosophical nonviolence and his concentration on 'civil rights' . . . had rendered him an essentially harmless leader." Davis says she and her peers never thought King would need their protection, or that he would be killed. "I don't think we had realized that his new notion of struggle—involving poor people of all colors throughout the world—could potentially represent a great threat to our enemy."[5]

King knew. As the nation's leading civil rights activist, he was accustomed to receiving death threats. His campaign to eliminate poverty and to end the war in Vietnam kept him a target of racists and right-wing radicals. In this speech, King said the answer to America's problems required no less than a complete restructuring of society. "America," he thundered, "you must be born again!"

DR. ABERNATHY, our distinguished vice president, fellow delegates to this, the tenth annual session of the Southern Christian Leadership Conference, my brothers and sisters from not only all over the South, but from all over the United States of America: ten years ago during the piercing chill of a January day and on the heels of the yearlong Montgomery bus boycott, a group of approximately one hundred Negro leaders from across the South assembled in this church and agreed on the need for an organization to be formed that could serve as a channel through which local protest organizations in the South could coordinate their protest activities. It was this meeting that gave birth to the Southern Christian Leadership Conference.

And when our organization was formed ten years ago, racial segregation was still a structured part of the architecture of Southern society. Negroes with the pangs of hunger and the anguish of thirst were denied access to the average lunch counter. The downtown restaurants were still off-limits for the black man. Negroes, burdened with the fatigue of travel, were still barred from the motels of the highways and the hotels of the cities. Negro boys and girls in dire need of recreational activities were not allowed to inhale the fresh air of the big city parks. Negroes in desperate need of allowing their mental buckets to sink deep into the wells of knowledge were confronted with a firm no when they sought to use the city libraries. Ten years ago, legislative halls of the South were still ringing loud with such words as "interposition" and "nullification." All types of conniving methods were still being used to keep the Negro from becoming a registered voter. A decade ago, not a single Negro entered the legislative chambers of the South except as a porter or a chauffeur. Ten years ago, all too many Negroes were still harried by day and haunted by night by a corroding sense of fear and a nagging sense of nobody-ness. [*Yeah*]

But things are different now. In assault after assault, we caused the sagging walls of segregation to come tumbling down. During this era, the entire edifice of segregation was profoundly shaken. This is an accomplishment whose consequences are deeply felt by every Southern Negro in his daily life. [*Oh yeah*] It is no longer possible to count the number of public establishments that are open to Negroes. Ten years ago, Negroes seemed almost

invisible to the larger society, and the facts of their harsh lives were unknown
to the majority of the nation. But today, civil rights is a dominating issue in
every state, crowding the pages of the press and the daily conversation of
white Americans. In this decade of change, the Negro stood up and confronted his oppressor. He faced the bullies and the guns, and the dogs and
the tear gas. He put himself squarely before the vicious mobs and moved
with strength and dignity toward them and decisively defeated them. [*Yes*]
And the courage with which he confronted enraged mobs dissolved the stereotype of the grinning, submissive Uncle Tom. [*Yes*] He came out of his
struggle integrated only slightly in the external society, but powerfully integrated within. This was a victory that had to precede all other gains.

In short, over the last ten years, the Negro decided to straighten his back
up [*Yes*], realizing that a man cannot ride your back unless it is bent. [*Yes,
that's right!*] We made our government write new laws to alter some of the
cruelest injustices that affected us. We made an indifferent and unconcerned
nation rise from lethargy and subpoenaed its conscience to appear before the
judgment seat of morality on the whole question of civil rights. We gained
manhood in the nation that had always called us "boy." It would be hypocritical indeed if I allowed modesty to forbid my saying that SCLC stood at the
forefront of all of the watershed movements that brought these monumental
changes in the South. For this, we can feel a legitimate pride. But in spite
of a decade of significant progress, the problem is far from solved. The deep
rumbling of discontent in our cities is indicative of the fact that the plant of
freedom has grown only a bud and not yet a flower.

And before discussing the awesome responsibilities that we face in the
days ahead, let us take an inventory of our programmatic action and activities over the past year. Last year as we met in Jackson, Mississippi, we were
painfully aware of the struggle of our brothers in Grenada, Mississippi. After
living for a hundred or more years under the yoke of total segregation, the
Negro citizens of this northern Delta hamlet banded together in nonviolent
warfare against racial discrimination under the leadership of our affiliate
chapter and organization there. The fact of this nondestructive rebellion was
as spectacular as were its results. In a few short weeks, the Grenada County
Movement challenged every aspect of the society's exploitative life. Stores
which denied employment were boycotted; voter registration increased by
thousands. We can never forget the courageous action of the people of Grenada, who moved our nation and its federal courts to powerful action on behalf of school integration, giving Grenada one of the most integrated school

systems in America. The battle is far from over, but the black people of Grenada have achieved forty of fifty-three demands through their persistent nonviolent efforts.

Slowly but surely, our Southern affiliates continued their building and organizing. Seventy-nine counties conducted voter registration drives, while double that number carried on political education and get-out-the-vote efforts. In spite of press opinions, our staff is still overwhelmingly a Southern-based staff. One hundred and five persons have worked across the South under the direction of Hosea Williams. What used to be primarily a voter registration staff is actually a multifaceted program dealing with the total life of the community, from farm cooperatives, business development, tutorials, credit unions, et cetera. Especially to be commended are those ninety-nine communities and their staffs which maintain regular mass meetings throughout the year.

Our Citizenship Education Program continues to lay the solid foundation of adult education and community organization upon which all social change must ultimately rest. This year, five hundred local leaders received training at Dorchester and ten community centers through our Citizenship Education Program. They were trained in literacy, consumer education, planned parenthood, and many other things. And this program, so ably directed by Mrs. Dorothy Cotton, Mrs. Septima Clark, and their staff of eight persons, continues to cover ten Southern states. One auxiliary feature of CEP is the aid which they have given to poor communities, poor counties, in receiving and establishing OEO projects. With the competent professional guidance of our marvelous staff member, Miss Mew Soong-Li, Lowndes and Wilcox counties in Alabama have pioneered in developing outstanding poverty programs totally controlled and operated by residents of the area.

Perhaps the area of greatest concentration of my efforts has been in the cities of Chicago and Cleveland. Chicago has been a wonderful proving ground for our work in the North. There have been no earth-shaking victories, but neither has there been failure. Our open-housing marches, which finally brought about an agreement which actually calls [on] the power structure of Chicago to capitulate to the civil rights movement, these marches and the agreement have finally begun to pay off. After the season of delay around election periods, the Leadership Conference, organized to meet our demands for an open city, has finally begun to implement the programs agreed to last summer.

But this is not the most important aspect of our work. As a result of our tenant union organizing, we have begun a four-million-dollar rehabilitation project, which will renovate deteriorating buildings and allow their tenants the opportunity to own their own homes. This pilot project was the inspiration for the new home-ownership bill, which Senator Percy introduced in Congress only recently.

The most dramatic success in Chicago has been Operation Breadbasket. Through Operation Breadbasket we have now achieved for the Negro community of Chicago more than twenty-two hundred new jobs with an income of approximately eighteen million dollars a year, new income to the Negro community. [applause] But not only have we gotten jobs through Operation Breadbasket in Chicago; there was another area through this economic program, and that was the development of financial institutions which were controlled by Negroes and which were sensitive to problems of economic deprivation of the Negro community. The two banks in Chicago that were interested in helping Negro businessmen were largely unable to loan much because of limited assets. Hi-Lo, one of the chain stores in Chicago, agreed to maintain substantial accounts in the two banks, thus increasing their ability to serve the needs of the Negro community. And I can say to you today that as a result of Operation Breadbasket in Chicago, both of these Negro-operated banks have now more than doubled their assets, and this has been done in less than a year by the work of Operation Breadbasket. [applause]

In addition, the ministers learned that Negro scavengers had been deprived of significant accounts in the ghetto. Whites controlled even the garbage of Negroes. Consequently, the chain stores agreed to contract with Negro scavengers to service at least the stores in Negro areas. Negro insect and rodent exterminators, as well as janitorial services, were likewise excluded from major contracts with chain stores. The chain stores also agreed to utilize these services. It also became apparent that chain stores advertised only rarely in Negro-owned community newspapers. This area of neglect was also negotiated, giving community newspapers regular, substantial accounts. And finally, the ministers found that Negro contractors, from painters to masons, from electricians to excavators, had also been forced to remain small by the monopolies of white contractors. Breadbasket negotiated agreements on new construction and rehabilitation work for the chain stores. These several interrelated aspects of economic development, all based on the power of organized consumers, hold great possibilities for dealing with the problems of Negroes in other Northern cities. The kinds of requests made by

Breadbasket in Chicago can be made not only of chain stores, but of almost any major industry in any city in the country.

And so Operation Breadbasket has a very simple program, but a powerful one. It simply says, "If you respect my dollar, you must respect my person." It simply says that we will no longer spend our money where we cannot get substantial jobs. [applause]

In Cleveland, Ohio, a group of ministers have formed an Operation Breadbasket through our program there and have moved against a major dairy company. Their requests include jobs, advertising in Negro newspapers, and depositing funds in Negro financial institutions. This effort resulted in something marvelous. I went to Cleveland just last week to sign the agreement with Sealtest. We went to get the facts about their employment; we discovered that they had four hundred forty-two employees and only forty-three were Negroes, yet the Negro population of Cleveland is thirty-five percent of the total population. They refused to give us all of the information that we requested, and we said, in substance, "Mr. Sealtest, we're sorry. We aren't going to burn your store down. We aren't going to throw any bricks in the window. But we are going to put picket signs around, and we are going to put leaflets out, and we are going to our pulpits and tell them not to sell Sealtest products, and not to purchase Sealtest products."

We did that. We went through the churches. Reverend Dr. Hoover, who pastors the largest church in Cleveland, who's here today, and all of the ministers got together and got behind this program. We went to every store in the ghetto and said, "You must take Sealtest products off of your counters. If not, we're going to boycott your whole store." [That's right!] A&P refused. We put picket lines around A&P; they have a hundred and some stores in Cleveland, and we picketed A&P and closed down eighteen of them in one day. Nobody went in A&P. [applause] The next day, Mr. A&P was calling on us, and Bob Brown, who is here on our board and who is a public relations man representing a number of firms, came in. They called him in because he worked for A&P, also; and they didn't know he worked for us, too. [laughter] Bob Brown sat down with A&P, and he said they said, "Now, Mr. Brown, what would you advise us to do." He said, "I would advise you to take Sealtest products off of all of your counters." A&P agreed next day not only to take Sealtest products off of the counters in the ghetto, but off of the counters of every A&P store in Cleveland, and they said to Sealtest, "If you don't reach an agreement with SCLC and Operation Breadbasket, we will take Sealtest products off of every A&P store in the state of Ohio."

The next day [applause] . . . the next day, the Sealtest people were talking nice [laughter]; they were very humble. And I am proud to say that I went to Cleveland just last Tuesday, and I sat down with the Sealtest people and some seventy ministers from Cleveland, and we signed the agreement. This effort resulted in a number of jobs, which will bring almost five hundred thousand dollars of new income to the Negro community a year. [applause] We also said to Sealtest, "The problem that we face is that the ghetto is a domestic colony that's constantly drained without being replenished. And you are always telling us to lift ourselves by our own bootstraps, and yet we are being robbed every day. Put something back in the ghetto." So along with our demand for jobs, we said, "We also demand that you put money in the Negro savings and loan association and that you take ads, advertise, in the Cleveland *Call & Post*, the Negro newspaper." So along with the new jobs, Sealtest has now deposited thousands of dollars in the Negro bank of Cleveland and has already started taking ads in the Negro newspaper in that city. This is the power of Operation Breadbasket. [applause]

Now, for fear that you may feel that it's limited to Chicago and Cleveland, let me say to you that we've gotten even more than that. In Atlanta, Georgia, Breadbasket has been equally successful in the South. Here the emphasis has been divided between governmental employment and private industry. And while I do not have time to go into the details, I want to commend the men who have been working with it here: the Reverend Bennett, the Reverend Joe Boone, the Reverend J. C. Ward, Reverend Dorsey, Reverend Greer, and I could go on down the line, and they have stood up along with all of the other ministers. But here is the story that's not printed in the newspapers in Atlanta: as a result of Operation Breadbasket, over the last three years, we have added about twenty-five million dollars of new income to the Negro community every year. [applause]

Now as you know, Operation Breadbasket has now gone national in the sense that we had a national conference in Chicago and agreed to launch a nationwide program, which you will hear more about.

Finally, SCLC has entered the field of housing. Under the leadership of attorney James Robinson, we have already contracted to build one hundred fifty-two units of low-income housing with apartments for the elderly on a choice downtown Atlanta site under the sponsorship of Ebenezer Baptist Church. This is the first project [applause], this is the first project of a proposed South-wide Housing Development Corporation, which we hope to develop in conjunction with SCLC, and through this corporation we hope to build housing from Mississippi to North Carolina using Negro work-men, Negro architects, Negro attorneys, and Negro financial institutions throughout. And it is our feeling that in the next two or three years, we can build right here in the South forty million dollars' worth of new housing for Negroes, and with millions and millions of dollars in income coming to the Negro community. [applause]

Now there are many other things that I could tell you, but time is pass-ing. This, in short, is an account of SCLC's work over the last year. It is a record of which we can all be proud.

With all the struggle and all the achievements, we must face the fact, however, that the Negro still lives in the basement of the Great Society. He is still at the bottom, despite the few who have penetrated to slightly higher levels. Even where the door has been forced partially open, mobility for the Negro is still sharply restricted. There is often no bottom at which to start, and when there is, there's almost no room at the top. In consequence, Ne-groes are still impoverished aliens in an affluent society. They are too poor even to rise with the society, too impoverished by the ages to be able to ascend by using their own resources. And the Negro did not do this himself; it was done to him. For more than half of his American history, he was en-slaved. Yet he built the spanning bridges and the grand mansions, the sturdy docks and stout factories of the South. His unpaid labor made cotton "king" and established America as a significant nation in international commerce. Even after his release from chattel slavery, the nation grew over him, sub-merging him. It became the richest, most powerful society in the history of man, but it left the Negro far behind.

And so we still have a long, long way to go before we reach the promised land of freedom. Yes, we have left the dusty soils of Egypt, and we have crossed a Red Sea that had for years been hardened by a long and piercing winter of massive resistance, but before we reach the majestic shores of the promised land, there will still be gigantic mountains of opposition ahead and prodigious hilltops of injustice. [Yes, that's right!] We still need some Paul Revere of conscience to alert every hamlet and every village of America that revolution is still at hand. Yes, we need a chart; we need a compass; indeed, we need some North Star to guide us into a future shrouded with impen-etrable uncertainties.

Now, in order to answer the question, "Where do we go from here?" which is our theme, we must first honestly recognize where we are now. When the Constitution was written, a strange formula to determine taxes and representation declared that the Negro was sixty percent of a person. Today another curious formula seems to declare he is fifty percent of a person. Of the good things in life, the Negro has approximately one half those of whites. Of the bad things of life, he has twice those of whites. Thus, half of all Negroes live in substandard housing. And Negroes have half the income of whites. When we turn to the negative experiences of life, the Negro has a double share: There are twice as many unemployed; the rate of infant mortality among Negroes is double that of whites; and there are twice as many Negroes dying in Vietnam as whites in proportion to their size in the population. [*Yes,* applause]

In other spheres, the figures are equally alarming. In elementary schools, Negroes lag one to three years behind whites, and their segregated schools [*Yeah*] receive substantially less money per student than the white schools. [*Those schools*] One-twentieth as many Negroes as whites attend college. Of employed Negroes, seventy-five percent hold menial jobs. This is where we are.

Where do we go from here? First, we must massively assert our dignity and worth. We must stand up amid a system that still oppresses us and develop an unassailable and majestic sense of values. We must no longer be ashamed of being black. [*All right!*] The job of arousing manhood within a people that have been taught for so many centuries that they are nobody is not easy.

Even semantics have conspired to make that which is black seem ugly and degrading. [*Yes*] In Roget's *Thesaurus* there are some one hundred twenty synonyms for blackness and at least sixty of them are offensive, such words as *blot, soot, grim, devil*, and *foul*. And there are some one hundred thirty-four synonyms for whiteness and all are favorable, expressed in such words as purity, cleanliness, chastity, and innocence. A white lie is better than a black lie. [*Yes*] The most degenerate member of a family is the "black sheep." [*Yes*] Ossie Davis has suggested that maybe the English language should be reconstructed so that teachers will not be forced to teach the Negro child sixty ways to despise himself, and thereby perpetuate his false sense of inferiority, and the white child 134 ways to adore himself, and thereby perpetuate his false sense of superiority. [applause] The tendency to ignore the Negro's contribution to American life and strip him of his personhood is as old as the earliest history books and as contemporary as the morning's newspaper. [*Yes*]

To offset this cultural homicide, the Negro must rise up with an affirmation

of his own Olympian manhood. [*Yes*] Any movement for the Negro's freedom that overlooks this necessity is only waiting to be buried. [*Yes*] As long
as the mind is enslaved, the body can never be free. [*Yes*] Psychological freedom, a firm sense of self-esteem, is the most powerful weapon against the
long night of physical slavery. No Lincolnian Emancipation Proclamation,
no Johnsonian civil rights bill can totally bring this kind of freedom. The
Negro will only be free when he reaches down to the inner depths of his own
being and signs with the pen and ink of assertive manhood his own emancipation proclamation. And with a spirit straining toward true self-esteem,
the Negro must boldly throw off the manacles of self-abnegation and say to
himself and to the world, "I am somebody. [*Oh yeah*] I am a person. I am a
man with dignity and honor. [*Go ahead*] I have a rich and noble history, however painful and exploited that history has been. Yes, I was a slave through
my foreparents [*That's right*], and now I'm not ashamed of that. I'm ashamed
of the people who were so sinful to make me a slave." [*Yes sir*] Yes [applause],
yes, we must stand up and say, "I'm black [*Yes sir*], but I'm black and beautiful." [*Yes*] This [applause], this self-affirmation is the black man's need, made
compelling [*All right*] by the white man's crimes against him. [*Yes*]

Now another basic challenge is to discover how to organize our strength
into economic and political power. Now no one can deny that the Negro is
in dire need of this kind of legitimate power. Indeed, one of the great problems that the Negro confronts is his lack of power. From the old plantations
of the South to the newer ghettos of the North, the Negro has been confined
to a life of voicelessness [*That's true*] and powerlessness. [*So true*] Stripped
of the right to make decisions concerning his life and destiny, he has been
subject to the authoritarian and sometimes whimsical decisions of the white
power structure. The plantation and the ghetto were created by those who
had power, both to confine those who had no power and to perpetuate their
powerlessness. Now the problem of transforming the ghetto, therefore, is a
problem of power, a confrontation between the forces of power demanding
change and the forces of power dedicated to the preserving of the status
quo. Now, power properly understood is nothing but the ability to achieve
purpose. It is the strength required to bring about social, political, and economic change. Walter Reuther defined power one day. He said, "Power is
the ability of a labor union like UAW to make the most powerful corporation
in the world, General Motors, say yes when it wants to say no. That's power."
[applause]

Now a lot of us are preachers, and all of us have our moral convictions and concerns, and so often we have problems with power. But there is nothing wrong with power if power is used correctly.

You see, what happened is that some of our philosophers got off base. And one of the great problems of history is that the concepts of love and power have usually been contrasted as opposites, polar opposites, so that love is identified with a resignation of power, and power with a denial of love. It was this misinterpretation that caused the philosopher Nietzsche, who was a philosopher of the will to power, to reject the Christian concept of love. It was this same misinterpretation which induced Christian theologians to reject Nietzsche's philosophy of the will to power in the name of the Christian idea of love.

Now, we got to get this thing right. What is needed is a realization that power without love is reckless and abusive, and that love without power is sentimental and anemic. [Yes] Power at its best [applause], power at its best is love [Yes] implementing the demands of justice, and justice at its best is love correcting everything that stands against love. [Speak!] And this is what we must see as we move on.

Now what has happened is that we've had it wrong and mixed up in our country, and this has led Negro Americans in the past to seek their goals through love and moral suasion devoid of power, and white Americans to seek their goals through power devoid of love and conscience. It is leading a few extremists today to advocate for Negroes the same destructive and conscienceless power that they have justly abhorred in whites. It is precisely this collision of immoral power with powerless morality which constitutes the major crisis of our times. [Yes]

Now we must develop progress, or rather, a program—and I can't stay on this long—that will drive the nation to a guaranteed annual income. Now, early in the century, this proposal would have been greeted with ridicule and denunciation as destructive of initiative and responsibility. At that time, economic status was considered the measure of the individual's abilities and talents. And in the thinking of that day, the absence of worldly goods indicated a want of industrious habits and moral fiber. We've come a long way in our understanding of human motivation and of the blind operation of our economic system. Now we realize that dislocations in the market operation of our economy and the prevalence of discrimination thrusts people into idleness and binds them in constant or frequent unemployment against their will. The poor are less often dismissed, I hope, from our conscience today by being branded as inferior and incompetent. We also know that no matter how dynamically the economy develops and expands, it does not eliminate all poverty.

The problem indicates that our emphasis must be twofold: We must create full employment, or we must create incomes. People must be made consumers by one method or the other. Once they are placed in this position, we need to be concerned that the potential of the individual is not wasted. New forms of work that enhance the social good will have to be devised for those for whom traditional jobs are not available. In 1879 Henry George anticipated this state of affairs when he wrote in *Progress and Poverty*:

> The fact is that the work which improves the condition of mankind, the work which extends knowledge and increases power, and enriches literature, and elevates thought, is not done to secure a living. It is not the work of slaves driven to their task either by the lash of a master or by animal necessities. It is the work of men who perform it for its own sake . . . In a state of society where want was abolished, work of this sort would be enormously increased.

And we are likely to find that the problem of housing and education, instead of preceding the elimination of poverty, will themselves be affected if poverty is first abolished. The poor, transformed into purchasers, will do a great deal on their own to alter housing decay. Negroes, who have a double disability, will have a greater effect on discrimination when they have the additional weapon of cash to use in their struggle.

Beyond these advantages, a host of positive psychological changes inevitably will result from widespread economic security. The dignity of the individual will flourish when the decisions concerning his life are in his own hands, when he has the assurance that his income is stable and certain, and when he knows that he has the means to seek self-improvement. Personal conflicts between husband, wife, and children will diminish when the unjust measurement of human worth on a scale of dollars is eliminated.

Now, our country can do this. John Kenneth Galbraith said that a guaranteed annual income could be done for about twenty billion dollars a year. And I say to you today, that if our nation can spend thirty-five billion dollars a year to fight an unjust, evil war in Vietnam, and twenty billion dollars to put a man on the moon, it can spend billions of dollars to put God's children on their own two feet right here on earth. [applause]

Now, let me rush on to say we must reaffirm our commitment to non-violence. And I want to stress this. The futility of violence in the struggle for racial justice has been tragically etched in all the recent Negro riots. Now, yesterday, I tried to analyze the riots and deal with the causes for them. Today I want to give the other side. There is something painfully sad about a riot. One sees screaming youngsters and angry adults fighting hopelessly and aimlessly against impossible odds. [*Yeah*] And deep down within them, you perceive a desire for self-destruction, a kind of suicidal longing. [*Yes*]

Occasionally, Negroes contend that the 1965 Watts riot and the other riots in various cities represented effective civil rights action. But those who express this view always end up with stumbling words when asked what concrete gains have been won as a result. At best, the riots have produced a little additional antipoverty money allotted by frightened government officials and a few water sprinklers to cool the children of the ghettos. It is something like improving the food in the prison while the people remain securely incarcerated behind bars. [*That's right*] Nowhere have the riots won any concrete improvement such as have the organized protest demonstrations.

And when one tries to pin down advocates of violence as to what acts would be effective, the answers are blatantly illogical. Sometimes they talk of overthrowing racist state and local governments and they talk about guerrilla warfare. They fail to see that no internal revolution has ever succeeded in overthrowing a government by violence unless the government had already lost the allegiance and effective control of its armed forces. Anyone in his right mind knows that this will not happen in the United States. In a violent racial situation, the power structure has the local police, the state troopers, the National Guard, and finally the army to call on, all of which are predominantly white. [*Yes*] Furthermore, few, if any, violent revolutions have been successful unless the violent minority had the sympathy and support of the nonresisting majority. Castro may have had only a few Cubans actually fighting with him and up in the hills [*Yes*], but he would have never overthrown the Batista regime unless he had had the sympathy of the vast majority of Cuban people. It is perfectly clear that a violent revolution on the part of American blacks would find no sympathy and support from the white population and very little from the majority of the Negroes themselves.

This is no time for romantic illusions and empty philosophical debates about freedom. This is a time for action. [*All right!*] What is needed is a strategy for change, a tactical program that will bring the Negro into the mainstream of American life as quickly as possible. So far, this has only been offered by the nonviolent movement. Without recognizing this, we will end up with solutions that don't solve, answers that don't answer, and explanations that don't explain. [applause]

And so I say to you today that I still stand by nonviolence. [Yes] And I am still convinced [applause], and I'm still convinced that it is the most potent weapon available to the Negro in his struggle for justice in this country.

And the other thing is, I'm concerned about a better world. I'm concerned about justice; I'm concerned about brotherhood; I'm concerned about truth. [That's right] And when one is concerned about that, he can never advocate violence. For through violence you may murder a murderer, but you can't murder murder. [Yes] Through violence you may murder a liar, but you can't establish truth. [That's right] Through violence you may murder a hater, but you can't murder hate through violence. [All right, that's right] Darkness cannot put out darkness; only light can do that. [applause]

And I say to you, I have also decided to stick with love, for I know that love is ultimately the only answer to mankind's problems. [Yes] And I'm going to talk about it everywhere I go. I know it isn't popular to talk about it in some circles today. [No] And I'm not talking about emotional bosh when I talk about love; I'm talking about a strong, demanding love. [Yes] For I have seen too much hate. [Yes] I've seen too much hate on the faces of sheriffs in the South. [Yea] I've seen hate on the faces of too many Klansmen and too many White Citizens Councillors in the South to want to hate, myself, because every time I see it, I know that it does something to their faces and their personalities, and I say to myself that hate is too great a burden to bear. [Yes, that's right] I have decided to love. [applause] If you are seeking the highest good, I think you can find it through love. And the beautiful thing is that we aren't moving wrong when we do it, because John was right, God is love. [Yes] He who hates does not know God, but he who loves has the key that unlocks the door to the meaning of ultimate reality.

And so I say to you today, my friends, that you may be able to speak with the tongues of men and angels [All right]; you may have the eloquence of articulate speech; but if you have not love, it means nothing. [That's right] Yes, you may have the gift of prophecy; you may have the gift of scientific prediction [Yes sir] and understand the behavior of molecules [All right]; you may break into the storehouse of nature [Yes sir] and bring forth many new insights; yes, you may ascend to the heights of academic achievement [Yes sir] so that you have all knowledge [Yes sir, yes]; and you may boast of your great institutions of learning and the boundless extent of your degrees; but if you have not love, all of these mean absolutely nothing. [*Yes*] You may even give your goods to feed the poor [*Yes sir*]; you may bestow great gifts to charity [*Speak*]; and you may tower high in philanthropy; but if you have not love, your charity means nothing. [*Yes sir*] You may even give your body to be burned and die the death of a martyr, and your split blood may be a symbol of honor for generations yet unborn, and thousands may praise you as one of history's greatest heroes; but if you have not love [*Yes, all right*], your blood was split in vain. What I'm trying to get you to see this morning is that a man may be self-centered in his self-denial and self-righteous in his self-sacrifice. His generosity may feed his ego, and his piety may feed his pride. [*Speak*] So without love, benevolence becomes egotism, and martyrdom becomes spiritual pride.

I want to say to you as I move to my conclusion, as we talk about "Where do we go from here?" that we must honestly face the fact that the movement must address itself to the question of restructuring the whole of American society. [*Yes*] There are forty million poor people here, and one day we must ask the question, "Why are there forty million poor people in America?" And when you begin to ask that question, you are raising a question about the economic system, about a broader distribution of wealth. When you ask that question, you begin to question the capitalistic economy. [*Yes*] And I'm simply saying that more and more, we've got to begin to ask questions about the whole society. We are called upon to help the discouraged beggars in life's marketplace. [*Yes*] But one day we must come to see that an edifice which produces beggars needs restructuring. [*All right*] It means that questions must be raised. And you see, my friends, when you deal with this, you begin to ask the question, "Who owns the oil?" [*Yes*] You begin to ask the question, "Who owns the iron ore?" [*Yes*] You begin to ask the question, "Why is it that people have to pay water bills in a world that's two-thirds water?" [*All right*] These are words that must be said. [*All right*]

Now, don't think you have me in a bind today. I'm not talking about communism. What I'm talking about is far beyond communism. [*Yeah*] My inspiration didn't come from Karl Marx [*Speak*]; my inspiration didn't come from Engels; my inspiration didn't come from Trotsky; my inspiration didn't come from Lenin. Yes, I read the *Communist Manifesto* and *Das Kapital* a long time ago [*Well*], and I saw that maybe Marx didn't follow Hegel enough. [*All right*] He took his dialectics, but he left out his idealism and his spiritualism.

And he went over to a German philosopher by the name of Feuerbach, and took his materialism and made it into a system that he called "dialectical materialism." [*Speak*] I have to reject that.

What I'm saying to you this morning is, communism forgets that *life* is individual. [*Yes*] Capitalism forgets that *life* is social. [*Yes, go ahead*] And the kingdom of brotherhood is found neither in the thesis of communism nor the antithesis of capitalism, but in a higher synthesis. [*Speak*, applause] It is found in a higher synthesis [*Come on*] that combines the truths of both. [*Yes*] Now, when I say questioning the whole society, it means ultimately coming to see that the problem of racism, the problem of economic exploitation, and the problem of war are all tied together. [*All right*] These are the triple evils that are interrelated.

And if you will let me be a preacher just a little bit. [*Speak*] One day [applause] . . . One night, a juror came to Jesus [*Yes sir*], and he wanted to know what he could do to be saved. [*Yea*] Jesus didn't get bogged down on the kind of isolated approach of what you shouldn't do. Jesus didn't say, "Now Nicodemus, you must stop lying." [*Oh yeah*] He didn't say, "Nicodemus, now you must not commit adultery." He didn't say, "Now Nicodemus, you must stop cheating if you are doing that." He didn't say, "Nicodemus, you must stop drinking liquor if you are doing that excessively." He said something altogether different, because Jesus realized something basic [*Yes*]: that if a man will lie, he will steal. [*Yes*] And if a man will steal, he will kill. [*Yes*] So instead of just getting bogged down on one thing, Jesus looked at him and said, "Nicodemus, you must be born again." [applause]

In other words, "Your whole structure [*Yes*] must be changed." [applause] A nation that will keep people in slavery for 244 years will "thingify" them and make them things. [*Speak*] And therefore, they will exploit them and poor people generally economically. [*Yes*] And a nation that will exploit economically will have to have foreign investments and everything else, and it will have to use its military might to protect them. All of these problems are tied together. [*Yes*, applause]

What I'm saying today is that we must go from this convention and say, "America, you must be born again!" [applause, *Oh yes*]

And so, I conclude by saying today that we have a task, and let us go out with a divine dissatisfaction. [*Yes*] Let us be dissatisfied until America will no longer have a high blood pressure of creeds and an anemia of deeds. [*All right*] Let us be dissatisfied [*Yes*] until the tragic walls that separate the outer city of wealth and comfort from the inner city of poverty and despair shall be crushed by the battering rams of the forces of justice. [Yes sir] Let us be dissatisfied [Yes] until those who live on the outskirts of hope are brought into the metropolis of daily security. Let us be dissatisfied [Yes] until slums are cast into the junk heaps of history [Yes], and every family will live in a decent, sanitary home. Let us be dissatisfied [Yes] until the dark yesterdays of segregated schools will be transformed into bright tomorrows of quality integrated education. Let us be dissatisfied until integration is not seen as a problem but as an opportunity to participate in the beauty of diversity. Let us be dissatisfied [All right] until men and women, however black they may be, will be judged on the basis of the content of their character, not on the basis of the color of their skin. [Yea] Let us be dissatisfied. [applause]

Let us be dissatisfied [Well] until every state capitol [Yes] will be housed by a governor who will do justly, who will love mercy, and who will walk humbly with his God. Let us be dissatisfied [applause] until from every city hall, justice will roll down like waters, and righteousness like a mighty stream. [Yes] Let us be dissatisfied [Yes] until that day when the lion and the lamb shall lie down together [Yes], and every man will sit under his own vine and fig tree, and none shall be afraid. Let us be dissatisfied [Yes], and men will recognize that out of one blood [Yes] God made all men to dwell upon the face of the earth. [Speak, sir] Let us be dissatisfied until that day when nobody will shout, "White Power!" when nobody will shout, "Black Power!" but everybody will talk about God's power and human power. [applause]

And I must confess, my friends [Yes sir], that the road ahead will not always be smooth. [Yes] There will still be rocky places of frustration [Yes] and meandering points of bewilderment. There will be inevitable setbacks here and there. [Yes] And there will be those moments when the buoyancy of hope will be transformed into the fatigue of despair. [Well] Our dreams will sometimes be shattered and our ethereal hopes blasted. [Yes] We may again, with tear-drenched eyes, have to stand before the bier of some coura- geous civil rights worker whose life will be snuffed out by the dastardly acts of bloodthirsty mobs. [Well] But difficult and painful as it is [Well], we must walk on in the days ahead with an audacious faith in the future. [Well] And as we continue our charted course, we may gain consolation from the words so nobly left by that great black bard, who was also a great freedom fighter of yesterday, James Weldon Johnson [Yes]:

Stony the road we trod [Yes],
Bitter the chastening rod
Felt in the days
When hope unborn had died. [Yes]
Yet with a steady beat,
Have not our weary feet
Come to the place
For which our fathers sighed?
We have come over a way
That with tears has been watered. [Well]
We have come treading our paths
Through the blood of the slaughtered.
Out from the gloomy past,
Till now we stand at last [Yes]
Where the bright gleam
Of our bright star is cast.

Let this affirmation be our ringing cry. [*Well*] It will give us the courage to face the uncertainties of the future. It will give our tired feet new strength as we continue our forward stride toward the city of freedom. [*Yes*] When our days become dreary with low-hovering clouds of despair [*Well*], and when our nights become darker than a thousand midnights [*Well*], let us remember [*Yes*] that there is a creative force in this universe working to pull down the gigantic mountains of evil [*Well*], a power that is able to make a way out of no way [*Yes*] and transform dark yesterdays into bright tomorrows. [*Speak!*]

Let us realize that the arc of the moral universe is long, but it bends toward justice. Let us realize that William Cullen Bryant is right: "Truth, crushed to earth, will rise again." Let us go out realizing that the Bible is right: "Be not deceived. God is not mocked. [*Oh yeah*] Whatsoever a man soweth [*Yes*], that [*Yes*] shall he also reap." This is our hope for the future, and with this faith we will be able to sing in some not too distant tomorrow, with a cosmic past tense, "We have overcome! [*Yes*] We have overcome! Deep in my heart, I did believe [*Yes*] we would overcome."

5.

ROY WILKINS
(1901–1981)

Speech on the National Advisory Commission
on Civil Disorders

National Press Club, Washington, D.C.—April 2, 1968

Roy Wilkins was one of the most powerful and influential civil rights leaders of the twentieth century. In the peak decades of the American civil
rights movement—the 1950s and '60s—Wilkins led the nation's oldest
and largest civil rights organization, the National Association for the Advancement of Colored People (NAACP). He helped oversee the NAACP's
landmark legal campaign against segregated schools. He worked closely
with President Lyndon Johnson to help pass groundbreaking civil rights
laws. But in the later 1960s, many younger African Americans grew impa-
tient with the seemingly slow pace of social change. They disdained older
moderates like Wilkins, who worked within the nation's power structures.
In turn, Wilkins denounced the revolutionary rhetoric of the Black Power
movement, calling it a new form of racism.

Wilkins worked as a journalist before joining the NAACP. In the course
of his civil rights career, he developed what the *New York Times* described
as a "mastery of the geography and mechanics of power in Washington."[1]
Wilkins used his organizational and political skills to expand the NAACP
from some twenty-five thousand members to nearly half a million people.
He traveled extensively to organize NAACP chapters, raise money, and

take part in demonstrations, while pressuring Congress and the courts to make good on the Constitution's promise of equality for all Americans.

Wilkins was well known and widely respected, but he did not possess the charisma of leaders such as Martin Luther King Jr. or Stokely Carmichael. "Roy wasn't the . . . one out front," veteran civil rights lawyer Joseph Rauh said. "He was the one in the back who got things done."[2] He was a complicated man. Historian Patricia Sullivan describes him as "ambitious, hard-working—the ultimate organization man." Yet, she writes, "He was also thin-skinned and could be petty and vindictive."[3]

Wilkins was born in 1901 in St. Louis, Missouri. His parents were both from the Deep South and were college graduates, which was unusual for blacks from that region at the time. Before Wilkins was born, his father moved the family to St. Louis from Mississippi looking for work. The only job his father could find was operating a brick kiln. Wilkins's mother died of tuberculosis when he was four years old, and his father sent him and his two siblings to live with relatives in St. Paul, Minnesota. Wilkins grew up there, living in a mostly Scandinavian neighborhood, attending an integrated high school, where he edited the student newspaper. While blacks were not the social equals of whites, Wilkins experienced little in the way of formal segregation. "I was sheltered," he said about the relatively benign racial climate in Minnesota. "A tremendous shock was waiting for me."[4]

Wilkins studied sociology at the University of Minnesota and worked on his college newspaper as well as a St. Paul weekly for African Americans. Meanwhile, he paid his way through school by working at a slaughterhouse and as a waiter on Pullman train cars. After school let out for the summer of 1920, "I lost my innocence on race once and for all."[5] Three black circus hands were lynched in Duluth, Minnesota, 150 miles north of the Twin Cities. The men were accused of raping a young white woman, although a doctor's report found no evidence to support the charge. The killings made national headlines. They stunned Wilkins into realizing, for the first time, how vulnerable he was as a black man in white America, even in a Northern state like Minnesota.

After graduating in 1923, Wilkins moved to Kansas for a job on the *Kansas City Call*, a black newspaper. He experienced Southern-style racism for the first time—segregated streetcars, churches, movie theaters, and the like. "Kansas City ate my heart out," Wilkins said. "It was a Jim Crow town through and through."[6] As a reporter and then as managing editor, Wilkins campaigned against racist laws and politicians. He became active in the local chapter of the NAACP, an organization his family in St. Paul had belonged to from its earliest days.

Wilkins's activism in Kansas City got the attention of Walter White, the national head of the NAACP. In 1931, White hired Wilkins to work at the organization's headquarters in New York. His first assignment was to conduct undercover research into poor working conditions for black laborers on a federally funded flood-control project in Mississippi. Wilkins's findings led to a federal investigation and improved conditions. In 1934, Wilkins took up the leadership of the NAACP's long-running crusade against lynching. The campaign was credited with raising national awareness about the atrocities and eventually ending the practice.

Wilkins was also deeply involved in organizing and raising money for the NAACP's decades-long legal assault on segregation. Starting in the 1930s, teams of NAACP lawyers filed lawsuits in courts across the land— and especially in the South—to fight discrimination in the voting booth, in housing and education, and in law enforcement. Wilkins was not a lawyer. He was the man who paid the bills, organized the staff, and drummed up public support. Still, he said his "crowning glory" was the 1954 U.S. Supreme Court decision *Brown v. Board of Education*, which banned public school segregation.[7]

The NAACP elevated Wilkins to the top post of executive director when longtime leader Walter White retired in 1955. Wilkins's tenure marked the high point of NAACP influence in American politics. As the 1960s unfolded, the NAACP fought for the right of activists to engage in nonviolent protests. It frequently supplied bail money and legal help to people who were arrested in demonstrations. Wilkins took part in many of the historic civil rights protest marches, including those in the South headed by King. Wilkins also helped organize the massive March on Washington in 1963. But historian Simon Hall says the NAACP under Wilkins was "lukewarm" to protest as a tactic. Wilkins and the organization preferred to labor within the political system, Hall says, "in an attempt to win support for progressive legislation by lobbying congressmen and by using litigation to strike down segregation laws."[8]

Wilkins cultivated an especially close relationship with President Johnson. He helped Johnson drive the historic 1964 Civil Rights Act and the 1965 Voting Rights Act through Congress. "[Johnson] called me before each of his major speeches on civil rights and after each civil rights crisis, and there were plenty," Wilkins wrote in his autobiography, *Standing*

Fast.[9] Johnson, according to one reporter, "needed an influential black he could trust as much as Mr. Wilkins needed the power of the presidency to push civil rights programs through Congress."[10]

But in the mid-1960s, young people on the front lines of the freedom struggle in the South were losing faith in the federal government. From their perspective, Johnson wasn't doing enough to protect them and the local African American activists who were getting beaten, jailed, and lynched by white racists. Stokely Carmichael and others called for a new, militant, "Black Power" movement. They encouraged armed self-defense and the exclusion of whites from formerly integrated civil rights groups.

Wilkins publicly condemned the Black Power slogan at the NAACP's 1966 national convention. He said it was "dangerous naïveté" to endorse racial separatism. He said that blacks should seek "legitimate" political power within the democratic system, "but it ought never to be ethnic or racial."[11] Black Power, Wilkins warned, would result in "black death."[12]

Roy Wilkins's nephew Roger Wilkins was an assistant attorney general in the Johnson administration and thirty years younger. "When I heard him utter the words 'Black Power means black death,' I knew he lost the youth," Roger Wilkins wrote. "Roy knew how to grab a headline, and he got it across the nation. I was sorry about it."[13]

Young activists branded Wilkins an Uncle Tom and a tool of the establishment. "We're putting down white help, not seeking it, like Wilkins does," one young black activist told a reporter. "Wilkins has made himself irrelevant to the blacks. Worse, he is helping our enemies."[14]

Wilkins responded to his critics with a "cool, understated disdain." In a 1969 interview, he said he understood and shared the impatience for change among younger African Americans. Nevertheless, Wilkins said, "They should have some idea of what it has taken to get them their right to raise hell. And before there's a final victory, it will take more than just loud talk."[15] In his autobiography, Wilkins dismissed the young and relentless critics. "There was nothing to do but wait them out," he wrote.[16] He had the ear of the president and the confidence of other powerful people in Washington, the only place, he believed, lasting change could really be accomplished.

When he retired from the NAACP in 1977, Wilkins was seventy-six years old. The civil rights movement, and Wilkins's own organization, had been through a decade of decline. But he was widely praised for the half century of tireless and often thankless work he contributed as a civil rights executive—a man who kept the engine of the freedom movement running. In 1969, Lyndon Johnson honored Wilkins with the Presidential Medal of Freedom. After Wilkins's death, Congress awarded him the Congressional Gold Medal.

Wilkins gave this speech in 1968 in response to the findings of the National Advisory Commission on Civil Disorders. The commission (also known as the Kerner Commission, after the chairman of the panel) examined the 1967 race riots in the United States. Its report famously declared, "Our nation is moving toward two societies, one black, one white—separate and unequal."[17] The report found that white racism was "essentially responsible" for creating black fury in the nation's ghettos.[18] President Johnson had created the commission and appointed Wilkins as one of its eleven members. But the president was unhappy with the Kerner Commission's findings and never formally accepted or acted on them. "I was disappointed with him," Wilkins wrote.[19]

The Sunday before the speech, Johnson surprised the nation by announcing that he would not seek reelection. His administration was crippled by the unpopular war in Vietnam and social divisions at home. Two days after Wilkins made this speech, Martin Luther King Jr. was assassinated in Memphis, Tennessee.

I MUST APOLOGIZE FOR THIS TALK. I write my own material, as the people in the entertainment world say. I don't think this is entertainment, but at least I write my own material. I don't say I don't trust my public relations man, but I think I can do it better. [*laughter*]

It's a great honor to be here today at the National Press Club and to have this opportunity of sharing with you an estimate of one or two phases of the report of the President's Commission on Civil Disorders. No one of the eleven members of the President's Commission imagined at their introduction meeting on July 29, 1967, that they would bring forth a report on March 1st, 1968, which would draw an introduction by a member of the press in these words: "Reading it is an ugly experience, but one that brings finally something like the relief of beginning. What had to be said has been said at last." Tom Wicker of the Washington bureau of the *New York Times* wrote that introduction to the widely circulated paperback edition. His "at last" referred to the principal distinction of this report from others of its kind, that is, it found white racism—what it called a "most fundamental matter"—the racial attitude and behavior of white Americans toward black Americans. "White racism," it went on to say, "is essentially responsible for the explosive mixture which has been accumulating in our cities since the end of World War II."

This indictment has been received with skepticism in many quarters of the white population, even with impassioned dissent. Yet it is true. The commission report, in the section on "Why did it happen," declares, "Race prejudice has shaped our history decisively in the past. It now threatens to do so again." Surely it is not necessary to remind this select and knowledgeable gathering that while the commission indictment goes only to World War Two, it might as well have gone back to 1619. For since the day the first slaves were landed 350 years ago next year, American life has been marked by the most subtle and sophisticated—as well as the most brutal—policies and practices of racial differentiation.

I need only remind the men here that it was not until 1952 that white official Washington, and black-protesting Washingtonians, agreed to abide by the decision in a test court action to determine, if one pleases, whether Negro American citizens could freely utilize all places of public accommodation in the capital city of the world's greatest democratic nation. The skeptics might turn also to the Constitution of the United States, Article One, Section Two, on the apportionment of representatives in the new Congress, where the phrase "other persons" occurs. Slaves, that is, were to be counted as three-fifths of a man.

Or, take the unthinking acceptance as a matter of course of the item related by the late George Sessions Perry, of the separate Negro school in his Texas hometown. The school was across the creek, and the only path over the water for the Negro schoolchildren was via a log, not a bridge. It was not until after several children had fallen into the water, and after annual petitions by Negro parents to the school board, that a footbridge was finally built. The inferior and often intolerable position of the Negro was so much a part of the mores of the majority population that many millions of them, in the North as well as in the South, are bewildered now as they were then at the charge of racism.

Obviously, it is not possible to discuss here a seven-hundred-page report on the 1967 riots in our cities. In addition to the indictment on racism, the keeping of law and order, in the light of approaching summer—a long hot summer, some say, and a long cool summer, others say—of 1968, merits some attention.

Frankly, the reports from over the country, and the incidents that have occurred thus far, are ominous in their portent. Too many officials in key state and local positions are interpreting "riot control" and "law and order" to mean a crackdown, racially, on Negro Americans—young and old, in the North, South, East and West. A story that we'll knock down is one in which an unnamed police chief is said to have told his mayor, "Last year, Mr. Mayor, we did it your way, and we spoiled them. This year, dammit, we're going to do it our way, and they'd better behave."

The policeman on the beat has a hard job. He must make split-second decisions which often involve his own life. He has to try to recall the Constitution and its Bill of Rights, together with state and local laws. He has to decide whether a Negro lad has committed, or is about to commit, a felony. Whether he is a prankish teenager or a dangerous drug addict. No one envies a policeman his job.

But in the racial tension stalking the land, our policemen must be doubly careful, must bend over backwards in racial situations. The commission report declares, almost invariably, the incident that ignites disorder arises from police action. It calls the role of the police "difficult" and "significant." In nineteen out of twenty city studies, the probers on the police question found Negroes complaining of a variety of matters, from physical and verbal abuse to discrimination in employment and the promotion of Negroes on police forces.

And just last week out of Oakland, California, the Oakland chapter of the NAACP announced an "Adopt a Cop" plan for the Negro community. And it said, with its tongue in its cheek, "Since we can't get into the police force, and they will not hire any Negro policeman, let's have the Negro community 'Adopt a Cop,' and get acquainted with the policemen who *are* on the force."

When policemen stop a Negro in a traffic matter, as they did in Watts in 1965, and in Newark in 1967, the wrong word, a faulty judgment, or some other surfacing of a white attitude, instead of a police attitude, can erupt into a disorder. Judging by reports, many governments are bent on legitimizing the past errors of the police in racial situations. Some incredible legislation has been proposed to absolve, automatically, law enforcement officers for any maiming or killing they may do in the course of a disturbance. Such proposals are nothing less than hunting licenses. Armored cars, personnel carriers, automatic weapons, tanks, and mounted weapon carriers are not riot-control equipment. They are weapons of destruction and have no place in an urban community.

Irrespective of the catchwords and the hot rhetoric of the would-be provocateurs, we are not at war in our cities. The weapons of warfare have no place there. Moreover, the type of mind that either condones or encourages warfare upon the Negro community has no place in public life. It is a menace to white citizens as well as to black. The adoption of its alleged reasoning would convert our country into a police state. Individual freedom would be no more.

But you say, "Must not law prevail?" Most certainly so. But with justice. Without justice, law is meaningless. Preserving civil peace, says the report, is the first responsibility of government. Individuals cannot be permitted to endanger the public peace and safety. Our society is founded on a rule of law, and that rule must prevail. And then the report warned solemnly that we must be careful not to sacrifice the rule of law in the name of order. And that, precisely, is what the crackdown theory on alleged Negro rioters would do: sacrifice the rule of law in the name of order.

Already this year, the nation has had a preview of the new force that is in prospect. At a Negro college in Orangeburg, South Carolina, three students were killed by shots fired *into* the campus by state policemen. The students were not out on the town. They were on their own campus. The state officers claimed they were being fired upon and they thought the fire came from the students. In Memphis, a march in support of the striking Negro rubbish collectors erupted into violence despite the nonviolent doctrine of the Reverend Dr. Martin Luther King Jr., who led the march. One teenager was killed. These two samples are two too many. If this type of action becomes general this summer, then the country is in for an uneasy season.

Now there is an attempt to justify stern riot-control measures by citing the wildly racist pronouncements of some vocal members of what may be termed the Black Bloc. A few of these, wounded deeply in spirit and intoxicated with their own words, or with the emotional response of their bands of followers, have called for destruction. They have declared war on white people. They have even issued uncamouflaged appeals for Negroes to get guns, *shoot* white people. They yell for burning down the town, and tearing up the town. They are so hurt, so outraged, and so frustrated that they preach the very thing that has brought them to their unhappy state—namely, racial hate.

It is easy for the uninformed white man on the street and for the white politician who bends with every wind to react in kind. And office holders, smugly intoning law and order, and that more chilling phrase, "crime in our streets," can push for an almost blank check in both funds and activity for law enforcement bodies. Our memories are so short, and our prejudices and fears are so long, that we already have forgotten that the official state probe of the 1967 Newark, New Jersey, riot condemned the police for the use of *excessive force*. Already we have forgotten that in Newark, the widely reported sniping by Negroes was found to be the police shooting at each other. We fail to remember that of twenty-six persons arrested for sniping in Detroit, twenty-three were freed promptly, without trial, for lack of evidence. Two were tried and acquitted, and the trial of one is still pending.

In the face of all this and much more that can be found in the commission report and in its as-yet-unpublished files, too many cities and states are permitting the far-out threats of a tiny sliver of the Negro population to convert our urban communities into battlefields, complete with troops, command posts, general headquarters, deployed weaponry, communication centers, and the horrifying war implements of destruction.

The separatists among Negroes are another minuscule but vocal minority. This preachment has become a comfort to both whites and blacks. It has been seized upon by those white people who secretly desire nothing more in this world, and more fervently, than that Negro Americans be completely separated off from the white population. There are jubilant rejoicings in white families and living rooms across the nation, as young, wounded, and misguided Negroes intone or shriek—as the case may be—that they want black neighborhoods controlled by black people. To many, many white people, this seems too good to be true. An unverified story from a northeastern city is that certain of the city fathers faced with the knotty problem of providing quality integrated public education quietly egged on several organized Negro groups who were yelling for black control and black teachers for black children. The whites never had it so good, psychologically. Here they can appear to be acceding reluctantly to a demand that all along has been their innermost wish. Thanks to a small but vociferous coterie of Negroes, no penalty is attached to white acquiescence, now, in racial separation.

The separatists are but an infinitesimal part of the 22 million Negroes in America. Prior efforts, just after the Civil War, and in the 1920s under the colorful Marcus Garvey, to stimulate Negro migration back to Africa were conspicuously unsuccessful. At the present time, with most of Africa free, the black Africans want their land for themselves.

The other day in Detroit, a handful of persons (of a number that would be disdained by a storefront church) proclaimed themselves a black nation, elected a Negro who is now a resident of communist China as president, and announced that it would seek the allocation of five Southern states, including

Alabama, Georgia, Mississippi, and Louisiana, to be the *new nation*. I hope none of you own any property in those states. [*laughter*] Although they announced boldly that they had never been citizens of the United States, they were vague on the question of whether they would renounce that which they deny they possess, namely their U.S. citizenship.

More tragic than this is the theory that has been sold to many young and ill-informed Negroes that the way to group strength is through a return to the very separation from the mainstream of life that has brought about their present weakness and disadvantage. These young people are, in reality, running away from the competition of life in the world of men. They seek, instead, regression into the comforting world of their accustomed ghettos. Here, they think, the rounded and emotional experience of "soul" will compensate for the harsh corners, the fast track, and the demanding standards of the white world outside.

They will come—softly, I hope—to disillusionment, for the world is the world. Standards are standards, not white or black. And people in the race of life are people, whatever their color. It is just as tough in Lagos, or Accra, or Nairobi, as it is in lower Manhattan, or in Pocatello, Idaho, or in New Orleans.

No, separatism and hate do not mark the path to racial peace and to mutual progress. We must have, instead, the implementation of the recommendations of the Commission on Civil Disorders. It found, and I quote, "pervasive discrimination and segregation" in the all-important areas of employment, housing, public education, the administration of justice, and health and welfare. These differentiations must be attacked with new and imaginative vigor and on a vast scale.

Our president, who stunned us all Sunday night, has pointed the way for the nation to proceed out of the thicket of racial injustice and conflict. If we Negroes had been asked to guess what Lyndon Baines Johnson would do on the nettlesome issue of racial and civil rights, ninety-nine percent of us would have looked at his place of origin, Texas, listened to his accent, which is far from that of New England, and shrugged our shoulders in negative resignation. Yet this man has been better in pronouncement and in performance on America's old and emotional problem of race than any other president in our history. [applause]

He has been forthright on racial discrimination in housing, in education, and employment. He has struck at poverty, the Negro's great enemy. He has sponsored legislative action aimed at the ills of the cities, where seventy percent of all Americans live and seventy-three percent of the Negroes live. To his credit, he has the Voting Rights Act of 1965, which has armed the Negro minority, in the states where they are an important element of the population, with the ballot as a weapon to speed their escalation toward full and participating citizenship.

To this vital ranging of the high and powerful office of the presidency behind the steps to racial justice must be added the encouraging findings of a poll by *Fortune* magazine, published in January 1968. More than seventy percent of the Negroes interviewed felt that the chances of solving the race problem were good and that the general situation was better today than five years ago. More than sixty percent were opposed to violence, with the percentage among young Southern Negroes up to eighty-five percent. Ninety-seven percent wanted what? Number one, more education for their children. Ninety-three percent wanted desegregation in employment and in schools. Eighty-seven percent wanted a better job. And sixty-nine percent, surprisingly, wanted better police protection where they live. And I say "surprisingly" because very few people understand that when we talk about crime in the streets, and crime by Negroes, we forget that most crime is committed against Negroes, not against white people. The rapes, the murders, the burglaries, the looting, the robberies are committed by Negroes on Negroes. And so this sixty-nine percent has asked for better police protection where they live.

So then, my friends, the course is clear. The commission report said we need not continue the movement toward two societies—one white, one black, separate and unequal. The alternative, it said, is not blind repression or capitulation to lawlessness. It is the realization of common opportunities for all within a single society. This alternative, it went on, will require a commitment to national action, compassionate, massive, and sustained, backed by the resources of the most powerful, and the richest, nation on earth. From every American, it will require new attitudes. And above all, new will.

The communications media, the press, radio, and television, can help create that new attitude, that new will. Understanding is essential, and understanding depends upon education. The commission report recognizes the vital role of the media in this explosive issue. It calls, as I and every other earnest Negro American now call, for skillful and dedicated education by the media, to the end that our founding dream of one, indivisible nation, with liberty and justice for all, becomes a reality.

6.

Benjamin E. Mays
(1894–1984)

Eulogy for Martin Luther King Jr.

Morehouse College, Atlanta, Georgia—April 9, 1968

Benjamin E. Mays was a prominent educator, minister, and civil rights activist. He said his life's greatest honor was that he was able to serve as a mentor to Martin Luther King Jr. For nearly three decades (1940–1967), Mays was president of Morehouse College, a respected black school for men in Atlanta. King was a Morehouse graduate and once described Mays as "my spiritual mentor and intellectual father."[1] Mays was a guiding influence to other notable Morehouse men, too, including Andrew Young and Julian Bond.

Benjamin Mays was the child of former slaves. He was born on an isolated South Carolina cotton farm in 1894. His parents were sharecroppers. The darkest years of Jim Crow segregation were just descending on the South; humiliation, mob violence, and lynching by whites were common threats for African Americans. Mays learned at an early age the searing lessons of racial inferiority. He had a vivid memory of being stopped with his father by a group of armed, white men on horseback. "I remember starting to cry," Mays wrote. "They cursed my father, drew their guns, and made him salute, made him take off his hat and bow down to them several times. Then they rode away. I was not yet five years old, but I have never forgotten them."[2]

Mays was the youngest of eight children. At the time, school terms for black farm children lasted only four winter months. Mays and his siblings spent the rest of the year working in the fields. Mays was eager for "book learning." Before he even started school, an older sister taught him the alphabet and how to count to one hundred. At the one-room Brickhouse School, Mays was such a devoted student he sometimes wept when bad weather kept him home.

As a young boy, Mays also discovered his power to move an audience through words. In his autobiography, *Born to Rebel*, he remembered reciting the Sermon on the Mount at age nine and getting a standing ovation from his church congregation.

Few black farm children in the South went beyond grade school. Mays's father initially resisted Benjamin's hunger to keep learning. But Mays prevailed, enrolling in the high school attached to all-black South Carolina State College. He graduated as class valedictorian in 1916. Mays attended Bates College in Maine, paying his tuition with scholarships, loans, and summer work as a Pullman railroad porter.

Over the next two decades, Mays taught at black colleges, became ordained as a Baptist minister, and earned his PhD in ethics and theology from the University of Chicago. In the early 1930s, Mays helped conduct an influential study of African American churches in the United States. In 1934 he became dean of the School of Religion at Howard University in Washington, D.C. In 1940, Mays was named president of Morehouse College.

Mays stressed academic excellence, leading Morehouse to become one of just four Georgia colleges to qualify for a chapter of the honor society Phi Beta Kappa. Mays fought for the integration of Atlanta's public schools and of all-white colleges, but he insisted on the continuing value of historically black institutions like Morehouse. Frank Prial of the *New York Times* described Mays as "a voice of moderation in the critical years of the civil rights movement." Prial says Mays "attacked white liberals who paid only lip service to racial equality, but he criticized, too, black extremists such as the Black Panthers."[3]

Mays's speaking style is credited with influencing Martin Luther King's legendary power of oratory. Mays favored the use of eloquent phrases, quotations, and names of heroic men and women from history. Mays has been described as an intellectual "whose speaking style, though full-voiced and dramatic, did not compromise his fundamentally reasoned interpretation of life and religion."[4]

Mays retired from Morehouse in 1967 and served on the Atlanta School Board for more than a decade. He died in 1984 at the age of eighty-nine. He and his wife, Sadie, had no children. In a newspaper obituary, Atlanta mayor Andrew Young remembered his former teacher as a "strong, tall, brisk-walking intellectual giant."[5]

Mays gave this eulogy for King at an open-air service on the Morehouse campus. The memorial followed King's funeral service at Ebenezer Baptist Church, where King had served as a co-pastor with his father. The crowd at Morehouse was estimated at more than 150,000 people, including King's widow and children. The event was broadcast live on national radio and television. Mays was seventy-three years old at the time. He and King had made an agreement, he explained, that if one should die, the other would give the homily at his funeral. Thus, the teacher spoke in memory of the student.

At the time of the memorial service, King's assassin was still at large. James Earl Ray was arrested two months later.

TO BE HONORED BY being requested to give the eulogy at the funeral of Dr. Martin Luther King Jr. is like asking one to eulogize his deceased son, so close and so precious was he to me. Our friendship goes back to his student days here at Morehouse. It is not an easy task. Nevertheless, I accept it with a sad heart and with full knowledge of my inadequacy to do justice to this good man. It was my desire that if I predeceased Dr. King, he would pay tribute to me on my final day. It was his wish that if he predeceased me, I would deliver the homily at *his* funeral. Fate has decreed that I eulogize him. I wish it might have been otherwise, for after all, I am three score years and ten, and Martin Luther is dead at thirty-nine. How strange.

God called the grandson of a slave on his father's side, and the grandson of a man born during the Civil War on his mother's side, and said to him, "Martin Luther, speak to America about war and peace. Speak to America about social justice and racial discrimination. Speak to America about its obligation to the poor. And speak to America about nonviolence."

Let it be thoroughly understood that our deceased brother did not embrace nonviolence out of fear or cowardice. Moral courage was one of his noblest virtues. As Mahatma Gandhi challenged the British Empire without a sword and won, Martin Luther King Jr. challenged the interracial injustice of his country without a gun. And he had faith to believe that he would win the battle for social justice. I make bold to assert that it took more courage for Martin Luther to practice nonviolence than it took his assassin to fire the fatal shot. The assassin is a coward. He committed his dastardly deed and fled. When Martin Luther disobeyed an unjust law, he accepted the consequences of his actions. He never ran away and he never begged for mercy. He returned to Birmingham jail to serve his time.

Perhaps he was more courageous than soldiers who fight and die on the battlefield. There is an element of compulsion in their dying. But when Martin Luther faced death, again and again, and finally embraced it, there was no external pressure. He was acting on an inner urge that drove him on. More courageous than those who advocate violence as a way out, for they carry weapons of destruction for defense. But Martin Luther faced the dogs, the police, jail, heavy criticism, and finally death. And he never carried a gun, not even a pocketknife to defend himself. He had only his faith in a just God to rely on, and his belief that "thrice is he armed who has his quarrels just." The faith that Browning writes about when he says:

> One who never turned his back but marched abreast forward,
> Never doubted the clouds would break,
> Never dreamed, though right were worsted, wrong would triumph,
> Held we fall to rise, are baffled to fight better,
> Sleep to wake.

Coupled with moral courage was Martin Luther King Jr.'s capacity to love people. Though deeply committed to a program of freedom for Negroes, he had a love and concern for all kinds of people. He drew no distinction between the high and the low. None between the rich and the poor. He believed, especially, that he was sent to champion the cause of the man farthest down. He would probably say, "If death had to come, I am sure there was no greater cause to die for than fighting to get a just wage for garbage collectors." This man was supra-race, supra-nation, supra-denomination, supra-class, and supra-culture. He belonged to the world and to mankind. Now he belongs to posterity.

But there is a dichotomy in all this. This man was loved by some and hated by others. If any man knew the meaning of suffering, King knew.

House bombed. Living day-by-day for thirteen years under constant threats of death. Maliciously accused of being a communist. Falsely accused of being insincere and seeking limelight for his own glory. Stabbed by a member of his own race. Slugged in a hotel lobby. Jailed thirty times. Occasionally deeply hurt because his friends betrayed him. And yet this man had no bitterness in his heart, no rancor in his soul, no revenge in his mind. And he went up and down the length and breadth of this world preaching nonviolence and the redemptive power of love.

He believed in all of his heart, mind, and soul that the way to peace and brotherhood is through nonviolence, love, and suffering. He was severely criticized for his opposition to the war in Vietnam. It must be said, however, that one could hardly expect a prophet of King's commitment to advocate nonviolence at home and violence in Vietnam. Nonviolence to King was total commitment, not only in solving the problems of race in the United States but in solving the problems of the world.

Surely, surely this man was called of God to his work. If Amos and Micah were prophets in the eighth century B.C., Martin Luther King Jr. was a prophet in the twentieth century. If Isaiah was called of God to prophesy in his day, Martin Luther was called of God to prophesy in his day. If Hosea was sent to preach love and forgiveness centuries ago, Martin Luther was sent to expound the doctrine of nonviolence and forgiveness in the third quarter of the twentieth century. If Jesus was called to preach the Gospel to the poor, Martin Luther was called to bring dignity to the common man. If a prophet is one who interprets in clear and intelligible language the will of God, Martin Luther King Jr. fits that designation. If a prophet is one who does not seek popular causes to espouse, but rather the causes which he thinks are right, Martin Luther qualifies on that score.

No, he was not ahead of his time. No man is ahead of his time. Every man is within his star. Each man must respond to the call of God in his lifetime and not somebody else's time. Jesus had to respond to the call of God in the first century A.D., and not in the twentieth century. He had but one life to live. Jesus couldn't wait. How long do you think Jesus would have had to wait for the constituted authorities to accept him? Twenty-five years? A hundred years? A thousand? Never? He died at thirty-three. He couldn't wait.

Paul, Copernicus, Martin Luther the Protestant reformer, Gandhi, and Nehru couldn't wait for another time. They had to act in their lifetime. No man is ahead of his time. Abraham, leaving his country in obedience to

God's call. Moses leading a rebellious people to the Promised Land. Jesus dying on a cross. Galileo on his knees recanting at seventy. Lincoln dying of an assassin's bullet. Woodrow Wilson crusading for a League of Nations. Martin Luther King Jr. fighting for justice for garbage collectors. None of these men were ahead of their time. With them, the time is always ripe to do that which is right [*Amen*] and that which needs to be done. [*That's right*]

Too bad, you say, Martin Luther Jr. died so young. I feel that way too. But as I have said many times before, it isn't how long one lives, but how well. Jesus died at thirty-three. Joan of Arc at nineteen. Byron and Burns at thirty-six. Keats and Marlowe at twenty-nine. And Shelley at thirty. Dunbar before thirty-five. John Fitzgerald Kennedy at forty-six. [*Yes*] William Rainey Harper at forty-nine. And Martin Luther King Jr. at thirty-nine. It isn't how long, but how well.

We all pray that the assassin will be apprehended and brought to justice. But make no mistake, the American people are, in part, responsible for Martin Luther King's death. [*That's right*] The assassin heard enough condemnation of King and Negroes to feel that he had public support. [*Tell it, yes sir*] He, he knew that there were millions of people in the United States who wished that King was dead. [*That's right*] He had support. [*Yes sir*]

The Memphis officials must bear some of the guilt for Martin Luther King's assassination. [*Yes sir*, applause] The strike should have been settled [*Yes sir*] several weeks ago. [*Yes*] The lowest-paid men in our society should not have to strike to get a decent wage. A century after Emancipation [*Speak, sir*], and after the enactment of the Thirteenth, Fourteenth, and Fifteenth Amendments [*Yes sir*], it should not have been necessary for Martin Luther King Jr. to stage marches in Montgomery, Birmingham, [*Yeah*] Selma, and go to jail thirty times, trying to achieve for his people those rights which people of lighter hue get by virtue of the fact that they are born white. [*Yes sir*]

We, too, are guilty of murder. [*Speak, sir*] It is a time for the American people to repent and make democracy equally, equally applicable to all Americans. What can we do? We and not the assassin, we and not the prejudiced, we and not the apostles of hate, we represent, here today, America at its best. [*All right*] We have the power to make democracy function so that Martin Luther King and his kind will not have to march.

What can we do? If we love Martin Luther King, and respect him, as this crowd surely testifies, let us see to it that he did not die in vain. [*Yes sir, amen,* applause] Let us see to it that we do not dishonor his name by trying to solve our problems through rioting in the streets. [*Amen*] Violence was foreign to his nature. [*Yes sir, that's right*] He warned that continued riots could produce a fascist state. But let us see to it, also, that the conditions that cause riots are promptly removed, as the president of the United States is trying to get us to do. Let black and white alike search their hearts. And if there be any prejudice in our hearts against any racial or ethnic group, let us exterminate it, and let us pray, as Martin Luther would pray if he could, "Father, forgive them, for they know not what they do." [*Amen, preach it*]

If we do this, Martin Luther King Jr. will have died a redemptive death for which all mankind will benefit. Morehouse will never be the same because Martin Luther came by here. And the nation and the world will be indebted to him for centuries to come. It is natural, therefore, that we here at Morehouse, and Doctor Gloster, would want to memorialize him to serve as an inspiration to all students who study in this center. I close by saying to you what Martin Luther King Jr. believed. If physical death was the price he had to pay to rid America of prejudice and injustice, nothing could be more redemptive. And, to paraphrase the words of the immortal John Fitzgerald Kennedy, permit me to say that Martin Luther King Jr.'s unfinished work on earth must truly be our own. [*Amen*, applause]

7.

KATHLEEN CLEAVER
(1945–)

Speech delivered at Memorial Service
for Bobby Hutton

Merritt Park, Oakland, California—April 12, 1968

Kathleen Cleaver was the first woman to become a highly visible leader in the militant Black Panther Party and one of the few women to emerge as a nationwide symbol of the Black Power movement. From 1967 to 1971, Cleaver was the Panthers' communications secretary. She worked closely with her husband, Eldridge Cleaver, and other Panther leaders to expand the ranks of the party nationwide, while fending off a secret FBI campaign to destroy the Panthers.[1]

Kathleen Neal was born in Dallas, Texas, in 1945. She grew up in a well-educated, middle-class family. Her father, a sociologist, joined the Foreign Service when Neal was a girl; she spent half her childhood living abroad. Neal attended a Quaker high school near Philadelphia and graduated with honors. She was a talented student, but in 1966 she dropped out of Barnard College in New York to work full time on civil rights issues with the Student Nonviolent Coordinating Committee (SNCC). The Black Power movement was on the rise, and Neal wanted to be a part of it. Like many young African Americans in the mid-1960s, she was fed up with what she considered the limited gains made by the civil rights movement. She embraced the potential of the Black Power movement to push

African Americans toward full self-determination and to contest, as she said, "the remaining legacy of racial slavery."[2]

At a SNCC conference in 1967, Neal met Eldridge Cleaver, a radical intellectual who was on parole from California's Soledad Prison. Cleaver had been convicted of rape and served nearly a decade in prison. He was completing a book of essays on race issues he wrote while in jail. Cleaver's *Soul on Ice* was published to significant acclaim and became a classic of Black Power literature. Kathleen says that at the SNCC conference, Eldridge "was thrilled to be around those civil rights organizers whose courage had inspired him from afar, and the revolutionary atmosphere he encountered among us captivated him."[3]

Kathleen Neal also captivated him. Eldridge convinced Kathleen to join him in San Francisco to work for the Black Panther Party. He had begun to work with the party as minister of information shortly after his release from prison. "What appealed to me about the Black Panther Party was that it took th[e] position of self-determination and articulated it in a local community structure," Kathleen Cleaver told Henry Louis Gates Jr. in a 1997 interview. "[It] had a program, had a platform and an implementation [strategy] through the statement of how blacks should exercise community control over education, housing, business, military service."[4] Kathleen and Eldridge married in December 1967.

As the most prominent woman in the Black Panther Party, Kathleen Cleaver was often asked about the role women played in the organization. She always responded that it was the same role as a man's. For Kathleen, the only relevant question was simply, "Where can I go to get involved in the revolutionary struggle?"[5] According to Cleaver, her activism was built on the work of a long line of African American women who had come before. In a 2001 essay, "Women, Power, and Revolution," Cleaver writes that while growing up, she was inspired by women like Gloria Richardson, Diane Nash, and Ruby Doris Robinson, all of whom led daring assaults on Southern segregation. According to Cleaver, "These women were unfurling a social revolution in the Deep South."[6]

Cleaver's mission was to unfurl a revolution in the rest of the United States. As she writes, "Those of us who were drawn to the early Black Panther Party were just one more insurgent band of young men and women who refused to tolerate the systematic violence and abuse being meted out to . . . blacks. When we looked at our situation, when we saw the violence, bad housing, unemployment, rotten education, unfair treatment in

the courts, as well as direct attacks from the police, our response was to
defend ourselves. We became part of that assault against the capitalist
powers."[7]

Kathleen Cleaver was a skilled organizer and Panther spokesperson.
She created the position of communications secretary based on what she
had seen activist Julian Bond do in SNCC. As Cleaver writes, "I organized
demonstrations. I wrote leaflets. I held press conferences. I attended
court hearings. I designed posters. I appeared on television programs, I
spoke at rallies."[8]

One of those rallies was held in honor of Bobby Hutton, a seventeen-
year-old Panther killed by police in an Oakland, California, shoot-out. In
her speech, Cleaver describes Hutton as a martyr for black liberation and
laments the tyranny of the criminal justice system. More than a thousand
people attended the memorial service in Oakland's Merritt Park. As Kathleen spoke, her husband Eldridge was in jail in nearby Vacaville. He had
fought the police alongside Hutton and had been wounded. He was arrested for violating his parole.

The gunfight was part of an escalating series of confrontations between Panthers and law enforcement officials.[9] Beginning in August 1967,
FBI director J. Edgar Hoover ordered a wide-ranging counterintelligence
program designed to "expose, disrupt, misdirect, discredit, or otherwise
neutralize" the Black Panther Party and other black liberation groups.[10]
The code name was COINTELPRO. Enlisting local law enforcement agencies nationwide, the FBI "declared war on the Panthers."[11] Their tactics
included infiltrating the party, sowing mistrust and conflict among members, and planting false and misleading stories in the media.[12] In 1968
alone, the police killed at least eight Panthers in Los Angeles, Oakland,
and Seattle. The next year they arrested 348 Panthers "for a range of of-
fenses, among them murder, rape, robbery, and assault."[13] In 1969, the
police and FBI killed at least ten other Panthers, including two in Chicago
who were shot in their sleep.[14]

Eldridge Cleaver continued to have his own troubles with the law. He
was released from the prison in Vacaville in June 1968 but was ordered to
return to jail at the end of November to serve out the rest of his original
prison sentence. On November 24, 1968, Eldridge disappeared, fleeing
first to Cuba and then to Algiers. Kathleen joined him there in June of
1969, just in time to give birth to their first child, Maceo. The next year,
she gave birth to a daughter, Joju. The Cleavers lived in exile until 1975,

when they decided to come home. Eldridge had undergone an enormous conversion, abandoning his revolutionary principles and embracing Christianity. He was ready to surrender, serve time, and move on.

In the late 1970s, Eldridge became well known as a politically conservative, born-again Christian. Kathleen, meanwhile, retained her radical views. The two separated in 1981, and she moved with her children to New Haven, where she earned her BA and law degrees from Yale University. Kathleen went on to practice law and to teach at several schools, including Emory University in Atlanta. Despite her own move into the ranks of the middle class, Cleaver has remained deeply critical of capitalism.

The Black Panther Party was all but dead by the end of 1971, destroyed in part by the FBI, in part by internal disagreements and confrontations. As the scholar Ward Churchill writes, "Both the relative inexperience of its leadership and the obvious youthfulness of the great majority of its members helped prevent the Party from mounting a mature response to the situation it confronted." However, Churchill continues, "The scale and intensity of the repression to which it was subject . . . make it doubtful that even the most seasoned group of activists would have done better."[15]

Kathleen Cleaver says another reason the Panthers failed to incite revolution in the United States has to do with capitalism itself. According to Cleaver, too many Americans had a financial stake in maintaining the status quo. "When you have people who are revolutionaries," she told Henry Louis Gates in 1997, "they repudiate the commitment to making money, and say, 'We want justice. We want change. We want truth. We want freedom.' Well, that's not going to work if the structure [of society] is based on financial rewards and financial incentives. So we were at odds with the way the system worked. We had a different idea. We said, 'Power to the people.' "[16]

MY FIRST REACTION UPON finding out about the attack upon the leadership of the Black Panther Party April 6th was that I was glad that I was not a widow for black liberation.

Here I have a message, a telegram that I think I'd like to read, from the widow of our greatest spokesman for black liberation, Malcolm X. It's to the family of Bobby James Hutton, in care of myself.

The question is not will it be nonviolence versus violence, but whether a human being can practice his God-given right to self-defense. Shot down like a common animal, he died a warrior for black liberation. If the generation before him had not been afraid, he perhaps would be alive today. Remember, like Solomon, there's a time for everything. A time to be born, a time to die; a time to love, a time to hate. A time to fight, and a time to retreat. For brotherhood and survival, remember Bobby. It could be your husband, your son, or your brother tomorrow. Crimes against an individual are often crimes against an entire nation. To his family: only time can eliminate the pain of losing him, but may he be remembered in the hearts and minds of all of us. Betty Shabazz.

Whatever path we seem to take, it always has one end: a racist bullet. A racist bullet murdered Malcolm X, murdered Martin Luther King, murdered Bobby Hutton. Attempted to murder Huey Newton; attempted to murder Eldridge Cleaver. From the streets, from the flying of this bullet in the air into the flesh of a black man, a whole structure proceeds: walls of courthouses, bars of jails, locked keys, billy clubs, police.

Everywhere you turn, you're encaged. The same police force, the very same police force that murdered Bobby Hutton in cold blood, deliberately, provided a funeral escort to the cemetery. The very same police force that attempted to assassinate Eldridge Cleaver is minding the highways from here to Vacaville, stacked deep. The town of Vacaville is closed down. There's double security on the penitentiary. Machine-gun guards in the church.

One bullet in the flesh is not enough; fifty policemen in the streets of West Oakland is not enough for them. Right over there in the parking lot they've got seven hundred policemen, waiting.

Huey Newton—there on the tenth floor of the Alameda County Courthouse—Huey Newton held the key to liberating the black people. He stated if the racist-dog policemen do not withdraw from the black community, cease their wanton murder and torture and brutality of black people, they will face the wrath of the armed people.

For the simple demand—basic human liberty—Huey Newton is in jail, charged with murder. Bobby Hutton is dead. Eldridge Cleaver is in jail, charged with three counts of assault with attempt to murder. David Hilliard, national captain of the party, is in jail, three counts of murder. And a series of other brothers in the Black Panther Party. This is only the first. They move against every leadership as it extends itself. As each group of leaders rises up their [inaudible], but they cannot stop [us] by wiping away our leaders. For every leader that's shot down, more spring up, until the people rise up as one man and fight and gain their liberation, and this is what this one man, Bobby Hutton, died for.

We lost something very precious when we lost Bobby Hutton. But Bobby Hutton didn't lose anything. Bobby Hutton took his stand; he gave his life. And here we are, we have our lives. He added something to them. It's up to us, to whether we can treasure that and carry that forward, or if we'll allow the walls of the jails and bullets of the racist dog police to increasingly intimidate and encircle and murder us until we degenerate into a state maintained purely by brute police power. This time, this day, is not far off. We have very little time. We are in a race against time.

Huey Newton, Eldridge Cleaver, and Bobby Hutton. Thank you.

8.

BOBBY SEALE
(1936–)

Speech delivered at the Kaleidoscope Theater

Los Angeles, California—April 16, 1968

Bobby Seale was chairman of the Black Panther Party during the most violent, tumultuous period of the Black Power movement. Beginning in late 1966, Seale helped expand the reach and influence of the Panthers from their home base of Oakland, California, to more than thirty cities nationwide. The Panthers engaged in militant rallies, hair-raising confrontations with police, and community service programs aimed at helping the poor. They preached armed self-defense against police brutality and revolution against white power structures, quickly topping the FBI's list of national threats.[1] For a time, Bobby Seale and the Black Panthers represented "the face of the new radicalism," historian Peniel Joseph writes. "Comprised of reformed troublemakers, college students and ex-cons, the Panthers brandished guns and law books in an effort—sometimes quixotic—to foment revolution from below."[2]

Bobby Seale was born in Dallas, Texas, in 1936. He says he "grew up just like any other [black] brother," in a family that never had much money.[3] The family eventually moved to Berkeley, California, and lived in a housing project that Seale remembers as crowded and dirty. As a teenager, Seale joined the air force but was discharged for bad conduct.

The turning point in Seale's life came in 1962, when he met Huey Newton, a fellow student at Merritt College in Oakland. Seale was deeply impressed with Newton's intellect, his revolutionary views on politics, and his willingness to use violence to change society. According to Seale, many left-wing activists he knew shied away from using weapons, but Newton said, "You must pick up guns, because guns are key."[4]

Bobby Seale and Huey Newton formed the Black Panther Party on October 15, 1966. Fed up with police brutality and the tyranny of poverty in black America, they devised a ten-point program to empower African Americans and give them control of their own communities. As they started to organize, Seale said, "We began to understand the unwritten law of force. They, the police, have guns, and what the law actually says ain't worth a damn. We started to think of a program that defines and offsets this physical fact of the ghetto. I view black people in America as a colonial people. Therefore we have to arm ourselves and make the colonial power give us our freedom."[5]

Many of the Panthers' demands were similar to those of mainstream civil rights leaders, including full employment, decent housing, and better schools. But other parts of the ten-point platform were far more radical. The Panthers wanted all African Americans released from jail because, they said, black people could not get fair and impartial trials in American courts. They also demanded an exemption of all black men from the draft. As Seale and Newton wrote, "We believe that Black people should not be forced to fight in the military service to defend a racist government that does not protect us. We will not fight and kill other people of color in the world who, like Black people, are being victimized by the White racist government of America."[6]

Malcolm X was their greatest inspiration, but Seale and Newton were also influenced by the ideas of Marx, Lenin, and Mao Tse-tung's *Little Red Book*. They raised money to buy guns by selling Mao's book—a guide for political revolution—to Berkeley college students.[7]

The Panthers' early activities included audacious "defense patrols." Seale and Newton organized small bands of Panthers to intercept police radio calls and learn when an arrest was taking place. The band then "rushed to the scene of the arrest, and, armed with a law book, informed the person being arrested of his constitutional rights." Newton continues, "Party members also carried loaded weapons, publicly displayed but not pointed toward anyone, and dressed in leather jackets and berets."[8]

These patrols displayed a courage and bravado that earned the Panthers local street credibility.

Bolder tactics quickly earned them national attention. The first was a daring march to the California Capitol in Sacramento, where legislators were considering a bill to restrict carrying loaded weapons in public. Brandishing guns, Bobby Seale and more than twenty other Panthers filed into the Capitol building to protest the bill. "As they marched grimly down the immaculate halls," wrote journalist Sol Stern, "secretaries and tourists gaped and then moved quickly out of the way. By the time they were halfway down the corridor, every reporter and cameraman in the building had gathered; they stayed in front of the Panthers, moving backward, snapping pictures as they went."[9] Confrontations like these, along with speeches that called for executing cops, led FBI director J. Edgar Hoover to describe the Panthers as the country's "most dangerous and violence-prone of all extremist groups."[10]

But within four years, the Panthers went into a steep and permanent decline. A combination of FBI sabotage, troubled finances, and internecine battles sapped their energy. Along with scores of other Panthers, Seale and Newton faced dogged harassment by police.[11] In late October 1967, Newton was arrested and charged with killing a white police officer during a traffic stop. He was found guilty of voluntary manslaughter. A massive "Free Huey" campaign brought the Panthers greater national attention and support, but Newton stayed in jail for almost three years until he was released pending a new trial. In his absence, Eldridge Cleaver helped lead the party in an even more militant and revolutionary direction.

Meanwhile, Seale faced his own legal battles. Seale had played a small role in the protests that rocked the 1968 Democratic National Convention in Chicago, yet he was indicted—along with seven white radicals—for conspiring to incite a riot. At his trial in Chicago in the fall of 1969, Seale refused to use the lawyer appointed to him by Judge Julius Hoffman. In a series of daily courtroom standoffs, Seale repeatedly disrupted court proceedings, demanding the right to represent himself and declaring Judge Hoffman a racist. Judge Hoffman finally ordered Seale to be "bound, shackled, and gagged for future courtroom proceedings."[12] On November 5, 1969, the judge declared a mistrial and then cited Seale on sixteen counts of contempt of court. He sentenced him to four years in prison. As Seale was hauled away by marshals, the audience in the courtroom shouted "Free Bobby! Free Bobby!"[13] In May 1971, Bobby Seale was acquitted when a new conspiracy trial ended in a hung jury. In 1970–71, Seale and a co-defendant also faced a first-degree murder charge in the case of a Panther operative who was tortured and killed for allegedly working as government spy. That trial also ended in a hung jury.

By the time Seale got out of jail, the Black Panther Party had been crippled by killings, arrests, and ugly turf battles. Seale himself was battle-weary. He eventually turned to local politics, running for mayor of Oakland in 1973 and nearly defeating the white Republican incumbent. Seale went on to lecture about his involvement in the Panthers and to sell his own cookbook, *Barbeque'n with Bobby*.

The violent showdowns and dramatic trials that defined the Black Panthers on the national stage overshadowed the urban "survival programs" they ran to help the poor. These included a free breakfast program that offered meals to as many as two hundred thousand children, free health clinics, clothing giveaways, and numerous other community-based initiatives. "What is often forgotten," Peniel Joseph argues, "is that cofounders Huey P. Newton and Bobby Seale were college students and fledgling community organizers who cared deeply about the survival of the black community."[14]

When Seale delivered this speech at the Kaleidoscope Theater in Los Angeles, he was mourning the death of one of the people who had come from that community, a young man named Bobby Hutton. Seale had become a mentor to Hutton in 1966, when Seale was running a youth-oriented antipoverty program in Oakland. At the age of sixteen, Hutton was the first person to officially join the Black Panther Party. Hutton was shot during a gunfight with police in Oakland on April 6, 1968, just two days after Martin Luther King Jr. was assassinated.

The event at the Kaleidoscope was sponsored by the Peace and Freedom Party. It featured the party's candidate for U.S. Senate from California, social critic Paul Jacobs, as well as comedian Dick Gregory. Six hundred people, many of them white, crammed into the theater to listen and to grieve.[15]

THE MEMORIAL THAT WE just left—or had—the other day in Oakland, California, in racist USA, was preceded by a funeral that was held for Brother Bobby Hutton. And at this funeral, one of the preachers there began to get himself uptight and began to check the situation out, doing his best not to do anymore Tomming, stated that there was a man—a little story he's told—a man who was wandering in the hills and in the woods, and he was looking for a spring that was supposed to have clear water where he could get a drink, because he was thirsty. He was very, very thirsty.

And he found a spring that was very, very muddy and dirty and filthy. The water wasn't clear, so he began to sit down and try to get in some clear, clean water, by trying to clear the spring out. He went through all kind of hassles and changes trying to clear the spring out, so he could get him a clear drink of water from the spring.

And another man came along and said, "What are you trying to do?" He says, "I am trying to get me a clear drink of water here. I've been thirsty for a long, long time, and I can't seem to get the dirt and the filth and the mud and the dirt that's here in this spring cleared out to get me a clear drink of water."

The man said, "Well the reason you can't do that," he says, "is because on top of the hill about a mile or two back, where you haven't checked out yet," he said, "there's a hog in the spring." He said, "There's a hog in the spring, and a lot of little pigs are running around too in the spring." All we want is a little freedom. All we want is a clear drink of water, but there's a hog in the spring." [applause, cheering]

Look, how should we try and how should we work to get the hog out of the spring? Now the spring has been running dirty for a long, long time for peoples in Vietnam, for peoples in Africa, our black brothers, for our black brothers and colored brothers and sisters in South America and Asia and the Caribbean, etc., throughout this world. Where three-quarters of the world who are nonwhite have been brutalized and beaten and exploited and colonialized, etc., by this racist power structure here in America. The hog has got to be removed from the spring. [applause]

You can sit by, and many times you might say, "Well, the spring is really not that dirty." But if you are so close to the hog and you have a tendency to sit by and think it's a game that's going on, while the hogs and the pigs dirty the spring, while you enjoy yourself, looking at the hogs and the pigs dirty the spring where the clear water is, where is the freedom that we want? And you think it's a game, you're jiving and you're shucking, you're shucking yourselves, and these young Black Panthers here and many others and many, many other thousands of people who are joining the Party now are concerned with removing that hog from the spring.

Now how do we do it? For a long, long time we struggled. Brother Martin

Luther King gave us a tactic, and this tactic, the tactic that he used, was exhausted. And it was exhausted with a racist bullet taking his life.

Brother Bobby Hutton, a member of the Black Panther Party, hasn't yet exhausted his means, but yet he was killed by the same kind of racist bullet. Pigs. Hungry, exploiting, robbing thuggish pigs. A whole power structure and all its racism.

We have to fight it, we have to deal with this hog. We have to deal with this pig. We have to deal with and understand the situation. We have to understand that when Huey P. Newton says that power is the ability to define phenomena and make it act in a desired manner, that when Huey P. Newton gives this functional definition of power, he's talking about power in the real sense. He's not talking about green power, which is a shuck.

Green power? Just ask the question: green power? As Huey P. Newton teaches, he says that the North had Yankee money and the South had Confederate money—both had green power. The North also had organized guns and force and the South also had organized guns and force. But the North using many, many black men and many, many slaves—ex-slaves, or slaves—outmaneuvered the South and had all the guns and force.

Power is the ability to define phenomena and make it act in the desired manner. The North defined the South's money as not being money anymore, and they burned it in the streets. The only power that was there was the organized guns and force.

It was the organized guns and force. Money is only a tool by which power is manipulated. We've seen this happen with the racist white power structure and what it's done to the world.

Racist America, the Congo, and oppressed people of South Africa. Africa, Liberia, Ghana, Guinea, South America. Cuba, where a valiant revolutionary struggle went down. China, where a most valiant revolutionary struggle went down against all forms of exploitation and is still going down in relation to the world's struggle, of black people and people to be free. All across this world we can see what racism is doing, and all across this world right here in America, you can see what black people are getting ready to do. To begin to stop racism.

Do I have to talk about the fact that Rockefeller's subsidiaries in the banking industry take out twenty-seven percent of the net profits out of South Africa? Do I have to talk about the fact that fifty-five percent of the surplus uranium that came to the United States from 1955 to 1962 came from South Africa, while a black man works in a mine making $260 a year

and a white man doing the same damn job makes $3,360 a year? Do we have
to go through these facts that are scattered throughout the world, these type
of examples to get you to understand what's going down? [applause]

Do I have to lay out to you again the platform of the program of the Black
Panther Party? Do I have to get you to understand what we mean by black
liberation in this country? Do we have to get you to understand the necessity
of black people taking up arms to defend themselves against racist attack in
this country? Well damn it, if I have to do it, we're going to do it. Here we
are, all right, come on now! [Audience member yells, cheering, applause]

Listen, in our program it states—if you haven't read it you begin to read
it, you begin to understand it. This program is not outlined for the white
community; it's outlined for the black community. Now, number one: we
want power to determine our own destiny in our own black communities.
Number two: we want full employment for our people. Number three: we
want decent housing fit for shelter of human beings. Number four: we want
an end to the robbery by the white men of the black people in the black
communities. Number five: we want decent education that teaches us about
the true nature of this racist, decadent system and education that teaches us
about our true history and our role in society and the world. Number six: we
want all black men to be exempt from military service. [applause] Number
seven: we want immediate end of police brutality and murder of black people. [applause] Number eight: we want all black men and women to be released from county jails, prisons, federal, state, what have you, because they
have not had fair trial, they have been tried by all-white juries. [applause]
Number nine: we want all people when brought to trial to be tried in a court
by their peer groups or people from their black community as defined by
your jive Constitution of the United States. [applause] Number ten, and
in summarization: we want some land, we want some bread, we want some
clothing, we want some education, we want some justice, and we want some
damn peace. [applause]

If I say I want peace, then you say, "Well, you should put down your
gun." But hasn't it occurred to you by now, after four hundred years of being
brutalized and murdered and lynched and maimed by guns and force on
the part of racists and the racist power structure in this country, it's damn
near time we picked up the gun to try to begin to get some peace, to defend
ourselves and our community from racist attacks by the pigs, to defend ourselves against racist attacks by Birchites, Minutemen, or Ku Klux Klansmen
or what have you?

Hasn't it occurred to you that it's damn near time we organize ourselves in some fashion to have some ability to begin to make racists and the racist power structure act in a desired manner, as we define the functional definition of what power is? The ability to define the situation—and we have been defining it. Now we must organize our black communities to also make the power structure of racism act in a desired manner.

And what is that desired manner? Politics, what is politics? What is politics? You think politics starts with a seat in the assembly? No, it doesn't. It's related to it, but it doesn't start there. Politics starts with a hungry stomach. Politics starts with a pig crushing us across our skull and murdering our people. Politics starts with the fact that we get a rotten education, and we get brainwashed and fooled into trick notion and trick knowledge and everything else that goes on with us in terms of the exploitation that goes down.

Politics starts with the fact that we want decent housing, fit for shelter of human beings! Now this is where politics starts. And black people now understand with the Black Panther Party that we are going to relate to politics in a real fashion. We are not going for no more jive verbal sincerity—at all. Don't give me Robert F. Kennedy, your jive shuck—"I think it is necessary here, that we come forth . . ." I don't want to hear it. [applause and laughter]

I'm tired of my black brother being brainwashed, to—"Kingfish, what did you think about John F. Kennedy or Robert Kennedy?" "Well, Andy, you know I'd go dere, boy, I think the boy is going to do something dere." Look, we are not going for that thing anymore. Robert F. Kennedy was well related to Robert Williams being put in a situation where he had to vamp from his country and split because he was being prosecuted by Robert F. Kennedy. [applause]

John F. Kennedy, John F. Kennedy did not send troops into Birmingham in 1963 until black people decided it was necessary for them to defend themselves. When Martin Luther King's motel was bombed, and the racists had been attacking us constantly in that particular area and all over this country, why didn't John F. Kennedy send some troops in? And he didn't send troops until *after* black people decide we're going to defend ourselves from racist attacks and went to the streets and whupped up a few racists' heads, then Robert—John F. Kennedy—decide to send in troops.

See, all that verbal "sincerity"—we learn from the past; we learn, so we are going to guide our feets by the lamps of the past, and we are going to make sure we aren't going to fall into more bags. So, peace and freedom, if you want to do something, get down to the nitty-gritty and don't miss no nits and grits. No more shucking and no more jiving with the McCarthys, with the "Lynchin'" Baines Johnsons, with the Governor Reagans, with the Robert F. Kennedy, right on down the line. No more shucking and jiving! [applause and whistles]

You want to support black liberation? You support the ten-part program of the Black Panther Party, that's what you support. [applause]

Freedom—we are not going to sit around and superficially and abstractly try to define freedom anymore. Black people, the mothers who scrub Miss Anne's kitchens and brought the shopping bags home full of the leftover ends. And the black brothers who try to do their best, who struggle in the system, who've been railroaded through the court system, et cetera. The black brothers on the block, young kids coming up, the crap that we get in the context of this racist system.

We are going to define our freedom, and we are going to define it by comparing with what we get in the future against what we don't have now. [applause] That's the way we are going to define our freedom. So, you are thrown into a position where you don't sit up to me and talking no more— [in a mocking voice] "I really feel for your situation." Uh, you know, "Really now, John, Negroes should be better off, but I really feel for your situation." I don't want to hear that crap. I "shouldn't be violent." OK, I shouldn't be violent. Some of you are so miseducated. Have we went into your communities and lynched you and murdered you? No. Racists have come into our communities throughout this country and lynched and murdered and brutalized us.

Have we gone into your community and intimidated you with any guns? No. Racists, pigs—cops, and racists have come in, intimidated and brutalized and murdered us. Did we design this racist power-structure system here that exploits and maims black people? No. They designed and used it against us; we didn't put it on you.

Now the next time you accuse us of [being] racist, you'd better check yourselves and see what the hell you're accusing. The Black Panther Party does not hate anybody because of the color of their skin. That's the game of the Ku Klux Klansmen, you check it out. [applause]

We will not, we will not stoop to the level of hating a person because of the color of their skin, because we understand where racism is manifested. It's not just manifested in some white man sitting in his community and saying, "You know, I don't like black people because of the color of their skin." Racism is manifested in the racist brutal murder and the racist bullet that killed Martin Luther King. The racist bullet that killed Bobby Hutton. The racist bullet that killed Medgar Evers. The racist bullet that killed and maimed and murdered black people across this country. The lynching. This is where racism is manifested, and you want to know what we hate? That's what we hate with a passion! [applause]

So where do you go from there? You look at the Black Panther Party; oh, they are going to attack you tomorrow. If you bring a gun down in a black community and started shooting at some black man, the brothers are going to shoot back. I'm sorry, you are going to get buckshot, twelve-oh, double-oh buck, .357 magnums. We're going to go for what we know. [applause and cheering]

Now you say we shouldn't. I say we're going to do it whether you like it or not. Now the rest of you who want to start dealing with the power structure on a level where you want to try to change the system, get on your gig. You'd better get on your gig. Because you are jiving. Before Watts, before the Black Rebellion in Watts, there were thirteen hundred cops; there's a little over six thousand pigs in this country now. And some seventy percent of them are directly concentrated in black communities controlling black people.

Oakland's pig force has been tripled since three and a half years ago, from three hundred fifty pigs to over a thousand pigs. San Francisco, doubling. Every major metropolis across this country, where black people live, the pig forces have been tripled, the national guards have been doubled. Now you check it out. Now who are they putting 'em out there for? For those of you out in Santa Monica? Don't be foolish. [laughter] They're out there for black people, with stunner guns and new equipment!

You understand politics enough to know that you've got to change that system. When Ronald Reagan sits up and chops up the little chicken feed or welfare programs at the same time, do you remember when he was doing that, he increased the highway patrolmen some fifteen hundred? You start thinking about seven or eight hundred dollars a month for a highway patrol- man salary—a month! Add that by twelve and you start thinking about the new cars and the new equipment, et cetera. And when Los Angeles County ask for forty-five or fifty or two hundred million dollars for the black com- munities so they can organize themselves, you know where it went to. It went to the increase of the Gestapo force that Reagan and the rest of these racist bastards and Lyndon Baines Johnson are putting all over this country. [applause]

So this is what we are dealing with: we're dealing with the reality. There's no more time to sit down and continue discussing as to whether or not the racist, white wall that black people are chained against is real or not. There's no more time to do that. It's time for you white people to get off in your white communities and begin to end racism, and we'll deal with it in our communities. [applause]

That's where you are going to work at. Don't come down in our communities trying to grow philodendrons and poppies, and don't come down in our communities talking about the "basic socioeconomic structure as it's related to the adverse condition that the black people is subjected to." Black brothers say, "I don't want to hear this crap. The best thing that you can do is get your hat, because I am thinking about robbing you." [laughter]

'Cause he don't want to hear it, and I don't blame him, so you stay in your *own* community. Because one of them brothers down there get to seeing you down there, he don't know. Some of them ain't run into the Panther Party, and they ain't been instructed not to rob you just yet. [laughter] The brother hasn't been instructed on the political relationship between you whites and the Peace and Freedom Party, et cetera.

So don't come down there. We'll take care of our community, 'cause we want *our* power in *our* community to determine our *own* destiny in our black communities. We want our own black police force chosen by black people, controlled [applause starts]—wait a minute, wait a minute—controlled by black people, and we're going to make one specific rule that while he's going be a member of the police department chosen from our black community, he's going to have to live in our black community in the areas that he patrols, because of this here. If he have to live there, he ain't going to be murdering and committing no police brutality 'cause he's got to come back home and sleep that night. [applause and cheering]

If that ain't giving a significant, symbolic understanding of having power to determine your own destiny in your own black community, I don't know what the hell is. That's a very significant point to start with. Point number seven of the program of the Black Panther Party deals specifically with the fact that black people should and do and are forming black self-defense groups to defend themselves against racist attacks on the part of the pig department and any other racists who come in our community.

So you see organized black brothers here, ready to do what they have to do to defend themselves against all forms of racist attacks. And this is where it's going. This is political. Power comes out of the barrel of a gun, and if you don't believe it, you jiving. You see that power structure up there? Where their power come from?

Every time they make a political decision upon any group of people's heads throughout this world or any local country or any local community and the people disagree with that political decision that's been made by the power structure, the power structure sends their guns and force to see that the political decisions that they've made is carried out.

Black people revolted in Watts; they revolved in Newark; they revolted in Detroit; they revolted all across this country. Rebellions, rebellions, rebellions. A hundred and fifteen rebellions before our black brother's death—King—and over a hundred-some-odd rebellions after his death. Those rebellions is the part and the voice of the people saying that we disagree with the oppressive conditions that we are in, and these oppressive conditions are caused by the political decisions that have been made on the part of the power structure. And each time, the power structure mobilizes guns and force to send in on the people.

So what should we do? Should we go there and sit in and slide in, roll in, jump in, beg in, pray in, wait in, boogaloo in? [laughter] No, because while we are doing all that and while we are singing "We Shall Overcome," some pig is keeping a beat on our head. "We shall [*beat*] overcome . . ." See what I mean? Crushing our skulls and we sitting there, "No, no, no." King has already said that "we shall overcome," so we are going to do it for real—overcome. [applause]

Now Mike is going to run for DA here. Mike says he's not a racist. As long as Mike doesn't act in a racist manner, we'll treat him as not acting like a racist, and that's that. We don't have to go through a long dissertation of bull crap, running around, concerning ourselves with whether or not the white wall, the white racist wall that we are chained against, is real or not. We are not going to talk about the molecular structure of the wall—"You know, the molecular structure of the wall really says, you know, that it's really ninety percent space, you know. Now is the wall really real or not?" And meanwhile these black men and all these black men up here with their arms chained against the wall saying, "You're damn right it's real. I want to get free from it." So the brother breaks one of the chains on the right. Newark, Detroit, Watts. Black rebellions across the country. A brother breaks the chain. Now are you still going to sit down and talk about whether or not the white racist wall is real or not? About the molecular and the atomic structure of it? No, you are not going to do it anymore, if you are not going to be a racist, you're not, 'cause you're going to pick up a crowbar, and you're going to start prying the rest of those spikes loose. Because we're coming off the wall, we're overcoming, we ain't jiving, it's going to be that way.

Every racist who comes into our community has to be driven out, by one means or another, and if you want to aid black liberation, you start working on some of them jive legislatures who supposedly represent you, who are jiving and shucking. You start working on that. [applause] And we come over here and say, "Look man, there's a special racist that's doing such and such and such and such," and we'll point it out 'cause we can define our situation. You come on down and get down to nitty-gritty and don't miss any nits or grits. It's time for you to move. Black people are on the move; all they need is organizing. We're coming. We're coming. We're coming!

We're not outnumbered. Around this world, black people and colored people are not outnumbered; we are outorganized by the racist, white power structure. *You* are outorganized. Antidraft demonstrators, don't tell me you don't know what police brutality is all about, when you were up there in Oakland in front of the draft office, the draft office that you were demonstrating against, what did that pig department do? They whupped your heads.

Right down here when they let LBJ come down here, they whupped your heads. And then you came to me, a black man, that says, "You know what, all that stuff he's talking about police brutality is really real, isn't it?" Uh huh. It's real as hell. [applause] We've been expressing it for four hundred years. [applause]

It's real. You disagree with the political decision that the power structure had made, the power structure sending violence and force upon your head. You see that, that it's basic political decision being carried out. You were there nonviolently. I mean you weren't violent, you were sitting there, and you were going to sit in front of the place real nonviolent-like, and you were going to say, "Well, you just have to arrest me."

The pigs didn't do that. They come down there with force and hit you upside your head. I was sitting in jail reading the racist *Oakland Tribune*, checking you out. I said, "I wonder what they learned." I just wondered. The brothers know. You noticed how you've got them big demonstrations going across the country, you was talking about them nonviolent, you didn't see that many black brothers in there, did you?

We've been knowing for four hundred years; we wasn't coming out there, we weren't coming out there at all. Besides, the rebellions that we've had in our communities, we would know what them pigs would do to us. Look, the platform of the program of the Black Panther Party only outlines the clear drink of water that we wanted, freedom. That's all. And we're saying that it's time—that it's time that people move forward to begin to stop racism, begin to deal with it. Now, [in a mocking voice] "How do I deal with it?"

Well you've been closer to the racists than we have! Start dealing with it. Learn! How do we deal with the racism that comes up on our heads? We're learning. The other night, we learned warfare through warfare from being attacked. In Oakland. The brothers did their best. The [police] had floodlights on their place. They put tear gas in that place, and they set a fire in the bottom of the basement. That's what they did. They forced some brothers in there by attacking them, and the brothers got off in there and went for what they knew.

AND WE LEARN WARFARE through warfare. We learn warfare through our brother's death—who died for our freedom, because he stuck with it, 'cause he believed in it. When Bobby Hutton walked out of that house, slightly before he walked out of the house, Eldridge Cleaver told him to take off all his clothes, man. Eldridge Cleaver's been in prison before, and he was quite hip to the racist system, and how they do things.

He said, "Because you won't get killed if you take off all your clothes." And young Bobby Hutton was just a little too modest and said, "Later for it, man," and didn't take off all his clothes. And the pigs say, "Now, nigger, run to the car—the squad car," and before he get there, they gunned him down.

Eldridge took off *all* of his clothes, every stitch, because he said, "If they shoot me and kill me . . . since we're being forced out. I can't see how to shoot 'cause of the water in my eyes, I can't see how to shoot with the floodlights, the tear gas is in here, and the fire is burning the place down, I've got to come out." He says, "So if they kill me, there won't be any bullet holes in my clothes." Eldridge is ready to leave that for you—that in case he did get murdered, you can understand racism in the real sense. Bobby Hutton left it for us.

Before Bobby Hutton died, before Bobby Hutton died, some five young brothers had been hit in Oakland, killed in Oakland. Young brothers—sixteen, seventeen, eighteen—three weeks prior to Bobby Hutton. Bobby Hutton made the sixth murder on the part of the pig department in a period of three, three and a half weeks. So this is the memorial for our black brother, Bobby Hutton.

Who is Bobby Hutton? Some of you probably might be thinking that we are saying that he's one of the first members that joined just because he got killed. That's not true. Bobby Hutton was one of the first members that joined. Even before the Black Panther Party was formed, I got Bobby Hutton a job at the local poverty program that I was working in—that I got fired at because I wouldn't go for the crap that they was putting down. Bobby Hutton took his money out of his pocket from that dollar-thirty-five-an-hour gig for thirty hours a week—and the gig is there to try to make him think that he shouldn't organize against the power structure but think the power structure is beautiful. Bobby Hutton took money out of his pocket to put the first officer up.

Huey P. Newton. Look, you read in the paper about a man committing a robbery or something and there's a shoot-out and someone is killed. You pass it off. But Huey P. Newton was stopped for a traffic ticket! And then a shoot-out occurred. That's a hell of a large gap that has to be filled! Especially when he's a political leader in the local community there; especially when we oppose the pig department. We patrol those cops up there with guns and force to make sure no brutality was committed. Huey P. Newton didn't murder anybody. If we wanted to murder a cop, we could have murdered them way back then—I'm talking about 1966, when we first started. They stopped Huey and held him down for twenty minutes! And tried to set him up for a killing, but they lost. The pigs lost. [applause]

Twenty minutes for a traffic ticket? It doesn't take twenty minutes to stop a man to give him a traffic citation. So we're going to have a trial in Oakland—May the sixth, that's Huey P. Newton's trial date, nine A.M. We say we want Huey P. Newton free, May sixth, nine A.M., Twelfth and Fallon, in Oakland. The national days of black protest to free Huey P. Newton, to free Eldridge Cleaver, to free David Hilliard, to free all the black political prisoners—Rap Brown, all of them, right in Oakland, fifty thousand in Oakland, May the sixth. Now how many of you coming up May sixth? [Yeah!]

Six days of trials, we are going to upset Oakland so bad, we're going to let the power structure know! Black people are going to be in the streets, black people are going to demonstrate. We can easily tell black people in Oakland to go home, and you know what they do? They go home.

We can easily tell black people to go to the streets, and you know what they do? They go to the streets. They say, "All right, the Black Panther Party is where it's at, and they want us to lead them politically, we're going to do that." So everybody should be in Oakland May the sixth for black protests against the power structure, to stand that we want Huey P. Newton to be set free, support black liberation, and we want Eldridge Cleaver free, et cetera. Fifty to a hundred thousand. Mayor Redding, Governor Reagan, Chief of Police Gaines in the City of Oakland, Cahill of San Francisco are all shook now because we've announced the fact that fifty thousand people—fifty thousand to a hundred thousand people are going to be in Oakland.

Now, is it so rough that you can't come there? What are you talking about? You demonstrated across this country a million strong. A million strong against the war in Vietnam. Now if you can't get up off your butts to come up *there* to demonstrate against the war against black people, then you're jiving and you're shucking me! [applause]

How many people we going to have up there to say, "We are going to stand for free Huey?" You want to stand up and say you're going to be there, or you want to sit down and contemplate it? May the sixth in the city of Oakland. Be there. [applause]

Now we want Huey free. We want to see where your money, where your mouth is at. You talk that talk, well get on up. 'Cause we say we're a winner and we are going to move on up. You got it? I want to thank you.

9.

ELLA BAKER
(1903–1986)

Speech to the Southern Conference Education Fund

New York City—April 24, 1968

Ella Baker was a master strategist and visionary in the civil rights movement. She was a guiding force for prominent movement leaders, such as Martin Luther King Jr. and Stokely Carmichael, and she fueled the work of several leading organizations in the freedom movement. Baker was regarded as a powerful and inspiring figure, but she consciously avoided the limelight. She believed that local African Americans could best lead themselves in their efforts to overturn Jim Crow segregation, rather than relying on charismatic preachers or outside experts. One activist praised Baker as "the mortar between the bricks," holding together the often unsettled foundations of the American civil rights struggle.[1]

Ella Josephine Baker was born in Norfolk, Virginia, in 1903 and raised in Littleton, North Carolina. She was the granddaughter of slaves, one of three children born into an extended family of modest means and strong social ideals. Her family valued faith, hard work, education, and duty to the community. Baker biographer Barbara Ransby says the family belonged to a particular class, "who saw themselves as representatives of the race to the white world and as role models for those less fortunate within the black community."[2] Baker's father was a railroad dining-car waiter. Her mother had been trained as a teacher. She managed the household, was active in church and women's groups, and groomed her children to be pious and respectable citizens. The family was hardly well-to-do, but they had much compared to the desperate poverty endured by so many other African Americans, and they believed much was expected of them in return. The drive to serve her people powered Ella Baker's life.

After attending the high school boarding program at all-black Shaw University in Raleigh, Baker got her BA in sociology from Shaw. She showed an early interest in activism, leading campus protests against strict social rules, such as a ban on silk stockings and the obligation to sing spirituals to visiting guests. After graduating in 1927, Baker moved to Harlem to live with a cousin and look for work. Although the Great Depression made jobs scarce, Baker thrived intellectually in the political and cultural ferment of the Harlem Renaissance. She helped organize the Young Negroes Cooperative League, a coalition of local cooperatives and buying clubs that banded together to increase their economic power. She was also involved in the federal Workers Education Project, the Harlem YWCA, the Women's Day Workers and Industrial Leagues, and other left-wing and pro-union organizations. Baker had many friends who were socialists and communists. She admired their principles and some of their organizing methods, but she never joined their parties.

In 1935, Baker went undercover to report on the dismal conditions of itinerant black domestic workers in New York. She posed as a job seeker among the black women who waited each morning on designated Bronx street corners for white women to hire them for a day of low-paid labor. The women workers were routinely approached by white men wanting to pay for sex. Baker co-authored an exposé titled "The Bronx Slave Market," which appeared in the NAACP's magazine, *Crisis*.

In 1940, Baker got a job working for the NAACP as a field organizer and later as a director of the organization's branches. For much of the 1940s, she traveled the South building membership and recruiting local leaders. Baker often spent half of each year on the road. Historian Charles M. Payne says Baker's vast travels for the NAACP were a kind of "practicum" in grassroots social change.[3] Early on, Baker recognized the dangers inherent in having well-educated outsiders arrive in local communities to organize. "Such a person gets to the point of believing that he *is* the movement," she said. "Such people get so involved with playing the game of being important that they exhaust themselves and their time and they don't do the work of actually organizing."[4] Over time, Baker began to chafe at the NAACP's bureaucracy and its egocentric national leader Walter White. She left the national organization in 1946 to care for a young niece but eventually took the helm of the New York City NAACP branch.

As the 1950s civil rights movement gathered steam in the South, Baker joined with New York activists Stanley Levison and Bayard Rustin to raise money in support of Martin Luther King Jr.'s Montgomery Improvement Association in Alabama and the group's city bus boycott. In 1957, Rustin and Baker traveled south to help the young King create a new organization that would coordinate protest activities across the region, the Southern Christian Leadership Conference (SCLC). Though Baker had misgivings about King's top-down leadership style, she signed on as the provisional director of the SCLC's voting rights campaign. With her years of ground-level organizing across the South, Baker had a wealth of local networks and connections to help spread the SCLC message.

After more than two years, Baker left the SCLC because she felt it had become excessively centered on King's persona and authority. Baker yearned for a genuinely grassroots, democratic way to make change. "It was the opportunity to dig in and work shoulder to shoulder with local activists that most appealed to Baker," Ransby writes. "Local people would be there long after she had gone. In the final analysis, [she felt] the major political decisions had to be theirs."[5]

In 1960, a wave of student-led lunch counter sit-ins offered new promise. Baker organized a youth conference at Shaw University that drew hundreds of young activists and established leaders, including King. Baker encouraged the young people to be their own leaders rather than get absorbed in existing organizations. At the end of the weekend, the conference-goers created a new group, the Student Nonviolent Coordinating Committee (SNCC). It brought together a new generation of organizers, including Stokely Carmichael, Bob Moses, Diane Nash, Julian Bond, and John Lewis. At fifty-seven years old, Baker was "the godmother of SNCC," urging the group to move deep into the rural South to recruit and support local leaders such as Fannie Lou Hamer of Ruleville, Mississippi. Baker's method, with the SNCC cadre and local Southern communities, was to create "conditions of possibility for others to find their voices and develop leadership."[6] With Baker's help, the Mississippi civil rights movement would become one of the most successful chapters of the freedom story in the South.

Ella Baker stayed involved in progressive politics and collective action well into her later years. But for a woman of such historical significance, Baker took pains to obscure her contributions. She remained true to her self-effacing style, leaving relatively few personal records or intimate interviews for historians and biographers to work with. She generally did not talk about her private life, even with colleagues. Few of her fellow activists knew about her twenty-year marriage to a hometown boyfriend that ended in divorce in late 1958. She'd kept her maiden name and was universally referred to as *Miss* Ella Baker. And although Baker had a reputation as a powerful orator, she "did not give many formal speeches before large audiences that were recorded by the media or published in manuscript form."[7] Baker died on her eighty-third birthday in her Harlem apartment. Her memorial service was attended by Stokely Carmichael, H. Rap Brown, Julian Bond, and others who considered themselves her movement "children."[8]

This speech was recorded at New York's Roosevelt Hotel at a dinner honoring Ella Baker. The event was sponsored by the Southern Conference Education Fund (SCEF). SCEF was an interracial civil rights group. Baker had worked with the organization from the late 1950s. It was headed by two of her closest friends, Anne and Carl Braden, who were white. The Bradens were journalists and radical activists from Louisville, Kentucky, who challenged racial oppression in their hometown and across the South. In 1954, the Bradens purchased a home on behalf of a black couple in a segregated white suburb of Louisville. Angry whites burned a cross on the lawn and finally bombed the house when the black occupants were away. Anne Braden was present at the testimonial dinner in New York. Baker mentions her, and also refers to the recently released report of the President's Commission on Civil Disorders. The commission had been appointed by President Lyndon Johnson to study the causes of rioting in African American urban neighborhoods in 1967.

The tribute dinner took place three weeks after King's assassination in Memphis. Brown attended the dinner, having been recently released from a Louisiana prison on a weapons charge. Carmichael was there, too, flanked by bodyguards because of the increasing controversy caused by his Black Power rhetoric. Historian Howard Zinn introduced Ella Baker as "one of the most consequential and yet one of the least honored people in America." Zinn continued: "She was always doing the nitty-gritty, down-in-the-earth work that other people were not doing. While all sorts of rhetoric was going on, all kinds of grandstanding was going on, that's what she was doing."[9]

I DON'T KNOW IF I can recall a point in my lifetime that I have been as near speechless as I am tonight. [laughter] I had said that I've had great difficulty trying to put down something to say. Not only because of tonight's occasion. But because, I suppose, like many people who have lived a long while, who've seen a lot of things take place, and who still want to see where we're going, I am among those who are finding it pretty difficult to talk these days, in the first place.

And tonight I am finding it even more difficult, because I must admit, I had not responded to this occasion in the way that apparently other people have responded. Maybe I am at fault. But when Anne asked me if the dinner this year might be "built around me," I said yes without any hesitation. Because I agreed with one other statement she made, namely, "That of course this has elements of using you, but if you're like me, you do not object to being used for a good cause." And as far as I was concerned, this was it. Because, irrespective of whatever else could take place tonight, to me, the most important reason for being here was for some people who did not know about SCEF to learn about its work, and for others of us who've been involved in its work to gain new life and new dedication to its support.

Now, maybe I was wrong in taking this position. Maybe I should've let my ego find some satisfaction in the fact that I was being honored. But I must admit to you that I have always found it very difficult to play that role. Because in my estimation, one must do what one's conscience bids them do. And from no one, except yourself, expect applause.

I have been introduced in various ways in my life. I have had the introductions—maybe I should be a little bit historical or reminisce a bit. I remember when I traveled for the NAACP in the early forties and throughout the South. I was weighing then about forty pounds less then I am weighing now. And I was twenty-seven years younger. And on many occasions, when I arrived in a place, because the people had been accustomed to seeing what we used to refer to facetiously as "bedecked" and "be-bosomed" ladies [laughter], and here I appeared, with neither bedecking nor not too much be-bosoming [laughter]. It was pretty difficult for some of the persons who had to introduce me to find a sense of security in presenting the speaker. [laughter] And, so, what they usually would say, after some words that maybe could be said about anybody, they said, "And here we have our national officer." And this of course meant, "Don't blame me if it isn't all right. It's the national office that sent her." [laughter]

But in '59, I went down to help them, in an effort to break through the barriers to voter registration in Caddo Parish, Louisiana. And among the things that we were doing, of course, was getting around to various sections of the community to try to get people to understand . . . what they would have to do in order to qualify to register, and to get them to come out to attempt to register. And on one occasion, after we had been around awhile, and my habits—my work habits—had become known, one of the dear brethren who introduced me, he said, "Now if this sister will give us a number on the PIE-ana [piano], and then we will have a few words from the old workhorse." [laughter] And this was what I was supposed to represent.

Now, I remember those instances, and I remember hundreds of other instances when I had the privilege of thinking, at least, that I spoke what people were thinking in their hearts. I remember one occasion, in the height of the world war—that war that was being fought in the Forties—I spoke at a church in Tampa, Florida. And there were, oh, a couple of hundred, about two hundred people present. And we were recruiting NAACP memberships. And out of that group we got about eighty that morning. And one sister got up and said afterwards, she said, "I'm joining because I know what this woman is saying. What she is saying, any mother can understand." Now, I wasn't a mother, but at least I was glad to know that in attempting to communicate, I had communicated with people in terms of their understanding and in terms of their drives.

A lot of nice things have been said about me tonight. But I said that my main concern for being here was because this was an occasion to call attention, again, to the work that SCEF is doing. You've heard it said that this is the thirtieth anniversary of its existence. And I know of no organization that can measure its effectiveness more effectively in terms of the repressions that it and its staff have suffered than SCEF. SCEF, as Anne has indicated, or at least . . . my meeting with Anne and Carl came at the time when they had been accused of a number of things, sedition among them, because they had bought a house, or bought a house and sold it to a Negro veteran, who had been unable to buy a home out of the ghetto. . . . And I met them.

I, then, was strictly a civil rights worker. You know, in the civil rights movement, there was not very much difference made, or distinction between, civil
rights and civil liberties. In fact, we may not have dwelt too well upon civil
liberties in those days. And after meeting Anne and Carl, one of the things
that became very clear was that those of us who were engaged—especially
the young people at that time—who were engaged in the nonviolent movement had not understood that the very laws that were being used against
them—like opposition to assembly, like exorbitant and unusual bail—these
were things that had to do with the civil-libertarian aspects of a struggle that
they knew very little of. But thanks to Anne Braden, especially, those who
had not known came out of the movement, I think, at least informed, and
I trust are now convinced that the struggle has to take on a double effort in
the direction of combating the violations of the civil liberties that we claim
to have as a result of being a part of the American system.

I've often felt that the marches were just, to a large extent, outlets for
people finding expression, and they assuaged their sense of guilt, or they
did away with any further need for involvement by becoming a part of the
march. No doubt they are a necessary part of dramatizing a situation. But
why march to Washington? Why not march to Long Island? Why not march
to Westchester? Why not march to the slums of New Jersey? Why not march
to Harlem? To Bedford-Stuyvesant? Not in terms of a physical march, but
in terms of recognizing that what is happening in these places, in terms of
poverty, is a responsibility that has to be dealt with by those who are not impoverished. In other words, those of us who have money have got to speak
to those who are in power in a way that they understand. Which is how?
Through the ballot. Through your pressure. And through the determination
that something has to be done.

Poverty. War. We are pretty well on the way to, at least, dealing with the
question of war. But beyond the question of the Vietnam War is the larger
question of what kind of foreign policy does the Vietnam War represent?
And what kind of foreign policy will there be after the Vietnam War? Does it
represent, as has been indicated in some of the things that we've read, that
our government has reached the point that it thinks in terms of being the
policemen for the rest of the world, against what they call the threat of communism? Or, is it truthfully said, as some of us think, that it is the representation of those who are in power, taking a position against the inherent right of
people to seek their own self-determination, in the ways that they think are
best suited to their problems? Does this represent the kind of foreign policy

that you and I, as citizens of our country, want to see followed? If so, that's one thing. But if not, what is our responsibility? Where does our responsibility begin? And where does it end?

When we come to the question of racism, this is the ticklish one. It has been said—and we must give credit where credit is due: the first to, perhaps, utter this were those who are now not very well received, the SNCC people. When they first said that we are in a racist culture, a racist society that is dominated by a racist philosophy, and an exploitation that to a large extent is based on racism, it wasn't heard. And now that it has been said, and perhaps to some extent documented by the President's Report on Urban—what is it called? [crowd responds] Urban Disorders, yes. We call them rebellions, somebody calls them riots, and the president's report refers to them as "urban disorders." [laughter] This report comes out and says that we are tending towards becoming two societies: one black, one white, separate and unequal. Now, the report hasn't said a thing that hasn't been said before, over and over and over again. But the great tragedy is that it wasn't heard. It was said each time there was a protest against racial segregation. It was said each time that people like Stokely Carmichael got his head beaten because he was trying to resist the racist aspects of the Southern society.

And then, we were much more eager for the fight against racism, because of what? It was over there. It was in the South. We could always point the finger. But when it begins to explode at our very doorsteps, what do we do? We get afraid. And we get fearful. That's understandable. It's understandable that you can be afraid of disorder. But that is not enough, to be afraid. There is a need to understand the reason *for* the disorder. Not an outbreak has taken place, but what there weren't some factors that had obtained for years and years, that had helped to create the climate, create the hatred, create the suppressed anger that made it necessary, in the minds of the people who gave vent to it the way they did, to do what they did.

This, you say, is condoning the rioters. It is not. It is an effort to say to people who say they would like to do something to save our country—it's an effort to say to you and to me—that we must understand what takes place at the riot level is a reflection of a lot of things that have not been on the surface before. And that have been festering like an old sore. And what happens with an old sore when it festers? Frequently, it infects the entire body. And we are now at that stage, I'm afraid.

One of the things about the question of racism that, or at least in talking to people the question that frequently has come up, recently with me is,

"Well, we are not guilty, personally." Of course you're not. I don't know that there's anybody in this room has carried on a campaign of racism per se. But I doubt that there's anybody in this room who has not, at some point, been guilty of supporting a racist culture. And we must search ourselves to find out how we have been guilty. Not for the sake of just wallowing in our guilt. But for the sake of facing the fact that the future of our culture, of our country, depends not so much on what black people do as it does depend on what white people do. This is a hard lesson for some of us. That the choice as to whether or not we will rid the country of racism is a choice that white America has to make.

But you say that when blacks call for separatism, they are guilty of racism in reverse. How many times have you listened when the separatism is echoed? What's behind the call for separatism? Many things are said. But in my estimation, there are times when the most radical makes the statement that "you can't expect anything from Whitey," what he's really saying is, "Show me." He's begging to be shown. Now how can you do it? I don't know. I wish I knew how you could show. But one thing is certain: you can't sit back and wait and say, "Well, if the blacks aren't going to work with me, I don't want to be bothered with them, and I don't want to interfere with their seceding." And if someone asks me, "Well what can I do?" I have only one answer: You have to do some things in terms of what you believe. And in terms of your own convictions. And if you're not going to be able to be motivated by your own conviction, and not wait for blacks to tell you where to move, then we are doomed.

I can assure you, I didn't intend this. But I listened to what was being said, and I listened to what was not said, when Stokely and Rap appeared before you. I know there was a great deal of, perhaps, apprehension as to whether or not things would turn out all right. [laughter] I understand that the hotel had raised questions of the possibility of riots. [laughter]

And I think what took place in connection with Rap's appearance in Maryland might be something of a lesson. He has been in jail for a number of weeks. And it was all started because of his appearance in Maryland— Cambridge, Maryland. And you remember all that was said. The story was to the effect that Rap Brown appeared, he spoke, and was followed by a riot. Maybe most of us know all the details, but some of us may not. And I'm going to just read you a couple of lines—if I can find a way to see— from a newspaper clipping that deals with the question of the Cambridge

riots. Before I read this, let me say, this represents a report that was prepared by a team of social scientists, headed by Dr. Robert Shellow, assistant
deputy director for research at the National Institute of Mental Health. And
it was prepared as part of the study on the urban disorders. But it wasn't included in there. We have some other documentation of it, but this will serve
the purpose.

> To the extent that Brown encouraged anybody to engage in precipitous or
> disorderly acts, the city officials are clearly the ones he influenced most.
> [crowd murmurs] Indeed, the existence of a riot existed for the most
> part in the minds of city officials. And to the extent that Negro disorders
> occurred, it can best be interpreted as a response to actions of the city
> officials. Brown was more a catalyst of white fears than of Negro an-
> tagonism; the disturbance more a product of white expectations than of
> Negro initiative. The 24-year-old Negro leader was indicted on charges
> of inciting to arson and riot.

I think the report points out that the school . . . the burning at the school
took place about four hours after he had been shot in the arm by a deputy
and after he had left. And that the people in the community really came out
and tried to help put out the school blaze. But there is the possibility that
the chief of police had decided that he was ready for a riot, and, so help
him, there had to be one. Those of us who are not ready for the burning
will go down to our city halls, go down to our mayors and our governors,
and even to our federal government, and question why so much artillery is
being bought and stacked and stocked, to deal with people who are fighting
against a repressive system that they have become victim to. The voice of
those who believe that life is more sacred than property must be heard now,
if at no other time. [applause]

One other thought, and that has to do with the whole question of repressive actions. I think it was this week that the twenty-fifth anniversary
of the Warsaw Ghetto—the resistance at the Warsaw Ghetto—took place
twenty-five years ago. Someone has said that those who fail to remember
history may live to experience history. What I am suggesting is that the trend
towards repressive measures against those who are resisting the war, those
who are resisting the racist repressions, those who are resisting the poverty
that they endure, those who are challenging the system, more and more the

repression is stepped up in terms of what? Eliminating those people in one way or the other, containing them. Rap Brown was sent to jail, not because he had been tried and found guilty of a crime, but because he was an easy target. And if we take the position that, "Sure, I don't believe in *that* kind of imprisonment, but you must remember what he said," then we aren't really understanding that the real issue is repression. Not repression for whom, but repression against anyone who violates or who is exercising what we say are our constitutional rights of freedom of speech.

10.

SHIRLEY CHISHOLM
(1924–2005)

Speech at Howard University

Washington, D.C.—April 21, 1969

Shirley Chisholm was the first African American woman elected to Congress, winning her seat in 1968 despite what she described as the "double drawback of being female and having skin darkened by melanin."[1] Her campaign slogan was, "Fighting Shirley Chisholm—Unbought and Unbossed." It was a credo she stuck to throughout fourteen years in Congress and in the 1972 presidential campaign, when she became the first black woman to seek a major-party nomination for the White House.

Born in Brooklyn, Shirley Anita St. Hill was the oldest of four girls whose parents had emigrated from the West Indies. At the age of three, she was sent to Barbados to be raised by her grandmother on the family farm. She was educated in the island's British-style school system and picked up traces of a British West Indian accent that would flavor her speech as an adult. At age ten, Shirley St. Hill rejoined her parents in Brooklyn. Her mother was a seamstress and domestic worker; her father was a baker and factory worker who admired black nationalist leader Marcus Garvey.

Shirley St. Hill attended a selective public high school in New York and earned high marks. At Brooklyn College, St. Hill joined the campus debate club, where she stood out as a skilled public speaker. She also became increasingly aware of the pervasive racial discrimination in the United States. St. Hill found that blacks were not welcome in campus social clubs and that white liberals who came to speak about racial problems often described African Americans as "another breed, less human than they."[2] Looking back, Chisholm told an interviewer: "In college, I became angry."[3] She grew skeptical of most politicians, especially those claiming to befriend the underprivileged. "Political organizations are formed to keep the powerful in power," St. Hill observed. Before long, she would challenge that system.

After graduating in 1946, Shirley St. Hill worked as a nursery school teacher and day care center director. In 1949, she married Jamaican immigrant Conrad Chisholm, a schoolteacher and private investigator. In 1952, Shirley Chisholm earned a graduate degree in early childhood education from Columbia University. Because of her debating skills, one of Chisholm's professors encouraged her to get into politics. She became active in the New York Democratic Party and in 1964 Chisholm won a landslide victory for a seat in the state assembly. Chisholm built a reputation as an independent and outspoken politician. In 1968, she defeated civil rights activist James Farmer to represent New York City's Twelfth Congressional District, which included parts of Manhattan, Brooklyn, and Queens.

Representative Chisholm waged her first campaign against Washington's power establishment within days of arriving at the Capitol. Ignoring the tradition that freshman lawmakers should be seen and not heard, she protested her assignment to an obscure committee on Forestry and Rural Villages. "Apparently all they know here in Washington about Brooklyn is that a tree grew there," she said. "I can think of no other reason for assigning me to the House Agriculture Committee."[4] When she was moved to the Veterans Affairs Committee, Chisholm noted approvingly that there were many more veterans than trees in her district.

When Chisholm ran for president in 1972, she campaigned neither as the black nor the female candidate—though she was proud to be both black and female—but the candidate of the people. Senator George McGovern easily defeated Chisholm and other contenders for the Democratic nomination, then lost to incumbent Republican president Richard Nixon in the general election. Chisholm's campaign was viewed, then as now, as largely symbolic. But she shrugged off the dismissive treatment her candidacy often got, predicting that future political campaigns by women and minorities would find a smoother path "because I helped pave it."[5] She also helped create institutions that would pry apart the gates of political exclusion, including the Congressional Black Caucus and the National Women's Political Caucus.

Chisholm retired from Congress in 1982. Historian Julie Gallagher says Chisholm was a tireless champion for women, working people, minorities, and the poor, but that she had few of the Washington networks or powerful allies needed to help pass meaningful legislation. "Chisholm's leadership remained an important symbol and inspiration to many, but as a legislator, she was not particularly successful," Gallagher wrote.[6] Still, Chisholm has been an inspiration to generations of women and African Americans, a trailblazer who helped open up American politics to women and minorities. Democratic representative Maxine Waters of California remembered Chisholm: "There she was—this feisty, articulate woman among all these white men—daring to speak her piece and challenge the system. It was awesome."[7]

One of Chisholm's former legislative aides remembered the spectacle that the diminutive congresswoman made as she strode the mostly male corridors of power. "Congress would only give secretarial or clerk positions to people like me," Laura W. Murphy wrote. "People would stare at [Chisholm] when she walked down the hall, because invariably a large entourage of professional staff women followed wherever she went."[8]

After leaving Congress, Chisholm taught at Mount Holyoke College and was an energetic supporter of the Reverend Jesse Jackson's 1984 and 1988 presidential campaigns. In 1993, she turned down President Bill Clinton's offer of an ambassadorship to Jamaica and settled on the Florida coast. Shirley Chisholm died in 2005.

When Chisholm gave this speech at Howard University in 1969, the campus had been through months of sometimes violent upheaval. The unrest sprang from a variety of factors: reaction to the killing of Martin Luther King Jr. a year earlier, protests against the war in Vietnam, the increasing militancy of the Black Power movement, and student clashes with Howard's administration over housing and academic issues. Speaking to a filled auditorium, Chisholm argued that "power concedes nothing" unless challenged, but that "Black Power" would never be more than a protest slogan unless African Americans took action from within the political system as well as out on the streets.

· · ·

GOOD AFTERNOON, STUDENTS. I usually speak extemporaneously because I like to see what is happening as I try to bring a message to you. But there's so many things that I have on my mind this afternoon, and in the interest of time, as well as to give you the opportunity to ask me any kind of questions you desire, I'm going to read my speech today. At another time, when I'm not so pressured, I will speak extemporaneously on many, many things that I want to bring to you from time to time.

While nothing is easy for the black man in America, neither is anything impossible. Like old man river, we are moving along, and we will continue to move resolutely until our goal of unequivocal equality is attained. We must not be docile, we must not be resigned, nor must we be inwardly bitter. We must see ourselves in an entirely new perspective, and we cannot sit in our homes waiting for someone to reach out and do things for us.

Every tomorrow has two handles. We can take hold of the handle of anxiety or the handle of faith. And the first battle is won, my brothers and sisters, when we fight for belief in ourselves and find that it has come to us while we are still battling. We must not allow petty things to color our lives and stimulate them into vast proportions of evil. To dwell on every slight and clutch it close to our breast and nourish it will corrode our thinking. We're on the move now, and as Frederick Douglass said, "Power concedes nothing without a struggle." It never has, and it never will.

The United States can no longer afford the luxury of costly morally, religiously, and ethically wrong racial discrimination. For America needs all of her citizens with their abilities developed to make a fuller contribution to the future. Many problems scream loudly in this country: the thousands of black citizens disenfranchised, living under degrading conditions; the millions of poor throughout this nation, white and black, who lack the bare rudiments for fruitful living; the rapidly growing numbers of children caught in a web of disillusionment which destroys their will to learn; the increasing numbers of aged who do not even look forward to rest or retirement.

And despite the historic legislation in our cities and our states, nearly eleven million black citizens today still live in basic ghetto communities of our cities. From decades of nonparticipation or only modest participation, the black man has within the last two years shifted his goal to full political participation for full American citizenship. And while on the picket line, at the lunch counter, and in the bus and the store boycott, the black man came face to face with the full breadth and weight of the power and influence exercised by local and state governments, intertwining and often stifling the protests.

Indeed, a principal by-product of the American civil rights movement has been the awakening of the black citizen to his awesome political potential. And just as the picket line and the lunch counter demonstrations and the boycotts were dramatic and effective weapons of protest for the civil rights movement, the polling place is the new phase in the new thrust of the black man's bid for equality of opportunity. "Power concedes nothing." How else can any man rise to power, and hold sway over millions or tens of thousands, except by smothering dissenting voices?

Freedom is an endless horizon, and there are many roads that lead to it. We must walk arm in arm with other men, and we must struggle toward goals which are commonly desired and sound. We must give and lend to the youth a stronger voice and encourage their individuality. We must look to the schools and constantly work for their improvement, because that is where the future leadership of the country will be coming from, to a large extent— particularly in the black communities.

The leaders of today in the black communities must be able to place the goal of freedom ahead of personal ambition. The truly dedicated leader follows what his conscience tells him is best for his people. For whatever else the black man is, he is American. Or whatever he is to become—integrated, unintegrated, or disintegrated—he will become it in America. Only a minority of black people have ever succumbed to the temptation to seek greener pastures of another country or another ideology.

You know, so often nowadays we hear people say that we should go back to Africa, we should establish ourselves in Africa, or we should do a lot of other things. Well, if people want to go back to Africa, or people want to go to Africa just like people want to go to Europe, that's their own personal business. And you do it voluntarily. I don't intend to go to Africa, I intend to stay here and fight, because the blood, sweat, and tears of our forefathers are rooted in the soil of this country. And the reason that Wall Street is the great financial center that it is today is because of the blood, sweat, and tears of your forefathers who worked in the tobacco and the cotton fields. And now because this nation is a mercantile nation, and is enjoying the efforts and the labor of many of our forefathers, many of us want to escape and many of us want to run away. We didn't ask to be brought here in the first place. We came here shackled in chains at our ankles and our wrists, and we were a cheap supply of labor, and we worked. We did many, many things.

And now that the problem is becoming a little bit too hot, everybody has all kinds of solutions for us. If you want to go to Africa willingly, you can go, just like other people in this country go to Europe, willingly. Nobody has to tell you or create something special for you. Our roots are here. Our blood and our sweat and our tears are here. And we're going to stay here. And we're going to fight.

For years, thousands of people from the European shores have been coming to this land. They came here hardly able to speak the English language. But they came here and acquired the technological know-how, and they acquired the necessary skills that enabled them to become assimilated in the American culture, and to move out and up into the American middle class. Hardly speakin' English.

But we who have been born here, we who have been citizens by birth, have not been able to become fully assimilated in the American culture because of an unmistakable and almost insurmountable barrier, that just will not disappear, because color doesn't disappear. And so, it behooves us to stay here and to fight. We have made this land, even though we have not been given the recognition, and nobody has to create any little nation or any little group, and send us scuttling off. We want to go, we go. Freedom of choice.

The black man's total commitment to America indicates that the prospect ahead does seem bright. It is true that we are angry about our present plight, for we measure this country not by her achievements but by her potential.

"Black Power." Oh how that phrase upsets so many people. Let me give you my definition of Black Power. Black Power is no different from any other kind of power in this country. Just as I told you a few moments ago, the people from European countries came here and found their way in the American scheme of things, after they were able to get a certain kind of economic and financial security. The next thing that they became interested in was to achieve power to control their own destinies. And so, for example, in New York City you had, at one time, the Germans in ascendency, then you had the Italians, then you had the Jewish people and the Irish—every other group moving out to get power to control their destinies.

But nobody had to label that as "White Power," because it was understood and assumed that it would always be White Power. Now that we are beginning to do what they have been telling us to do for a long time—take ourselves up by our bootstraps and begin to consolidate our efforts and move out like every other group has moved out in America—everybody is so hysterical and panic stricken because of the adjective that precedes the word power—"black." You know it would have been hoped in this country that we would never have to use the word "black" before the word "power," because America has been built on a series of immigrants coming into this land, rising up and moving out in terms of achieving power to control their lives.

But you see, they made one mistake. They thought that, because we had been relegated for such a long time to a subservient position, and that we had accepted, rather docilely, the position of second-class citizenship, that we would never rise up, that we would never speak out. And so, when we began to say to the world, in our own way, that we too know and understand what other groups have been doing for a long time in this country. Consolidating and using our power and our efforts to move up—and we want the world to know that it is Black Power, because we have learned what other groups have been learning and doing for a long time in this country. And people just have to get used to that word, "Black Power."

It is, indeed, a reality that is gaining in emotional intensity, if not always rational clarity. The harnessing and the solidification of Afro-American power, however, is constantly being dissipated with factionalism. Internal struggle for power by one group over another. This behavior is no different from that of the whites. But we as a people cannot afford the luxury of fighting among ourselves if we are going to make real progress.

And black people will gain only as much as they can through their ability to organize independent bases of economic and political power—through boycotts, electoral activity, rent strikes, et cetera. Black power is concerned with organizing the rage of black people. Organizing the rage. And it's putting new hard questions and demands to white America. We will build a new sense of community among our people. We will foster a bond between those who have made it and those on the bottom.

As Charles Hamilton says, "Alienation will be overcome, and trust will be restored." And let us remember that a great people are not affected by each puff of wind that blows ill. We must fight, constantly, for belief in ourselves. And above all we must harken back to the days of darkness, when Frederick Douglass, the great abolitionist, even in those times, echoed the famous phrase that has come realistically to haunt the black people today

in America, as they fight to enter the political, economic, and social mainstream of these United States, the land of their birth. And that phrase is,
"Power concedes nothing."

Let me say to you, my brothers and sisters, that until we can organize to
create black unity with an economic base, until we can develop a plan for
action to achieve the goals to make us totally independent, and not have
to look to the Man in order to live, we're not liberated. We must become
doers, and producers, in the system, in order to be able to control our own
destinies. We have the potential, but we must consolidate all of our strength
for eventual liberation.

And the black man's responsibility today is to establish his own values
and his own goals. In doing so, he will be affecting the larger American
society, of which he's a part. The black man and the black woman cannot,
however, act alone. They must act within a community or family, job, and
neighborhood. Let us not kid ourselves into thinking that the white man is
suddenly going to make the choice readily available. The new day will come
with honest black pride, and unified black action and education, politics,
and economics. Why it has taken us so long to discover this simple approach
is one of the mysteries of the twentieth century. The Jews, the Poles, and
the Slovaks discovered this phenomenon years ago. Compassion and understanding may moralize the system periodically, but it will never make it
honest, just, and decent for us. Only the application of real economic and
political power can achieve that goal.

"Black is beautiful." You hear that phrase a great deal. Black is beautiful
in what you do to contribute to the building of a strong black community
throughout this country. The time, now, is to counteract the poison that has
inflicted ignorance and hatred in the American social and political body. In
seeking your identity, you can explore your African heritage, not simply by
adopting the outward manifestations of African dress and appearance, but
by going beyond the roots of that superficial type of thing, that many of us
might be doing, to learn about contemporary Africa and its people.

I talk with so many people who affect these manifestations, and they
don't know anything about Africa. Learn about contemporary Africa and its
people. And appreciate that you and they have tremendous historical and
cultural links, that there is much that we can offer to each other's growth.
Nineteen sixty-eight has clearly and painfully demonstrated the degree of
stress and alienation that afflicts all of our institutions. Our young people
have questioned the validity of traditional university education. They and

many of their elders have fought against the tragic depletion of human and material resources in a complex Asian conflict that seems only to attract simple answers. The fabric of our incomplete nationhood has been torn down the seam of black/white confrontation in this country.

We need a liberated and developing black community in America that, once it has fully discovered its inherent worth and power, turns to the even greater task of protecting and enlarging upon its triumphs by further enriching an American culture that already has drawn so much from the black life stream. We need black businessmen who can rise beyond the local tax-and-spend, and make dollars as well as sense for a black community that plays a full part in all levels of government. And there can be no understanding of the recent rioting in northern black ghettos, or any realistic analysis of its impact upon the civil rights movement in the nation, without the realization that black citizens have just, pressing, and long-neglected grievances.

We do not erupt simply for exercise. We do not curse imaginary obstacles and procedures. Our resentments are not the product of a momentary flare-up but of years of postponement, denial, insult, and abuse. The conscience of political democracy cries out for an end to false democracy. It is just and inevitable that black Americans are tired of being governed by laws they had no part in making and by officials in whose choice they have no voice. It is idiotic to labor under the old white-supremacist supposition that a white man knows what's good for the black man. The nonwhite American is saying we no longer want tokens which will only take us on a subway ride. We want some bread, some meat, and a slice—not a sliver—of the pie, the same ways any other ethnic group receives under this system.

In humanitarian terms, the war on poverty must be fought wherever it is found. Part of the battle must be fought with the establishment of the hundred-dollar-per-week minimum for all Americans, so that subsidization by welfare authorities is drastically reduced and a man is paid a decent, living wage in today's automated society. In today's most affluent society, if you please. The goal must be $2.50 per hour—a national minimum for all Americans. This reduces poverty.

More crassly put, we will be able to get more people off welfare and relief rolls and on to tax rolls. We can get them out of the alleys of society and into the mainstream of productive society, and productive employment, where they can support themselves and their dependents, with dignity and pride. Where they can contribute to the growth and strength of the nation's economy.

The war on poverty must be fought with the inalienable right of every working American. The right to collective bargaining to protect themselves from human exploitation and human abuse. The grape worker in California, the migrant farm worker in New York, the rural blacks working in the South, the nonprofessional service workers in institutions are examples of the system which, year in and year out, relegates these people to the most shameful, subservient conditions as part of the labor force—the most important force, which keeps American business moving in this country. Our job is not to make poverty more endurable but to get rid of it!

The poor whites and the hungry blacks in the rural South—there's a serious question of the capacity of the American system itself to provide a decent living for the unfavored. And I think we can, if we will move forward in the way of plain justice, just plain justice, and decency, for the low man on the totem pole in America. It does no good to have the right to sit in the front of a bus if you don't have the bus fare. Or the right to sit down at a lunch counter and buy a cup of coffee if you don't have the dime to pay for it. As one leader said, "A mouth full of civil rights and an empty stomach, or a banner reading 'We shall overcome' on a wall that is full of holes or a floor where the rats are playing games with each other [inaudible] . . ."

Yes, the revolution of 1968–69 is about freedom, my friends. It's activists who speak to ghetto towns and tell it like it is. It's about parents who refuse to go on having their children programmed to deny their black identity in order to enter a society where the basic color scheme is white. It is about manhood and the assertion of self. The keys to the new mood in black America are the feelings that the nation does not really wish to do away with its dual society. Well, blacks then must have the dominant role in determining their own destiny. The nonviolent tactic has not always prevented the brutalization of the inhabitants of the ghetto, where the black people resisted, or the brutality of the Bull Connors, the dogs and the cattle prods, the murderers and the church bombings, as they insisted upon their rights as free men. Or as they demanded for their children a human dignity which American racism sought to deny all black people.

These are all testimonies that we will not turn back. [This nation], if it desires to grow, if it wants to continue to remain among the leading nations of this world, it is going to have to make sure that it utilizes the fullest of all the capacities of all of its citizens. There is no more time. Time's running out. There is no more time for debate in the Congress on civil rights bills. No more time for rich bishops to keep the church doors closed. No more time for unions to discriminate against black and Puerto Rican workers, both overtly and covertly.

We are living in an epoch of liberation of oppressed and deprived people in this country, which has always said it wants to make the world safe for democracy. Charity begins at home first. And the reality of the two Americas—one white, comfortable, and free; and the other black, fettered, and poor—must now become in reality the dream that the late Dr. Martin Luther King gave his life for. This greatest man, this saint must not be permitted to have died in vain. We've seen fit to introduce a bill in Congress to make his birth a national holiday, when every American will cease to work on this day to take stock of himself and the concept of human brotherhood. And every American shall see that a nation of men of different origins can abide together in peace, democracy, and equality.

In conclusion, let me say that the hour is late. Jargon is of no use any longer. We have been analyzed, surveyed, graphed, depicted. We have loads of documents and information on us as a people, on the shelves of the different departments of this country. Everyone knows about us. We don't need that anymore. The time now is for action.

Young people, I believe in you. I truly believe in you. I happen to feel that, although I'm approaching middle age—I'm now forty-four, and they say that in four years I'll be called a middle-aged woman—I don't feel like that. I happen to feel this community is going to be ultimately saved by the students, the young people. We may not always approve of some of your methods, because we realize that youth is often in a hurry and wants to get things done. But we know that you are tuned in to what's wrong with a country that has been talking about democracy but has not been practicing it. So allow me, as one of those who are moving into the middle-age category, to give you some ideas and suggestions. I know from time to time we will disagree, but healthy disagreement is all right. I know that you are going to be the inheritors of this country. And so we've got to depend on you even though you may not always agree with everything that we say. Thank you for giving me the opportunity to bring you this message.

11.

ANGELA Y. DAVIS
(1944–)

Speech delivered at the Embassy Auditorium

Los Angeles, California—June 9, 1972

Angela Davis was an international symbol of black revolution in the early 1970s. Organizing on behalf of three black prisoners accused of murder, Davis herself wound up behind bars, charged with criminal conspiracy, kidnapping, and first-degree murder. A massive, worldwide movement formed to free Davis from jail, and she was eventually cleared of all charges. The experience solidified her already deep determination to fight for radical change in America.

Angela Davis was born in 1944 and grew up in segregated Birmingham, Alabama. Her neighborhood was the target of such frequent attacks by the Ku Klux Klan it was dubbed "dynamite hill."[1] Davis won a scholarship to attend a private high school in New York's Greenwich Village, where she became close friends with two women—Margaret Burnham and Bettina Aptheker—who would one day work to help free her from jail. As teenagers, the three formed a socialist club called Advance and participated in local demonstrations to support the burgeoning civil rights movement down South.[2]

Davis graduated from Brandeis University with highest honors and a deep interest in Marxism. She went on to study at Goethe University in

Germany and to pursue a doctorate in philosophy at the University of California, San Diego, where her mentor, the radical philosopher Herbert Marcuse, was teaching.[3]

Davis first made national news in 1969 when California's Republican governor, Ronald Reagan, tried to get her fired from her teaching job at the University of California–Los Angeles (UCLA). Davis had declared herself a communist, and Reagan, a fervent anticommunist, was appalled. Students and faculty came to Davis's defense, but Reagan prevailed. On June 19, 1970, he issued a memorandum declaring that "Angela Davis, Professor of Philosophy, will no longer be a part of the UCLA staff. As the head of the Board of Regents, I, nor the board, will not tolerate any Communist activities at any state institution. Communists are an endangerment to this wonderful system of government that we all share and are proud of."[4]

While fighting for her job at UCLA, Davis was also active in several militant black organizations, including the Black Panther Political Party (which later became the Los Angeles chapter of SNCC). Working with these groups, Davis encountered what she says was a "constant problem" in her political life: sexism. "I was criticized very heavily for doing a 'man's' job," Davis wrote. Male organizers discouraged Davis from seeking leadership roles. They insisted that "a woman was supposed to 'inspire' her man and educate his children."[5] Davis rejected these ideas as "absurd"[6] and continued to organize.

In early 1970, Davis helped spearhead a movement to free the "Soledad Brothers" from a California prison. The three unrelated black men— Fleeta Drumgo, John Clutchette, and George Jackson—were accused of killing a Soledad Prison guard. Supporters believed they were being persecuted for their political views. The "brothers" had become radicalized in prison, reading Marx, studying black nationalism, and agitating for prison reform.[7]

Just days after their indictment, Angela Davis called a press conference announcing the new Soledad Brothers Defense Committee in Southern California. "The situation in Soledad is part of a continuous pattern in the black community," she told reporters. "Three black men who are known for their attempt within the prison to organize the inmates towards some form of united struggle against the real causes of our oppression, those three men are . . . singled out, and indicted for murder." Davis announced that a demonstration would be held the next day and said, "We are calling for basic structural changes within the prison system, and we are also attempting to build a movement directed towards the liberation of political prisoners."[8]

On August 7, 1970, George Jackson's younger brother Jonathan smuggled guns into a Marin County courthouse, handed them to several prisoners, and took five hostages. When Jonathan tried to escape with the group, guards opened fire. Four people were killed, including Jonathan Jackson and the presiding judge, who was white. The FBI learned that the guns were registered to Angela Davis. Davis maintained that Jonathan had taken the guns without her knowing, but when a warrant was issued for her arrest, she went into hiding. On August 18, J. Edgar Hoover put her on the FBI's Ten Most Wanted list, calling her "armed and dangerous."[9] The FBI caught Davis two months later in New York City. She was extradited to California.

Once Davis was jailed, "support for Angela did not have to be generated," wrote Bettina Aptheker. "It had to be organized."[10] Scores of black newspapers across the country called for her unconditional release. Black writers in New York formed a support committee. Singer Aretha Franklin offered to post her bail. "I'm going to set Angela free," she said. "Not because I believe in communism but because she's a black woman who wants freedom for all black people."[11]

The mainstream press remained circumspect. In an editorial following her capture in New York, the New York Times said "the tragedy" of Angela Davis "is that one who might have made a significant contribution to the nation's normal political debate and to its needed processes of peaceful change became so alienated that she finally went over to revolutionary words and perhaps even worse."[12]

Angela Davis spent sixteen months in jail awaiting trial for conspiracy, kidnapping, and murder. She became a cultural icon. Historian Robin D.G. Kelley writes, " 'Free Angela' posters, buttons, and T-shirts became as much a part of the changing urban landscape as liquor stores and 'soul food' restaurants. Tall, lean, with a raised fist and an Afro, a flashing smile, and an aura of confidence, Angela Davis offered the African-American community a striking image to rally around. To her many supporters— young and old, male and female—she was a young, beautiful, militant intellectual boldly challenging 'the system.' "[13] Davis also had wide international appeal. Along with hundreds of local committees, at least sixty-seven committees in foreign countries were working for her release.[14]

Davis was finally granted bail in February 1972, after a change in California state law (not related to her case). Davis was stoical during her thirteen-week trial. When the jury acquitted her of all charges, on June 4, 1972, she grabbed a close friend and broke into sobs.[15]

Five days after the trial ended, Angela Davis delivered this speech at a victory rally at the Embassy Auditorium in Los Angeles. It marked the first stop on a nationwide tour to thank her supporters. The place was packed; some 1,500 people showed up to hear her speak, many of them white.[16] Davis told her fans she was surprised by the role history had thrust upon her and that she would do her best to live up their expectations.

In her speech, Davis also talks about the death of George Jackson. He was shot by a guard while being held at San Quentin Prison on August 21, 1971. As Davis mentions, Jackson's murder helped spark the deadliest prison riot in American history, at Attica Prison in New York. What Davis doesn't say is that Jackson's death, which occurred while she was still in jail, was a heartbreaking personal loss. Jackson and Davis had been exchanging letters for more than a year and were deeply in love.[17] His death cemented her resolve to "fight for the cause George died defending."[18]

Davis did go on to fight for the reform and abolition of prisons and against all types of oppression. She also continued to teach and write about philosophy, feminism, and other issues of social justice. In 1990, Davis settled into a position at the University of California–Santa Cruz, where she was awarded the Presidential Chair in African American and Feminist Studies. She retired from the university in 2008, but remains a scholar, mentor, and political activist.

Reflecting on this last role, Davis once wrote, "For me revolution was never an interim 'thing-to-do' before settling down; it was no fashionable club with newly minted jargon, or new kind of social life—made thrilling by risk and confrontation. Revolution is a serious thing. . . . When one commits oneself to the struggle, it must be for a lifetime."[19]

IT'S REALLY A WONDERFUL feeling to be back among the people. [cheers and applause] To be back among all of you who fought so long and so hard, among all of you who actually achieved my freedom. And I really wish you could have been there in the courtroom at the moment when those three "not guilty" verdicts were pronounced, because that victory was just as much yours as it was mine. [*Right on!* applause] And as we laughed and cried, these were expressions of our joy as we witnessed what was a real people's victory, and in spirit you were all there at that moment.

Over the last few days, I've been literally overwhelmed with congratulations and expressions of solidarity, whether it's been in meetings or on the streets or in restaurants; in the black and brown communities in northern California, wherever I've gone, I've been greeted with hugs and kisses, and it's really been beautiful. Even in a city like San Jose, among the white population, many many people have come out and have congratulated me and have told me that, actually, they were behind us all the time. [applause] And during these last days, I have sensed a real feeling of unity and togetherness and a kind of collective enthusiasm which I have rarely experienced on such a massive scale.

And in the midst of all of this, it's sort of difficult for me to grasp that I am the person around whom all of this enthusiasm has emerged. Yet because of it, I feel that I have a special responsibility—a special responsibility to you who have stood with me in struggle. But sometimes, I have to admit, when I'm off by myself and I reflect on everything that has happened over the last two years, I really wonder whether or not I will be able to meet the role which history has cut out for me, which you have cut out for me, but I promise I am going to try. That, I promise. [applause]

When it all started—and I'm speaking of myself—when I experienced the first stirrings of a commitment to the cause of freedom, the last thing I envisioned at that time were ambitions to become a figure known to great numbers of people. At that time, I was simply aspiring to do everything I could to give my meager talents and energies to the cause of my people, to the cause of black people and brown people and to all racially oppressed, and economically oppressed people in this country and throughout the globe. But history doesn't always conform to our own personal desires. It doesn't always conform to the blueprints we set up for our lives.

My life, and the lives of my family, my mother, my comrades, my friends, has really been drastically transformed over the last two years. For what happened was that as our movement—and particularly our movement right here in Los Angeles, our movement to free political prisoners, our movement to free all oppressed people—as that movement began to grow and become stronger and develop in breadth, it just so happened that I was the one who, one of the ones who was singled out by the government's finger of repression. It just so happened that I was destined to become yet another symbol of what the government intends to do—what the government in this state would do to every person who refuses to be its passive, submissive subject. [applause]

But then came the surge of a massive popular resistance, then came thousands and thousands and hundreds of thousands of people who were rising up to save me as we had tried to rise up and save the Soledad Brothers and other political prisoners. And what happened was that the government's plan, the government's project of repression fell apart; it backfired. The government could not, through me, terrorize people who would openly demonstrate their opposition to racism, to war, to poverty, to repression.

And on the contrary, people let it be known that they would not be manipulated by terror. They would stand behind all their sisters and brothers who had been caught in the government's web of repression. I was one of those who was entrapped in that web. And the thousands and millions of people throughout the world came together in struggle and saved me from the fate the government had planned as an example to all of you who were disposed to resist. You intervened and saved my life, and now I am back among you, and as I was wrested away from you in struggle, so likewise I return in struggle. [applause] I return in struggle with a very simple message, a very simple message: We've just begun our fight. [applause] We've just begun.

And while we celebrate the victory of my own acquittal, and also of the release on appeal of a very beautiful brother from a Texas prison. I don't know if you know him, his name is Leotis Johnson. [applause] He was a SNCC, SCLC organizer in Texas and was framed up on a marijuana charge. He was released just a few days ago after having spent four years, four years in a Texas prison. We have to celebrate that victory, too, but as we celebrate these victories, we must also be about the business of transforming our joy, our enthusiasm into an even deeper commitment to all our sisters and brothers who do not yet have cause to celebrate.

And as I say this, I remember very, very vividly the hundreds of women who were with me in the New York Women's House of Detention, most of them black and brown women, all of them from the poorest strata of this society. I remember the women in the sterile cells of Marin County Jail, and the women in the dimly lit, windowless cells in Santa Clara County. There is still the savage inhumanity of Soledad Prison. One Soledad brother, our brother George, has been murdered. The two who survived were recently acquitted, but hundreds more are awaiting our aid and solidarity.

There are hundreds and thousands of Soledad Brothers, or San Quentin

Brothers, or Folsom Brothers, of CIW sisters, all of whom are prisoners of an insanely criminal social order. So let us celebrate, but let us celebrate in the only way that is compatible with all the pain and suffering that so many of our sisters and brothers must face each morning as they awake to the oppressive sight of impenetrable concrete and steel. As they awake to the harsh banging of heavy iron doors opening and closing at the push of a button. As they awake each morning to the inevitable jangling of the keepers' keys— keys which are a constant reminder that freedom is so near, yet so far away. Millenniums and millenniums away.

So let us celebrate in the only way that is fitting. Let the joy of victory be the foundation of an undying vow, a renewed commitment to the cause of freedom. For we know now that victories are possible, though the struggles they demand are long and arduous. So let our elation merge with a pledge to carry on this fight until a time when all the antiquated ugliness and brutality of jails and prisons linger on only as a mere memory of a nightmare. For our vow will be fulfilled only when we or our children or our grandchildren will have succeeded in seizing the reins of history, in determining the destiny of mankind and creating a society where prisons are unheard of because the racism and the exploitative economic arrangement which reproduces want for the many and wealth for the few will have become relics of a past era. [applause]

It has been said many times that one can learn a great deal about a society by looking towards its prisons. Look towards its dungeons, and there you will see in concentrated and microcosmic form the sickness of the entire system. And today in the United States of America in nineteen hundred and seventy-two, there is something that is particularly revealing about the analogy between the prison and the larger society of which it is a reflection. For in a painfully real sense we are all prisoners of a society whose bombastic proclamations of freedom and justice for all are nothing but meaningless rhetoric.

For this society's accumulated wealth, its scientific achievements are swallowed up by the avarice of a few capitalists and by insane projects of war and other irrational ventures. We are imprisoned in a society where there is so much wealth and so many sophisticated scientific and technological skills that anyone with just a little bit of common sense can see the insanity of a continued existence of ghettos and barrios and the poverty which is there. [applause]

For when we see the rockets taking off towards the moon and the B-52s raining destruction and death on the people of Vietnam, we know that something is wrong. We know that all we have to do is to redirect that wealth and that energy and channel it into food for the hungry and to clothes for the needy, into schools, hospitals, housing, and all the material things that are necessary [applause], all the material things that are necessary in order for human beings to lead decent, comfortable lives, in order to lead lives which are devoid of all the pressures of racism, and, yes, male supremacist attitudes and institutions, and all the other means with which the rulers manipulate the people. For only then can freedom take on a truly human meaning. Only then can we be free to live and to love and be creative human beings. [applause]

In this society, in the United States of America today, we are surrounded by the very wealth and the scientific achievements which hold forth a promise of freedom. Freedom is so near, yet at the same time it is so far away. And this thought invokes in me the same sensation I felt as I reflected on my own condition in a jail in New York City. For from my cell I could look down upon the crowded streets of Greenwich Village, almost tasting the freedom of movement and the freedom of space which had been taken from me and all my sisters in captivity.

It was so near but at the same time so far away, because somebody was holding the keys that would open the gates to freedom. Our condition here and now—the condition of all of us who are brown and black and working women and men—bears a very striking similarity to the condition of the prisoner. The wealth and the technology around us tells us that a free, humane, harmonious society lies very near. But at the same time, it is so far away, because someone is holding the keys, and that someone refuses to open the gates to freedom. Like the prisoner, we are locked up with the ugliness of racism and poverty and war and all the attendant mental frustrations and manipulations.

We're also locked up with our dreams and visions of freedom, and with the knowledge that if we only had the keys—if we could only seize them from the keepers, from the Standard Oils, the General Motors, and all the giant corporations, and of course from their protectors, the government—if we could only get our hands on those keys, we could transform these visions and these dreams into reality. [applause] Our situation bears a very excruciating similarity to the situation of the prisoner, and we must never forget this. For if we do, we will lose our desire for freedom and our will to struggle for liberation.

As black people, as brown people, as people of color, as working men and women in general, we know and we experience the agony of the struggle for existence each day. We are locked into that struggle. The parallels between our lives and the lives of our sisters and brothers behind bars are very clear. Yet there is a terrifying difference in degree between life on this side of the bars and life on the other side. And just as we must learn from the similarities and acquire an awareness of all the forces which oppress us out here, it is equally important that we understand that the plight of the prisoner unfolds in the rock-bottom realms of human existence.

Our sisters and brothers down there need our help and our solidarity in their collective strivings and struggles in the same elemental way that we all need fresh air and nourishment and shelter. And when I say this, I mean it to be taken quite literally, because I recall too well that in the bleak silence and solitude of a Marin County isolation cell, you, the people, were my only hope, my only promise of life.

Martin Luther King told us what he saw when he went to the mountaintop. He told us of visions of a new world of freedom and harmony, told us of the sisterhood and brotherhood of humankind. Doctor King described it far more eloquently than I could ever attempt to do. But there's also the foot of the mountain, and there are also the regions beneath the surface. And I am returning from a descent together with thousands and thousands of our sisters and brothers into the ugly depths of society. I want to try to tell you a little something about those regions. I want to attempt to persuade you to join in the struggle to give life and breath to those who live sealed away from everything that resembles human decency. Listen for a moment to George Jackson's description of life in Soledad Prison's O-Wing:

> This place destroys the logical processes of the mind. A man's thoughts become completely disorganized. The noise, madness streaming from every throat, frustrated sounds from the bars, metallic sounds from the walls, the steel trays, the iron beds bolted to the wall, the hollow sounds from a cast iron sink, a toilet, the smells, the human waste thrown at us, unwashed bodies, the rotten food. One can understand the depression felt by an inmate on max row. He's fallen as far as he can get into the social trap. Relief is so distant that it is very easy for him to lose his hopes. It's worse than Vietnam. And the guards with the carbines, and their sticks and tear gas are there to preserve this terror, to preserve it at any cost.

This in fact is what they told us at the trial in San Jose. I'd like to read a passage from our cross examination of one Sergeant Murphy, who was being questioned about San Quentin's policy about preventing escapes.

> Question: And to be certain I understand the significance of that policy, sir, does that policy mean that if people are attempting to escape, and if they have hostages, and if the guards are able at all to prevent that escape, that they are to prevent that escape even if it means that every hostage is killed?
>
> Answer: That is correct.
>
> Question: And that means whether they're holding one judge or five judges, or one woman or twenty women, or one child or twenty children, that the policy of San Quentin guards is that at all costs they must prevent the escape. Is that right?
>
> Answer: That also includes the officers that work in the institution, sir.
>
> Question: Alright. Even if they are holding other officers who work in the institution, that should not deter the San Quentin correctional officers from preventing an escape at all costs. Is that right?
>
> Answer: That is correct.
>
> Question: In other words, it is more important to prevent the escape than to save human life. Is that correct?
>
> Answer: Yes, sir. [*Ooh! Right!* applause]

You can find this in the official court records of the trial. This Sergeant Murphy told us that day why San Quentin guards were so eager to pump their bullets into the bodies of Jonathan Jackson, William Christmas, James McClain, and Ruchell Magee even if it meant that a judge, a DA, and women jurors might also be felled by their bullets. The terror of life in prison, its awesome presence in the society at large, could not be disturbed. Murphy called the prison by its rightful name. He captured the essence of the sociopolitical function of prisons today, for he was talking about a self-perpetuating system of terror. For prisons are political weapons; they function as means of containing elements in this society which threaten the stability of the larger system.

In prisons, people who are actually or potentially disruptive of the status quo are confined, contained, punished, and in some cases, forced to undergo psychological treatment by mind-altering drugs. This is happening in the state of California. The prison system is a weapon of repression. The government views young black and brown people as actually and potentially the most rebellious elements of this society. And thus the jails and prisons of this society are overflowing with young people of color. Anyone who has seen the streets of ghettos and barrios can already understand how easily a sister or a brother can fall victim to the police who are always there *en masse*.

Depending on the area, this country's prison population contains from forty-five percent to eighty-five percent people of color. Nationally, sixty percent of all women prisoners are black. And tens of thousands of prisoners in city and county jails have never been convicted of any crime; they're simply there, victims—they're there under the control of insensitive, incompetent, and often blatantly racist public defenders who insist that they plead guilty even though they know that their client is just as innocent as they are. And for those who have committed a crime, we have to seek out the root cause. And we seek this cause not in them as individuals, but in the capitalist system that produces the need for crime in the first place. [applause]

As one student of the prisons system has said, "Thus the materially hungry must steal to survive, and the spiritually hungry commit antisocial acts because their human needs cannot be met in a property-oriented state. It is a fair estimate," he goes on to say, "that somewhere around 90 percent of the crimes committed would not be considered crimes or would not occur in a people-oriented society." In October 1970, a prisoner who had taken part in the Tombs rebellion in New York gave the following answers to questions put to him by a newsman.

Question: What is your name?
Answer: I am a revolutionary.
Question: What are you charged with?
Answer: I was born black. [applause]
Question: How long have you been in?
Answer: I've had trouble since the day I was born. [applause]

Once our sisters and brothers are entrapped inside these massive medieval fortresses and dungeons, whether for nothing at all or whether for frame-up political charges, whether for trying to escape their misery through a petty property crime, through narcotics or prostitution, they are caught in a vicious circle.

For if on the other side of the walls they try to continue or to begin to be men and women, the brutality they face, the brutality they must face, increases with mounting speed. I remember very well the women in the house of detention in New York who vowed to leave the heroin alone which was beginning to destroy their lives. Women who vowed to stand up and fight a system which had driven them to illusory escape through drugs. Women who began to outwardly exhibit their new commitment and their new transformation. And these were the women whom the worst of the matrons sought out, to punish them, and to put them in the hole.

George Jackson was murdered by mindless, carbine-toting San Quentin guards because he refused, he resisted, and he helped to teach his fellow prisoners that there was hope through struggle. And now in San Quentin— in San Quentin's Adjustment Center, which is a euphemistic term for the worst of the worst in prison—there are six more brothers who are facing charges of murder stemming from that day when George was killed. There was Fleeta Drumgo, who as a Soledad Brother was recently acquitted from similar frame-up charges. There are Hugo Pinell, Larry Spain, Luis Talamantez, David Johnson, and Willie Tate.

As I was saved and freed by the people, so we must save and free these beautiful, struggling brothers. [applause] We must save them. And we must also save and free Ruchell Magee. And Wesley Robert Wells, who has spent over forty years of his life in California's prison system because he refused to submit, because he was a man. We must save, right here in Southern California, Gary Lawton. And Geronimo Ortega, and Ricardo Chavez. And all of our sisters and brothers who must live with and struggle together against the terrible realities of captivity.

My freedom was achieved as the outcome of a massive people's struggle. Young people and older people, black, brown, Asian, Native American, and white people, students, and workers. The people seized the keys which opened the gates to freedom. And we've just begun. The momentum of this movement must be sustained, and it must be increased. Let us try to seize more keys and open more gates and bring out more sisters and brothers so that they can join the ranks of our struggle out here. [applause]

In building a prison movement, we must not forget our brothers who are suffering in military prisons and the stockades on bases throughout the country and across the globe. Let us not forget Billy Dean Smith. [applause] Billy Dean Smith, one of our black brothers who is now awaiting court-martial in Fort Ord, California. In Vietnam, this courageous brother from this city—from Watts, in fact, I think—would not follow orders. For he refused, he refused to murder the Vietnamese, whom he knew as his comrades in the struggle for liberation. [applause] He would not follow orders.

And of course in the eyes of his superior, he was a very, very dangerous example to the other GIs. He had to be eliminated. So he was falsely accused with killing two white officers in Vietnam. In Biên Hòa, Vietnam. We must free Billy Dean Smith. We must free Billy Dean Smith and all his brothers and comrades who are imprisoned in the military. [applause]

We must be about the business of building a movement so strong and so powerful that it will not only free individuals like me—like the Soledad Brothers, the San Quentin Six, Billy Dean Smith—but one which will begin to attack the very foundations of the prison system itself. [applause]

And in doing this, the prison movement must be integrated into our struggles for black and brown liberation and to our struggles for an end to material want and need. A very long struggle awaits us. And we know that it would be very romantic and idealistic to entertain immediate goals of tearing down all the walls of all the jails and prisons throughout this country. We should take on the task of freeing as many of our sisters and brothers as possible. And at the same time, we must demand the ultimate abolition of the prison system along with the revolutionary transformation of this society. [applause] However, however, within the context of fighting for fundamental changes, there is something else we must do.

We must try to alter the very fabric of life behind walls as much as is possible through struggle, and there are a thousand concrete issues around which we can build this movement: uncensored and unlimited mail privileges, visits of the prisoners' choice, minimum wage levels in prison, adequate medical care—and for women this is particularly important when you consider that in some prisons a woman, a pregnant woman has to fight just to get one glass of milk per day. I saw this in New York. There are other issues. Literature must be uncensored. Prisoners must have the right to school themselves as they see fit. If they wish to learn about Marxism, Leninism, and about socialist revolution, then they should have the right to do it. [applause]

This is their right, and they should have the full flexibility to do so. There should be no more "kangaroo courts" behind prison walls. [applause] There should be no more kangaroo courts wherein one can be charged with a simple violation of prison regulations and end up spending the rest of one's life there simply because the parole board would have it that way. [applause] And there must be an end, there must be an end to the tormenting, indeterminate sentence policy with which a prisoner like George Jackson could be sentenced from one year to life after having been convicted of stealing a mere seventy-five dollars. [applause]

For if you talk to any prisoner in the state of California and in other states where the indeterminate sentence law prevails, they will inevitably say that this is the most grueling aspect of life in prison. Going before a board of ex-cops, ex–narcotics agents, ex–FBI agents, and ex–prison guards and, year after year after year after year, being told to wait it out until next time.

These are just a few of the issues that we are going to have to deal with. And all of them, every single one of them, is the kind of issue which any decent human being should be able to understand.

The need, the very urgent need to join our sisters and brothers behind bars in their struggle was brought home during the rebellion and the massacre at Attica last year.

And I would like to close by reading a brief passage from a set of reflections I wrote in Marin County Jail upon hearing of the Attica revolt and massacre.

The damage has been done, scores of men—some yet nameless—are dead. Unknown numbers are wounded. By now it would seem more people should realize that such explosions of repression are not isolated aberrations in a society, not terribly disturbing. For we have witnessed Birmingham and Orangeburg, Jackson State, Kent State, My Lai, and San Quentin August 21st. The list is unending.

None of these explosions emerged out of nothing. Rather, they all crystallized and attested to profound and extensive social infirmities.

But Attica was different from these other episodes in one very important respect. For this time, the authorities were indicted by the very events themselves; they were caught red-handed in their lies. They were publicly exposed when to justify that massacre—a massacre which was led by Governor Rockefeller and agreed to by President Nixon—when they hastened to falsify what had occurred.

Perhaps this in itself has pulled greater numbers of people from their socially inflicted slumber. Many have already expressed outrage, but outrage is not enough. Governments and prison bureaucracies must be subjected to fears and unqualified criticism for their harsh and murderous repression. But even this is not enough, for this is not yet the root of the matter. People must take a forthright stand in active support of prisoners and their grievances. They must try to comprehend the eminently human content of prisoners' stirrings and struggles. For it is justice that we seek, and many of us can already envision a world unblemished by poverty and alienation, one where the prison would be but a vague memory, a relic of the past.

But we also have immediate demands for justice right now, for fairness, and for room to think and live and act. Thank you.

12.

VERNON E. JORDAN JR.
(1935–)

Speech delivered at the National Press Club

Washington, D.C.—February 14, 1978

Vernon Jordan was a powerful civil rights leader with unprecedented access to America's business and government elite. From 1971 to 1981, Jordan served as president of the National Urban League, a mainstream civil rights organization dedicated to attacking urban poverty through programs that included job training and early childhood education. Its funding came from the federal government, foundations, and private corporations. Jordan's tremendous skills as a public speaker, organizer, political operator, and fund-raiser helped make him the civil rights movement's "ambassador to the establishment, a man of the boardrooms and the rarefied world of power and money."[1]

Jordan was born in 1935 and raised in the segregated world of Atlanta, Georgia. His father was a postal worker and his mother ran a successful catering business. The family lived in the nation's first government-funded housing project, populated by a mix of hardworking, ambitious African Americans. Jordan's mother raised her three sons to believe they could do anything. As Jordan recalls in his 2001 memoir, *Jordan Can Read!*, his mother nicknamed him "Man." She always addressed him that way, even in the letters she wrote him when he was away at camp or in college.

In an era when whites routinely called black men "boy," Jordan said his mother's nickname for him "was her positive way to counteract what she knew would be the outside world's—the white world's—view of me even after I had officially passed into manhood."[2]

Jordan did not fail his mother. He excelled in school and was a talented public speaker from an early age. In the late 1940s, his father took him to an NAACP mass meeting where the nation's most famous civil rights lawyer, Thurgood Marshall, was speaking. As Jordan recalls, Marshall's "determination and confidence that blacks would gain their civil rights were so thrilling that I said to my father as we were walking from the church, 'Daddy, I'm going to be a lawyer like Thurgood Marshall.' "[3] Jordan says his father looked at him like he was crazy, but Jordan was quite serious.

Jordan graduated from high school in 1953 and enrolled at DePauw University, a virtually all-white school in Indiana. While his college-bound friends headed for the historically black Howard University, Jordan was drawn to the challenge of trying something completely different and, as he wrote, going places where blacks weren't expected to go. The decision was, in part, "a natural outgrowth of my desire to change the way blacks lived in the United States."[4]

Nevertheless, when it was time for Jordan to choose a law school, there was no doubt it would be Howard University, Thurgood Marshall's alma mater. Howard was the intellectual hub of the NAACP's decades-long court battle to outlaw segregation. Jordan earned his law degree in 1960 and moved back to Atlanta to begin his career as a civil rights attorney. He took a job with one of the city's most revered civil rights lawyers, Donald Hollowell. Jordan quickly found himself on the front lines of the fight to end Jim Crow discrimination. Hollowell represented two black students suing the University of Georgia to be allowed in. When they won the case, it fell to Jordan to escort one of them, Charlayne Hunter, through a menacing mob of students (Charlayne Hunter-Gault would later become a prominent journalist). The image of Jordan's towering, six-four body shielding Hunter from assault is one of the classic photos of the civil rights era. For Jordan, this and other photographs capture not just the "ugliness of the scene," but also the "great dignity that stood in marked contrast to the baseness of those who came out to jeer."[5]

After a year clerking for Hollowell, Jordan was recruited by the NAACP to serve as the organization's Georgia field director. It was a high-profile position that involved opening new branches, expanding membership, and organizing boycotts and demonstrations. Jordan excelled at the job and, over the next decade, moved steadily into positions of greater power and responsibility in the national civil rights movement. In 1964, he joined the Southern Regional Council and became director of its Voter Education Project. As *Time* magazine later reported, "By 1968 the South had nearly 2 million new black voters, the number of black elected officials in the region had jumped almost eightfold, to 564, and Vernon Jordan was a nationally known civil rights leader."[6] In 1970 Jordan was tapped to run the United Negro College Fund, an organization that raises money to fund a consortium of black colleges nationwide. One year later, Jordan was recruited to head up the National Urban League.

Jordan was president of the Urban League for ten years. In that time he controlled an annual budget of more than $100 million. The federal government supplied much of the money, thanks in part to Jordan's close ties to the administrations of presidents Richard Nixon and Jimmy Carter. Jordan sometimes played tennis on the White House courts with Nixon aide John Ehrlichman, a practice that infuriated some militant civil rights activists who disliked the Republican White House. A young man who worked at the league headquarters in New York City confronted Jordan about it one day. He said he couldn't work for Jordan knowing he played tennis with Ehrlichman. According to Jordan, he asked the man how much he earned and the man told him $27,000 a year, a middle-class salary at the time. Jordan said, "You know what? I'm down there playing tennis with John Ehrlichman so you can continue to be a $27,000-a-year militant giving me hell about it."[7] Jordan's response to the man reflected one of his basic beliefs: "It is possible, and sometimes absolutely imperative, to work with people with whom you have fundamental disagreements. Very little would be accomplished in the world—in government, business, family, anywhere—if this were not true."[8] In Jordan's view, his tennis games at the White House helped to keep federal dollars flowing to the Urban League.

As Jordan expanded his efforts to raise money from corporate America, he was recruited to serve on the boards of several major firms, including Bankers Trust and Celanese Corporation, a chemical company. His decision to accept these lucrative positions drew scorn from militants such as the writer Amiri Baraka, who called the Urban League "a vehicle for allowing the interests and thinking of white racist monopoly capital to penetrate the black movement."[9] But Jordan believed that real racial equality would elude African Americans so long as they remained on the margins of the business world. Besides, Jordan reasoned in his memoir, "Why should we just be the beneficiaries of corporate largesse but not have a say in how that largesse would be distributed? If members of corporate America could be on our boards, why couldn't we be on theirs?"[10]

As head of the Urban League, Jordan often spoke about the crucial need for black economic advancement. In this speech, delivered at the National Press Club in 1978, Jordan says his focus on the nation's economic problems and urban policies has drawn criticism from people on the left and the right who argue that civil rights leaders should stay focused on civil rights, rather than other national issues. Jordan responds that civil rights, alone, will not allow African Americans to advance: "The masses of black people did not witness significant changes in their lives because of the rights they won in the 1960s. We were poor then, we are poor today. We were disadvantaged then, we remain so today."

Two years after delivering this speech, Jordan was shot and nearly killed by a white racist in Fort Wayne, Indiana. He spent months recovering, but was eventually able to resume a full life. In 1981, after a decade at the helm of the Urban League and twenty years in the civil rights movement, Jordan retired from his role as public servant to join a powerful private law firm in Washington, D.C. He was again criticized for selling out the cause. Jordan said he wasn't abandoning the principles of the movement, just his role as a leader.

The suggestion that he should have remained in the movement irked Jordan. The point of the black freedom struggle was "to remove barriers and let black people listen to that voice inside that tells them what their honorable life's pursuit should be. No black movement worth its salt would ever attempt to still that voice," he wrote in his memoir. Sounding a theme he once heard from Ruth Simmons, the first black woman to run an Ivy League school, he wrote, "Everything in the world belongs to black people, and there is much in this world. . . . There are 30 million black people in America, and there is a role and a function (perhaps even several over a lifetime) for each of us."[11]

In the fall of 2001, Jordan went on a national tour to promote his memoir. He said one reason he wrote the book was that "people in America think I was born on January 20, 1993," the day Bill Clinton was sworn in as president.[12] Jordan and Clinton had been friends for more than a decade, and Jordan was one of the president's closest confidants. Their relationship—and Jordan's influence—drew a great deal of press. Jordan headed Clinton's 1992 transition team and served as an unofficial adviser for the rest of Clinton's presidency. Jordan struggled to protect his reputation when he allegedly tried to help Clinton cover up a sex scandal that engulfed the White House in 1998. Jordan was never convicted of wrongdoing. Since 2000, he has served as a senior managing director at the investment firm Lazard Ltd. in New York.

MR. PRESIDENT, DEAREST GUESTS, ladies and gentlemen, it's a great pleasure to be with you here today and to be at the National Press Club again. I'd like to wish all of you, especially the ladies, Happy Valentine's Day.

I may disappoint many among you today, because while I will discuss some aspects of the administration's policies, I have not come to Washington today to criticize President Carter, nor do I intend to play the game of issuing a score card on the administration's record. I'd like to talk about something that's even more important in the long run, something that is increasingly a topic of press discussion. I know it's "soft" news, less sexy than attacking political leaders or making proposals to bring peace in the Middle East. But there is so much misunderstanding of the proper role of civil rights agencies that I think it is important to discuss it in this forum today.

Some weeks back, I was a guest on William Buckley's *Firing Line*, and the one theme he kept coming back to and later devoted several columns to was this: Why do civil rights leaders concentrate on national economic policy, urban policies, and other issues when their proper role is to stick to civil rights? I thought this was a theme peculiar to the specific ideological viewpoint Buckley and other conservatives cling to. By the way, this new concern for civil rights is heartening. Back in the sixties, the same people were upset because civil rights seemed to infringe on property rights, to which they give higher priority. Since most black leaders favor expanded government efforts and increased domestic spending, I could see where there would now be a reluctance to see greater black involvement in issues perceived as general economic ones.

But since then, I have come across liberals who make the same point. They've told me that blacks—as blacks—shouldn't be taking public positions on energy, tax cuts, unemployment, and other key issues. We should be concentrating on the moral aspects of securing full civil rights for minorities and leave the other issues to experts more qualified to deal with them, they say. Two Sundays ago, the *New York Times* made that point in effect when it said, and I quote:

> Increasingly, black leaders have taken up economic issues and other matters whose relationship to the welfare of minorities, while real, is not as direct or as clear cut as before. In so doing, those leaders have raised difficult questions about whom they represent, who their allies are, and whether the moral banner they once held so high still carries the same inspiration.

Today I hope to answer some of those difficult questions.

Frankly, I find it difficult to understand why sophisticated analysts—people presumably familiar with the realities of American life—should have doubts about the changed direction of the civil rights movement. It would seem self-evident that changing conditions demand changed strategy and tactics. In the 1950s and '60s, the basic thrust of blacks and other minorities was to achieve the equality under the law that had been denied them. Eating at the lunch counter, the right to sit anywhere on the bus, the right to drink water, rather than "colored" water, the right to vote or to check into a hotel are all easily understandable. The denial of those simple rights was an affront to human rights and to the democratic system.

The issues then were clear-cut. The actors in the civil rights drama were clearly identified. The good guys and the bad guys. The good guys marched peacefully, were nonviolent, suffered death, violence, jail, and other indignities. The bad guys looked mean and acted mean. They used cattle prods, water hoses, and dogs on women and children. The bad guys promised never, "No, not one," massive resistance, and segregation today, tomorrow, and forever. Behind the discussion about what the real nature of today's civil rights movement should be is a lingering nostalgia for those good old days of clear-cut moral decisions and easily defined issues.

But that phase of the movement is over. The basic rights were won through judicial decisions, legislation, and executive orders. But the reality behind those rights has not kept pace. Black people today can check into any hotel in America, but most do not have the wherewithal to check out. It is too often forgotten that the 1963 March on Washington was for more than just abstract rights. It was for jobs and freedom. To a large extent, we won the freedoms, but we still do not have the jobs. There are today a half million more black people unemployed than at the time of the March on Washington in 1963. So economics was always a part of the civil rights movement's concerns. So, too, were housing, urban policies, health, and a whole range of issues that affected blacks disproportionately because we were and are disproportionately poor, in bad housing, in bad health, and in deteriorating urban centers.

But are those properly civil rights issues? Yes they are. Because the disproportionate disadvantage borne by blacks and other minorities is the heritage of centuries of oppression. It is the residue of a society that practiced institutional discrimination and racism. It is the result of a complex web of federal, local, and private sector practices that operated to the exclusion of blacks and their interests. The rights granted in the 1960s left that structure largely intact. The National Urban League's report on the state of black America 1978 documents the fact that black progress has been limited. In the report's words, "There is a disturbing duality of the black economy, a slowly growing black middle class, and an increasingly jobless lower economic class."

So despite some gains in employment and in education, the masses of black people did not witness significant changes in their lives because of the rights they won in the 1960s. We were poor then; we are poor today. We were disadvantaged then; we remain so today.

There is a moral dimension in this. We are saying to the American people, "You cannot simply say, 'You have your rights. We won't discriminate in an overt fashion anymore,' and then just walk away from the problem." We are saying that there is a moral imperative to right the wrongs of the past.

Black people were placed on a lower track and continue to struggle for survival on that same track. We are saying that the rights granted in the sixties are hollow unless we are given the opportunity to compete on the same track as whites. The reluctance of our society to understand the simple point that black people want equality in *real* life and not just on the law books is mute testimony to the undercurrent of racism that still survives in America.

So I would contend there is a straight line that runs through the civil rights movement's history, a line of concern with improving the life chances of black people. Economics, urban policy, and related issues were always at the forefront of our concerns, but the first line of attack had to be [against] overtly discriminatory barriers. Once those barriers were lowered, we could then pursue our basic goal of achieving black equality in the realities of American life. And that is why civil rights leadership has in the 1970s become so concerned with jobs and urban policy, to mention just two basic areas. To some, it may seem as though we are now no different from any other group asking for an improved economy, for urban revitalization, or for similar goals, but we *are* different.

We bring a specifically black viewpoint and experience to those issues, and we are concerned with bringing to the nation's attention the simple fact that generalized answers to national problems will perpetuate black disadvantage. Let me illustrate this. The unemployment rate is supposed to be trending downward, the overall official rates are now at 6.3 percent level. There is a widespread feeling that unemployment is coming under control and is no longer the pressing problem it was a while back when a tenth of the labor force was out of work. But from a black perspective, that's not true at all. The black unemployment rate is not only well over double the white rate, but it is slightly higher than it was a year ago. The white rate has improved; the black rate has continued to rise. We don't even discuss here how the official statistics don't include many of the black unemployed, at all. My point is that while white Americans are talking about how well the economic recovery is progressing, black people in America are still in an economic depression.

Urban revitalization is another issue demanding a black perspective. Many people say the cities can be restored to economic health by attracting the middle class back. But what about the largely poor, black urban population? Not a word. The implication is that they'll have to be moved out somewhere else. Some of the urban proposals I've heard remind me of the old urban renewal programs that became tagged "black removal" because blacks were bulldozed out of their homes to make way for luxury housing and for office centers.

Let me quote that *Times* article again. It says: "The National Urban League denounced the presidential plan for a $25 billion tax cut. At first glance, it might seem that a reduction would benefit minorities by expanding the economy." Well, first glances are very misleading. The National Urban League opposes the tax cut because it would not solve the problems of minorities. There is little evidence to conclude that the job-stimulation effect of the tax cut would trickle down to minorities. We think the white unemployment rate would drop a little but the high, astronomically high, black rate would be largely unaffected.

There are those who believe in John Kennedy's phrase that a rising tide lifts all boats, but we must remind them that a rising tide lifts only those boats in the water, and black people are in the dry dock of this economy. Rather than scatter $25 billion to the winds, we want that money, or a large part of it, used to create jobs directly, either in public service employment, in public works, or in creative incentives to private industry to hire and train the unemployed. A broad tax cut would not only defeat our goal of lowering black unemployment, but would create a large deficit that would, in itself, become the excuse for not undertaking urban programs the nation needs.

But then there is something else in those tax proposals, something virtually no one has latched on to. The administration is proposing to extend investment tax credit to new construction as well as to machinery. What that means is that the government, through the tax laws, would offer incentives to industry to accelerate the abandonment of older cities. In effect, it is a subsidy to increase black unemployment. It is ironic that this proposal comes at a time when the administration is about to announce its national urban policy. Whatever positive measures that policy will include are likely to be offset by tax policies that drain more jobs from the cities. In the light of this, how can anyone claim that civil rights leaders ought to be tending to the business of fighting for abstract civil rights when our constituents face economic policies that leave them destitute, without jobs, without the human dignity we preach to other nations?

Civil rights don't take place in a vacuum. They are meaningful only in the real world—the world where people have to survive to work, to raise their families, to instill in their children hope for the future and the skills to function in a society where a broad back and the desire to work are no longer enough. That is why we are concerned with tax cuts, with energy, with a multitude of issues some white people think are not the concern of blacks. That is why we see our present efforts as being the logical outcome of those struggles for basic rights of the 1960s. And that is why we insist there is a vital, moral component to the current struggle.

The *Times* story asks whether the moral banner they once held so high still carries the same inspiration. And the unequivocal answer is, "Yes it does." It does because the struggle for equality is identical with the struggle for jobs, for housing, for education, for urban vitality. When a third of the poor are drawn from a tenth of the population, that's a moral issue. When a third of the jobless are drawn from a tenth of the population, that's a moral issue. When public and private policies strangle the cities in which the majority of blacks live, that's a moral issue. When a nation that subjected its black people first to slavery and then to persistent oppression and now subjects them to disproportionate disadvantage, that's a moral issue. And it is a moral issue when people label limited affirmative action to help blacks overcome past and present discriminatory practices as reverse discrimination.

Every statistic in any field shows continued white advantage. Where is this "reverse discrimination"? In an economy where blacks with some college have the same unemployment rates as white high school dropouts, where blacks with some high school education have double the unemployment rates of whites who never got past elementary school. It's a moral issue when welfare is labeled a black program while the majority of welfare recipients are white. It's a moral issue when every halting step of black progress is fought, when policies that would perpetuate a system that locks blacks into the bottom of our society are proposed. And it is that moral factor that continues to distinguish the civil rights movement. It is that moral factor that makes our views on tax policy different from those of clearly defined interest groups. And it is that moral factor so many people refuse to acknowledge today. Their refusal is based on the desire to avoid the necessary steps to modify the function of our society in a way that would help blacks and other minorities overcome their present disadvantage. Steps like a national full employment policy, a Marshall Plan for the cities, a national health plan, and others.

And what we ask for ourselves, in a spirit of enlightened self-interest, and in a spirit of desperate need, will also benefit the white poor. Everything we got in the sixties, everything we won through bitter struggles and moral suasion helped more white people than black people.

So I'm here today to say that the moral banner is still unfurled. It still waves high above the current struggle. The issues are more complex, and the resistance more entrenched. But the civil rights movement is still about the business of bringing America's minorities into the mainstream of our national life, with all of the rewards and responsibilities others take for granted. In the 1960s, we fought, bled, and died to build an open, pluralistic, integrated society. In the 1970s, that is still our goal, that is still our moral burden.

Thank you very much.

13.

DOROTHY I. HEIGHT
(1912–2010)

Speech delivered at the first Scholarly Conference
on Black Women

Washington, D.C.—November 13, 1979

Dorothy Height was one of the most powerful women in the long civil rights struggle. Through her leadership in the Young Women's Christian Association (YWCA), the Delta Sigma Theta sorority, and the National Council of Negro Women, along with countless other councils and committees, Height spent most of the twentieth century fighting poverty, racism, and sexism. Her work ranged from leading fair-wage battles in the 1930s, to organizing voter registration drives in the 1960s, to initiating nationwide black family reunions in the 1980s and '90s. Height pursued her ambitions with the vigor of a missionary, deeply believing that her duty as a Christian was to help people who suffered from discrimination and poverty.

Height was born in 1912 and raised in Rankin, Pennsylvania, a small steel town near Pittsburgh. Her father was a successful building contractor and painter, her mother a nurse and housekeeper. Her parents were marginally active in Republican politics, but as Height notes in her 2003 memoir, *Open Wide the Freedom Gates*, the major political parties had little to offer African Americans during a time when "lynching and unemployment were realities of everyday life." Rather, Height wrote, "Negro

Americans gained ground through the kind of self-help that had charac-
terized our struggle since slavery—by creating our own organizations to
meet our needs."[1] According to Cornel West and Henry Louis Gates Jr.,
Height epitomized the middle-class "club women" who ran these crucial organizations. "White-gloved, wearing hats and pearls, these women
cut an exemplary, no-nonsense figure for the community. Through their
organizations, they could provide for the sick and the destitute, care for
orphaned children, [and] establish beneficiary societies when no one else
could."[2]

Height inherited the role of "club woman" from her mother, who belonged to the Pennsylvania Federation of Colored Women's Clubs and
brought young Dorothy to every meeting. "There I saw women working,
organizing, teaching themselves." What she observed left Height with
a deep and lasting impression of how to get things done, as well as a
profound sense of belonging. "Since those early days," she wrote, "I've
never doubted my place in the sisterhood."[3]

Height was a talented student and exemplary orator. She graduated
from high school in 1929 and won a national public speaking contest that
earned her a four-year scholarship to college. Height applied to Barnard College in New York but was turned away because the school had
reached its quota of two black students per year. Instead, Height enrolled
at New York University, where she earned a BA in three years. She used
the fourth year of her scholarship to earn a master's degree in educational psychology.

Once out of school, Height took various jobs serving poor commu-
nities around New York City. During the dark years of the Depression,
Height's skills as a savvy and effective organizer were much in demand.
She was hired, at age twenty-three, as a personnel supervisor in New
York's Welfare Administration and soon found herself in charge of sev-
eral thousand workers and an array of special projects. During this time,
Height was also an active member of many different local and national
youth councils. By 1937, she was an officer of the United Christian Youth
Movement of North America, president of the New York State Christian
Youth Council, chair of the Harlem Youth Council, and an officer of the
National Youth Congress.

Height recalled the 1930s as the most politically vibrant era of the
twentieth century for young people. "We really believed," she said, "that
we were building a new world."[4] Her goals were ambitious: "Laws to

prevent lynching, the breakdown of segregation in the armed forces, free access to public accommodations, equal opportunity in education and employment, security for the aged and infirm, protection for children, reform of the criminal justice system, an end to bias and discrimination in housing, and recognition of women's rights," she wrote. Height worked for decades to try to achieve these goals. Looking back, she wrote, "I was determined to make America worthy of her stated ideals."[5]

In the fall of 1937, when Height was twenty-five, she met the most powerful black woman of the New Deal era, Mary McLeod Bethune. The daughter of former slaves, Bethune managed to get an education, start a college for African American women, and become an influential adviser to President Franklin D. Roosevelt. In 1935, Bethune launched the National Council of Negro Women (NCNW). The new organization aimed to unite disparate black women's groups into one powerful entity devoted to ending racial and gender discrimination and improving the lives of black women and their families. Bethune was hosting a meeting of the NCNW at the Harlem YWCA, where Height had just taken a job. Bethune's friend First Lady Eleanor Roosevelt was on hand to address the group. Bethune noticed Height's poise and ability and recruited her on the spot to the NCNW.

The meeting changed Height's life. "On that fall day, the redoubtable Mary McLeod Bethune put her hand on me," Height recalled. "She drew me into her dazzling orbit of people in power and people in poverty. I remember how she made her fingers into a fist to illustrate for the women the significance of working together to eliminate injustice. 'The freedom gates are half ajar,' she said. 'We must pry them fully open.' "[6]

Height worked closely with Bethune for nearly two decades, helping to build the NCNW into "one of the most vocal and visible organizations advocating the rights of black women."[7] In 1957, two years after her mentor died, Height was elected president of the organization. She served in that role until she retired in 1998. She remained chair and president emeritus of the NCNW until her death in 2010.

As head of the NCNW, Height was the only woman chosen to serve on an elite committee of civil rights leaders formed in 1960. The group met on a regular basis in New York City to discuss issues in the movement and generate philanthropic support. Eventually calling itself the Council for United Civil Rights Leadership, the group included Martin Luther King Jr., Roy Wilkins, and A. Philip Randolph. Despite Height's inclusion in the

Big Six, as it became known, women were treated as junior members in the movement.

During the planning stage of the 1963 March on Washington, the male organizers refused to appoint a woman to speak at the massive rally. According to Height, organizer Bayard Rustin said that women were well represented in all the groups that would be attending the rally and therefore didn't need to have their own speaker. Height protested the decision but lost. "I've never seen a more immovable force," Height recalled. "We could not get women's participation taken seriously."[8] Height and her peers learned a crucial lesson: "If we did not demand our rights, we were not going to get them," she wrote. After the March on Washington, Height said, "women became much more aware and much more aggressive in facing up to sexism in our dealings with the male leadership in the movement."[9]

Dorothy Height was given numerous honors and awards for her achievements. They include thirty-six honorary degrees from universities, ranging from Howard to Harvard, as well as the Presidential Medal of Freedom, which President Bill Clinton awarded her in 1994. A decade later, President George W. Bush presented Dorothy Height with the Congressional Gold Medal, the highest civilian award given by the United States Congress. At the award ceremony, former labor secretary Alexis Herman observed that Height can often be seen in historic civil rights photographs, standing alongside icons such as Martin Luther King Jr., Robert F. Kennedy, and the activist John Lewis. When Height was asked why she appears in so many of these images, Height said "I learned to stand in the center so I wouldn't be elbowed out of the picture."[10]

Height gave this speech at a 1979 symposium on the legacy of the NCNW. She recounts the organization's achievements under her leadership, and argues that women formed the backbone of the civil rights movement even when, she says, "our story has not been told." Some one thousand people attended the conference, which marked the official opening of the Bethune Museum and Archives for Black Women in Washington, D.C. It is the first institution devoted exclusively to black women's history.

Height ends her speech by urging audience members to rededicate themselves to community service because, she says, "What we did in '79 is not going to be good enough in the eighties." For Height, that meant launching a major new initiative in the 1980s that focused on strengthening

black families. In 1986, the NCNW organized the first Black Family Re-
union celebration, a massive day-long festival on the Mall in Washington,
D.C., that brought together multiple generations of black families to celebrate their heritage. The event drew more than 200,000 people, and soon
there were reunions in major cities from Los Angeles to Philadelphia. By
1992, more than 10 million people had attended one of the celebrations.
Height's idea was to remind African Americans of the traditional values
that had enabled them to overcome historic discrimination, and to share
practical information for getting ahead. "We are not a problem people,"
she explained in her 2003 memoir, "we are a people with problems." The
Black Family Reunions were meant to "awaken people to their rights, responsibilities, and opportunities. . . . I know we have black people—though
some people may not yet know this themselves—who are leaders. With
the right kind of encouragement, these people could show their brothers
and sisters the way."[11]

I CAME INTO OFFICE at a time when we were struggling very hard as black
women in this country, seeking to get hold of our organization and to hold
our heads high in the society around us. One of the things that had confronted us was that we were the inheritors of a great organization headed by
Mrs. Bethune, and we did not have tax-exempt status. And I think there are
people in this room who remember, as I do, how we stood on the floor and
said, "If it means we have to give up political action, let's not worry about it."
And we struggled on. We could not get any contributions based upon the
person's being exempt.

So one of the first things that we did was to seek a way to give us the
chance to expand our program so that the political activity that we can never
give up would somehow be in balance with the rest of it. And I think the
educational foundation that was established—and Daisy Lampkin served as
its chair and Dorothy Ferebee followed her—was a means through which we
were able to initiate new kinds of program activities. And one of the first of
these was the Bethune House here in Washington, the first 221-D.C. housing program sponsored by a nongovernmental organization.

But it was very shortly thereafter that the country was caught up in something else. It was moving towards what we had said in the NAACP, we would
be "free by '63." But little did we know the events that would somehow step
up around us. [Previous speaker] Mrs. Mason has referred to Rosa Parks,

and you know the story of Montgomery. And you know what that did to the whole nation and what it set in motion: the sit-ins, the pray-ins, all the different kind of things that were happening. And in the middle of all of that as the things began to move, the Taconic Foundation, under the leadership of Stephen Currier, wanted to know what could be done to help deal with the problems of the black community, and the black family. And they called together Roy Wilkins and Whitney Young, and Martin Luther King Jr., James Farmer, C. Eric Lincoln—who had written a book on the black Muslims—A. Philip Randolph, Jack Greenberg—who was with the NAACP Legal Defense Fund—and me. And made us pledge that we would somehow stay together, never send a substitute but come ourselves to each meeting, and that we would dedicate one day every six weeks to thinking together about where we were.

And I remember that each one took an assignment. I took the assignment of organizations because I was interested in organizations. And one of the significant things that I think we often forget is that black people and black women have been as shut out of volunteer opportunities on boards and committees and organizations outside of their own [communities]—they've been just as shut out there as we are out of jobs. And so I began to work with that kind of study. And someone else took housing, and away we went. And then suddenly something happened: Medgar Evers was assassinated. And, on the morning after his assassination, Stephen Currier called us all back together again, and he said, "We've been thinking of ourselves as a kind of united civil rights leadership." But he said, "What we need to do now is to see how this country can be brought to a realization that it cannot exist with this kind of thing happening, and what all this signifies."

He sent out telegrams to a hundred people to meet at the Carlisle Hotel the next morning. Ninety-some persons appeared, and he had each of us tell the story of the organization and its driving. Roy Wilkins had to leave for the funeral of Medgar Evers. And then after that, the rest of us all had a chance to talk. I had to say what it meant to black women that we were a part of the whole civil rights movement, that we were a civil rights organization, really, under the leadership of women. And that we had had a major hand in that whole beginning with the significant male leadership, to point out that we had to add to that great group that started, the Student Nonviolent Coordinating Committee, no matter what it was doing or who agreed with its tactics or not. Because as women, we could not see our children and our youth struggling and have them on the outside of our effort.

And after we had each told the stories, Stephen Currier made an appeal. He received pledges of some $800,000 for the civil rights movement. Those organizations that were tax-exempt could reap the full benefits. We were not tax-exempt, but we did have the educational arm, which was the educational foundation. So that as contributions were made, we received $50,000 from that civil rights pot. And I think I have to add there that another piece of money that came to us through the civil rights effort was from Martin Luther King Jr., who when he received the Nobel Peace Prize came back and he said to all of us around the table, "I have to give every organization its piece." I think we know a lot about Doctor King, but I think that's a little-known story of how he shared with each of those organizations.

From that little spark, we were asked also to perform another function, because we did have an educational foundation. We were asked to become the trustees for the funds the NAACP—which was not tax-exempt—gathered for the Evers children. And I'll always remember how Mrs. Lampkin, when the time came, said to us, "It is good that we did this, because those were lean days at many points." But we held that money and the interest, and it all went to that family and those children, because it was what people who had expressed their concern wanted them to have.

So that in a sense the civil rights movement and our role in it shaped the task of anyone carrying leadership in the organization. It meant—and I look over here and I see Arnetta Wallace—that on a certain day after the four little girls were murdered in Birmingham, that we descended into Birmingham, fourteen heads of national women's organizations, members of the National Council of Negro Women. And we were there, we marched through the bayonets, and we felt the tension in the city.

Dr. Ferebee and I were there in Selma long before the Selma march. We went down at the time that Prathia Wynn and James Forman called us and said, "Three hundred children are in jail here and nobody knows where they are. We need some outside voice that will come in and help us to get that story out." And we got there just as the three hundred children were released from jail, and some of their pictures looked like the children in Cambodia because they were bare bones; they had been denied food and services. And when we asked them, "What have you been having?" one little boy said, "We've been eating boll weevil gravy." And when I looked at some of the children, I said to them, "You say so many bad things about people here. Don't you think there are some good white people?" And the little boy who had said the most looked up, and he said—he looked at Dr. Ferebee and me, and he said, "Well, there must be some." [laughter] But you know, it was a driving thing to think that you live in a country where a child of one race would say, "There must be somebody of the other race who's decent."

And all of that kept pushing us. We went to Atlanta and brought together representatives—young women—who had been the victims of law enforcement officers in the jails. We heard them tell about the vaginal searches by orderlies who dipped their gloves in Lysol. We heard them tell about how they banded together so that they would not be raped by the officers all around them. And we found ourselves, little by little, pulling together all our forces to say, "What is there we can do?" And I remember the meeting that we had in Atlanta, when we were talking about this, because we brought together white women's groups also, that they might know what was happening as well.

And I'll never forget; we called it the Women's Inter-organizational Committee, because we didn't know what to call it. We didn't want to say it was a civil rights meeting. And when the meeting was over, one of the women said, "Well, you know, the initials of what we call [ourselves] is WIC. And it if means that if each one of us, no matter whether we are black or white, should go back into her community and be like a wick, lighted, that could be—that little bit of light, that could make a difference." And out of that, the whole concept of WICS was developed.

And when we were called upon to reach young women in poverty, the very coalition we had put together became the one that Sargent Shriver could call upon to help recruit young women for the Job Corps. And someone said, "What shall we call it?" And I remember Helen Racklin saying, "Well we already have WIC," so we called it Women in Community Service.

In other words, the National Council of Negro Women has been there even when our story has not been told. You may remember that in the summer of 1963, there was a great march on Washington. We were there. We did something that we were asked not to do, but it was too late when we heard they were asking that no one meet after the march on Washington. We held a meeting called After the March, What? And out of that meeting, there came a molding of some new spirits and new interests. So that by 1964, when Bob Moses called for the summer in Mississippi, the freedom schools, we had a coalition of women already working together, and those women went down into Mississippi on Wednesdays. Etta Barnett is one of them, who is here tonight.

And we went in interracial teams with an idea that was designed by Polly

Cowan, that we would go in to see what was happening to young people in the freedom schools. But that we would always carry our talents and we would always do something that would be significant. So out of Wednesdays in Mississippi, we began to build bridges of understanding between black and white women in the South and black and white women in communities across the country. And one of the significant things that had happened in that Atlanta meeting I mentioned was that we asked the women who were there, because so much was being said about, you know, "Yankees stay home! Don't interfere with what's going on in the South." We asked them a question: "Does it help you or does it hinder you to have a national organization come in?" And the women, Clarice Harvey, speaking for one group of women said, "We're from Jackson, Mississippi. We are black and white women. We are seeing each other here and knowing each other for the first time. But we know one thing, we will never be apart again." And then she said, "Don't give up. A national organization is like a long-handled spoon: you can come in and stir us up and get us moving."

I always thought that that was a good demonstration of what Mrs. Bethune had in mind, in saying that, when you think about it, there is no such thing as just being local when you're part of a national movement. And that that sense of being a part of a national movement came through in some very real ways. We had, after that, workshops in Mississippi, which got us into housing—into housing with low-income families. We were working with hunger, pig banks—we established pig banks and pig agreements with families. Because the people we saw in the workshops in Mississippi said to us, "We are concerned about our rights, but we have no jobs and our children have to eat." And so we helped them to see how to plant gardens, how to—I don't know, you don't grow pigs, (laughter) raise pigs, I guess—how to deal with pigs, and we taught them how to feed them. And some of those people said to us afterwards, "We learned through those pigs that it makes a difference what you eat. And many of us have never had the food that we needed."

Today, the National Council of Negro Women is able to report that we have assets that are some four to five million dollars. But we could not have even thought about this before 1965 when we got our tax exemption. December 1, 1965. There's a recent report just released on philanthropy to women's organizations. And it cites five organizations, and we rank third in terms of organizations who have received substantial support from foundations. In 1966, when the Ford Foundation made us a grant of $300,000, that was the most that it or any other foundation had given to a women's organization. Nineteen sixty-six! Just think of that. So it shows you where women's groups were.

Out of that experience, we learned one thing: that the council, in order to do the job, had to have the supporting services of staff. We had to have staff who could understand that they were part of an organization that is essentially volunteer, but that their job was to be a part of a partnership and to be supportive. And so today across this country, in some twenty locations, we have moved to the point where we have staff working at many different levels. There are one hundred forty-six of them. There are seventy-two who will be in this convention. But the important thing is not their numbers, nor that there are jobs, but it is the realization that where black women are in a society requires that we have the capability to work at our needs, not after hours but all through the day. That some of that continuity has to come through the kind of devoted, skilled work that staff give: disciplined and directed but responsive to the interests and concerns of the volunteers and the membership of the National Council of Negro Women.

I think another piece of movement I'd like to mention that I think has affected us over these years came because we were working to put [a statue of] Mrs. Bethune in Lincoln Park. When we started out in 1960, people said this was, you know, just something that we were discussing. But how could we stand to see Abraham Lincoln with a slave at his knee, put there by the emancipated group in 1874 with the funds raised by the newly emancipated citizens, and not try to place on the other end of that park a memorial that would say black people have made a contribution in American life? Charlotte Scott gave the first five dollars she earned in her freedom to start the Emancipation Group. And so we called upon people across the country to respond.

In the course of things, Abraham Lincoln was turned around so that his back would not face Mrs. Bethune. [laughter] Every time we say that, the Interior Department corrects us and says, "He was not turned around; he was repositioned." [laughter and applause]

Another movement that hit us very hard was the movement of women. And when you ask me the question that you've asked us all about—[Which was worse,] racism or sexism?—I have to say that the International Women's Year found itself with a unique contribution, not only of our domestic work, but of our international interests and the things that we have tried to do. Because it was at that time, at the hundredth anniversary of Mrs. Bethune's birth, that we were determined that we would make and expand on the international interests. There's so many things. Mrs. Mason and I were in Haiti working in the name of the National Council of Negro Women to get the vote for women there. I thought for a moment it was Mrs. Bethune's administration, and I asked Vivian today, and she said no, it was Dr. Ferebee's administration. But they all used the same techniques. I was then president of Delta Sigma Theta, and we were called and asked to go. Vivian represented the council; Laura Lovely, [inaudible] Kappa Alpha, and I, Delta Sigma Theta, and when we said, "Where are the funds?" They said, "Oh, well, of course we know your groups will see that you get there." [laughter] And they did, but that's the way the council was represented for years and years. For we went into our pockets, and when you got there you said, "I represent the National Council of Negro Women." [laughter and applause] And you were proud to do it!

So it was to be understood that in the International Women's Year we would get support to have at Mexico City a group of women from Africa and from the Caribbean. And then we had the chance to bring them back with us to let them see the pig banks, to go to visit the housing, to visit people, and then to join us for the hundredth-birthday celebration of Mary McLeod Bethune at Bethune-Cookman College. And I tell you, that is an occasion that we will never forget.

But it also heightened the fact that we are part of a whole women's movement. I think very strongly that no group has more right to say that than we. Bill Trent tells a story that's a favorite of mine. He says that Mrs. Bethune once had a meeting in Memphis, and she'd asked a nationally known black male to make the keynote address. And as he stood, he looked at the women and he said, "If you women would be as concerned about what you put *in* your heads, as you are about what you have *on* your heads, our race would be better off." And he said, at that point, Mrs. Bethune rose and said, "Thank you, sir. You have said quite enough." [laughter and applause] "The women will decide what they have on their heads *and* what they put in their heads." [laughter and applause]

Now, I think any organization that follows that has to be concerned about women. But when you ask me the question about race and sex, I want to add something else that I saw recently in a poster. And that poster was a woman who had two chains; she was chained down with two very heavy pieces of stone, with chains on her legs. And the heading underneath was "Double Trouble." And the idea that it reflected was, take one away—one said "racism" and the other said "sexism"—take one away and she is still tied down.

Take the other away and leave that one, she's still tied down. The only way she will make it: they both have to be eliminated. [applause] And I think that as we move into our convention with an idea of imperatives for the Eighties, we need to work very hard to eliminate both racism and sexism.

Two things I want to say about our internal life. One is that the spirit of collaboration and cooperation that has been expressed in the wider society has also touched us. In 1969, we had a meeting at Nassau, in which the national organizations comprising the National Council of Negro Women said, "It is so important to build this power that we must get every member we can in our organizations to become a direct member. And that small amount that each one contributes each year can help us to build our strength." We're far from achieving that goal, but seven of our national organizations, even this year, have called upon their members to do this, and it is coming in steadily. Because, you know, as I think it was Billie Holiday [who] said it, "Mama may have and Papa may have, but God bless the child that's got his own." [applause]

Now, because as proud as we are of what we have achieved, the fact is that today we have about a ninety-nine-percent batting average in our request for government and foundation support. But we are concerned that we also keep building that internal support, because those funds come, but they're earmarked; you're not free to use them. It is what we do ourselves that makes the difference. Now the other thing that is a characteristic we've been working on is the realization that with revenue sharing, with the new federalism, with everything moving to the states, black women had better learn to get themselves together in those states, because [applause] decisions are being made in the states. And while we considered clustering areas and regions, we now are trying to see that we look at the status of black women in each of the states and try to amass our power there.

So, you see, we are in the state of still becoming. We have so far to go. But I remember two things that were said this morning that have kind of stayed with me all day. It was what Jeanetta Welch Brown said when she said [there's been] a lot of talk about some of the early days—and each of us could tell you a whole lot of things—but what she said came through to me: "There's been a lot of suffering that has gone into building the National Council of Negro Women." A lot of people in many places have put a lot into it. And then Sue Bailey Thurman, remember what she said in her message: "This is an organization of women with caring hearts." I look back and realize that I've been a part of the council since 1937. And I don't think that outside of my mother and my church, there's been anything, any person of greater influence than Mary McLeod Bethune. And the thing I'm sure, if we could all say it as a trio, we would want to say about the National Council of Negro Women is that its greatest source of strength is the depth of the vision of the dream that Mrs. Bethune left with us.

Who except a great dreamer could be born of slave parents, could struggle in the fields of South Carolina, and leave a legacy that begins with the words, "I leave you love"? And if you take this message, it seems to me that when we look to what's to happen in the future, it isn't going to be just by, you know, designating this post or that post or this staff or that volunteer or this whatever. It's going to be the extent to which all of us rededicate ourselves—whether we are members of the council or not—to the idea of seeing how caring hearts take hold of a mission and keep it relevant, because what we did in '79 is not going to be good enough in the eighties.

14.

JAMES H. CONE
(1938–)

"The Relationship of the Christian Faith to Political Praxis"

Princeton Theological Seminary,
Princeton, New Jersey—March 12, 1980

Theologian James Cone is the main architect of black liberation theology, a strand of Christianity that grew out of the Black Power movement and interprets the Bible through the lens of the African American freedom struggle. Cone's first book, *Black Theology and Black Power*, was published in 1969 and, as one critic wrote, "sparked an historic and unprecedented shift in African-American religious and theological thought."[1] Scores of African American churches adopted its principles. Cone published his second book the following year, expanding on the ideas of black liberation theology and declaring, "Any message that is not related to the liberation of the poor in a society is not Christ's message. Any theology that is indifferent to the theme of liberation is not Christian theology."[2]

Among the early adherents to black liberation theology was the reverend Jeremiah Wright, President Barack Obama's former pastor. In 1972, Wright took over Trinity United Church of Christ on the South Side of Chicago and turned it into a massive institution, offering numerous programs for the poor. During the 2008 presidential election, Wright was depicted as a dangerous militant for sermons he delivered that condemned white

America for racism. In a 2003 sermon, he said, "The government gives [African Americans] the drugs, builds bigger prisons, passes a three-strike law, and then wants us to sing 'God Bless America'? No, no, no, not 'God Bless America'—'God Damn America.' "[3] Obama had been close to Wright for years, but there was no evidence he shared all of Wright's beliefs. Nevertheless, in the heat of a close primary campaign, Obama was forced to repudiate his pastor to avoid alienating white voters. At the time of the controversy, Cone said Trinity was the "best representation" of black liberation theology and that if Wright's sermons were offensive, it was because he "speaks the truth in harsh, blunt terms."[4]

James Cone was born in Arkansas in 1938 and raised in the small, segregated town of Bearden. It was a place where the white people "tried to make us believe that God created black people to be white people's servants,"[5] Cone said. Cone's father, Charlie, supported the family as a woodcutter. In the early 1950s, Charlie sued the local school board to desegregate Bearden's public schools. Under segregation the "colored" schools were invariably inferior to the white schools. Whites threatened to lynch Charlie Cone for his action, and it took several more years for the Bearden schools to desegregate. But Charlie Cone's brave move left a deep impression on his son. Cone said later, "No person has influenced me more than my father in his courage, sense of self, and the clarity of his commitment to end racial injustice."[6]

Cone's mother, Lucille, was a powerful orator in the family's African Methodist Episcopal church, and her example also left its mark on Cone. He says she "gave me the gift of speech and faith [in the church], which is where I discovered my own voice."[7] Cone felt protected from the daily onslaught of racism when he was in church, a place he says "affirmed your somebody-ness in a society that treated you as nobodies." In Cone's church, the preachers "always let us know that segregation was against God's will."[8] They focused their sermons on Bible passages that reinforced this message.

Cone felt his own call to the ministry when he was sixteen years old. At age seventeen he enrolled in college and became a pastor. Cone received his BA from Philander Smith College in Little Rock in 1958 and, several years later, a master's in divinity from Garrett Theological Seminary in Evanston, Illinois. He earned his PhD in systematic theology from Northwestern University in 1965. Cone was on the faculty at Adrian College in Michigan from 1966 to 1969, a time of tremendous racial upheaval in the United States. It was during that period that his ideas about black liberation theology began to crystallize.

As a young minister and theologian, Cone was deeply swayed by Martin Luther King Jr.'s nonviolent approach to black liberation. But Malcolm X's declaration that Christianity was a white man's religion led Cone to question his own theological perspective. Violent white backlash in the South and police brutality and urban unrest in the North in the late 1960s further tested Cone's faith. As he told the *New Yorker* in 2008, "It was the riots in Detroit, in Newark, both in '67—that was what shook me. I said to myself, 'I have to have a theology that speaks to the hurt in my community. I want a theology that would empower people to be more creative. To be just as aggressive as they are in the riots, but more constructive.' "[9] Cone wrote *Black Theology and Black Power* during the aftermath of Martin Luther King Jr.'s 1968 assassination. According to one account, it took Cone just a month to complete the book. He described the process as a "conversion experience,"[10] and said it was like he had a fire inside him.[11]

Since 1969, Cone has published ten books and more than a hundred articles about black liberation theology, expanding and refining his ideas in response to an array of thoughtful critics and the changing times. Martin Luther King Jr. and Malcolm X remain his abiding influences. Cone says, "I am an African-American theologian whose perspective on the Christian religion was shaped by Martin King and whose black consciousness was defined by Malcolm X."[12] For Cone, black liberation theology is a fusion of their two philosophies. "I wanted to bring Martin and Malcolm together," he says, "so we can fight for justice as Martin King said but love ourselves as Malcolm X said." Cone continues: "Malcolm said the worst crime white people have committed is to teach black people to hate themselves; that's why we kill each other in the ghettoes, et cetera. Black theology is bringing Martin and Malcolm together, teaching us how to be both unapologetically black and Christian at the same time."

Cone has taught at Union Theological Seminary in New York City since 1969. He won tenure early in his career and in 1987 was named Charles A. Briggs Distinguished Professor of Systematic Theology. Cone has won numerous awards and widespread praise for his groundbreaking work. Religious scholar C. Eric Lincoln said Cone "transcends the black revolution and offers to America, and to the church, a key to understanding more about the [Christian] faith than we have ever undertaken to learn."[13]

Cone is a forceful critic of white theologians who don't speak out against racism. "Their silence stems partly from a distorted understanding of what the Gospel means in a racially broken world," Cone said in a 2006 interview. "White theologians have not succeeded in making an empathetic bond with the pains and hurts of people of color." Cone speculates that, if their own children or parents were suffering discrimination, these theologians "would not only write passionately against it, but would make their rejection of injustice an essential part of their reflection on the Gospel." Cone concludes, "Of all the evils that exist in society, racism is one of the most intractable, because it is so difficult to name and so easy to deny."[14]

In this lecture, which Cone delivered at the Princeton Theological Seminary in 1980, he explains how black liberation theology grew out of the Black Power movement, and the connection between Christian faith and the political struggle for justice, freedom, and equality.

THANK YOU VERY MUCH. I'm very pleased to be here today and to share in this occasion with you.

The theme of my lecture is Christian faith and political praxis. In this lecture, my concern is to examine the relationship of the Christian faith to political praxis, with special reference to the concrete realities of oppressed and oppressor whites and blacks, and the church's responsibility to preach and to live the Gospel of Jesus Christ in a highly industrialized and capitalistic society.

What is the Christian faith? And what does it have to say about the rich and the poor, and the social, economic, and political conditions that determine that relationship? To answer this question is not easy in North America, because we live in a society that claims to separate church and state, religion and politics. Christianity, it is often said, is concerned with spiritual reality, but not with the material conditions of people. This view of the Christian faith is commonly held inside and outside of organized churches, thereby supporting the conservative role that religion has often played in politics.

If the Christian faith is no more than the cultural and political intrigues of rulers transformed into theological categories, then Karl Marx is right in his contention that "Religion is the opiate of the people" and therefore should be eliminated with other legitimizing agencies in an oppressive society.

But if religion generally, and the Christian faith in particular, is an imaginative and apocalyptic vision about the creation of a new humanity that is derived from the historical and the political struggles of oppressed peoples, then to describe it as a sedative is to misunderstand religion's essential nature and its later revolutionary and humanizing thrust in society.

When the meaning of the Christian faith is derived from the bottom and not from the top of those on the socioeconomic ladder, from people who are engaged in the fight for justice and not from those who seek to maintain the status quo, then something radical and revolutionary happens to the function of the holy in the context of the secular.

Viewed from the perspective of oppressed people's struggle for freedom, the holy becomes a radical challenge to the legitimacy of the secular structures of power by creating eschatological images about a vision of experience that is not confined to the values of this world.

This strange and revolutionary character of the Christian faith—that is, this is the strange and revolutionary character of the Christian faith that is often misunderstood by church and nonchurch people alike. When we permit ourselves to experience the root meaning of the biblical message and to hear the claims that it lays upon all who would dare to be Christian in this world, then we will see the radical difference between the established churches and the truth of the gospel. For inherent in the Christian gospel is the refusal to accept the things that are as the things that ought to be. This great refusal is what makes Christianity what it is and thus infuses in its very nature a radicality that can never accept the world as it is.

This radical perspective of the biblical faith has not always been presented as an essential part of the Christian Gospel. At least since the time of the emperor Constantine and his making Christianity the official religion of the Roman state, the chief interpreters of the Christian tradition have advocated a spiritual view of the Gospel that separated the confession of faith from the practice of political justice. Whether we speak of Augustine's identification of slavery with the sins of the slave, Luther's stand against the peasants' revolt, the white Americans' church endorsement of black slavery, or contemporary European and American theological indifference toward the political embodiment of the Gospel, it is unquestionably clear that the dominant representatives of the Christian tradition, both Protestant and Catholic alike, have contributed to the political oppression of humanity by defending the economic interests of the rich against the poor.

When the Gospel is spiritualized so as to render it invisible, the important economic distinctions between the haves and the have-nots, the dialectical relation between faith and the practice of political justice, is also obscured. Recently, this assumed separation between faith and political praxis has been seriously challenged by the appearance of liberation theology in North and South America, Asia, and Africa. Whether we speak of black theology, feminist theology, or African theology, liberation theology in all forms rejects the dichotomy between spiritual and physical salvation, between faith and political praxis, and insists upon their dialectical relationship.

Liberation theology has been created by people who consciously seek to speak to and for the victims of economic and political injustice as represented in racism, classism, and sexism. The advocates of this new theology are intolerant of any perspective of Christianity that fails to relate the Gospel of Jesus to the economic and social conditions of people. They contend that the Gospel embraces the whole human person in society, in work, and in play. This means that the Gospel is inseparably connected with the bodily liberation of the poor. Because I am a black North American theologian, whose political and religious consciousness has been shaped in and by black people's historical fight for justice, I agree with my theological colleagues in Asia, Africa, and Latin America, who contend that the Gospel cannot be separated from the concrete struggles of freedom among the oppressed of the land. Indeed, this theological conviction has been an essential and integral part of the black religious tradition from its beginning, and it was reinforced on my theological consciousness during the civil rights movement, and in the context of the rise of Black Power.

The civil rights movement of the 1950s and '60s, which was created and largely centered in the black churches, with Martin Luther King Jr. as its charismatic leader, demonstrated the continuing relevancy of black religion in the struggle for political and social justice. Not only were political strategy sessions held in the context of black church worship, but many black ministers withdrew from former denominational ties in order to devote full time to sit-ins, freedom rides, and other political activities. But the increasing violence of the existing structures in North American society, as well as black people's determination to exert their freedom in opposition to it, led many black civil rights workers to question Martin King's uncompromising devotion to the principle of nonviolence. Thus, in the context of the James Meredith march in Mississippi, spring 1966, and in light of the years of carefully organized violence of white society structures, Willy Rich sounded the cry of "Black Power!" And Stokely Carmichael and others enthusiastically accepted the intellectual and political challenge to define its social relevance in American society.

Black theology was born in response to the rise of Black Power and in the context of the organization of the National Committee of Negro Churchmen. From the very beginning, black theology was interpreted as the theological arm of Black Power, with the responsibility to define the religious meaning of our prior political commitment to black liberation. The initial move in this direction was the publication of the Black Power Statement, July 1966, in which an ad hoc ecumenical group of black church people defended the right of black people to empower themselves against the encroachment of white racism. Following the Black Power Statement, many black church people began to move away from Martin King's rigid commitment to nonviolence and to express their solidarity with James Forman's Marxist and revolutionary black manifesto: "Although we respected the integrity of Martin King's commitment to the struggle for justice, we nonetheless felt that his nonviolent method for radical change in society structures was not radical enough; and also, too dependent upon the possibility of change in the hearts of white oppressors."

The problem of King's assumption was that it did not take seriously enough Henry Holland Garnett's claim that if slaves would be free, they must themselves strike the blow. The theological meaning of Garnett's assertion for black Christians had to be worked out in the historical context of white violence. As black people were being systematically exterminated through the American military structures, dramatically symbolized in the Watts, Detroit, and Newark abortive insurrections, we black theologians had to ask, what has the Gospel to do with life and death and the struggle of people to be free in an extreme situation of oppression?

The existential and political implications of this question forced us to take a new look at the theological enterprise. And we concluded that the beginning and the end of the Christian faith is found in the struggle for justice on behalf of the victims of oppressive society structures. Whatever else theology might be, we contended that it must take sides with the victims, who are economically and politically oppressed. If theology does not side with the victims of injustice, how then can it represent the victim, Jesus of Nazareth, who was crucified because he was a threat to the political and religious structures of his time?

That insight impressed itself upon our consciousness to such a degree that we began to speak of a black theology of liberation. Our central concern was to show that the Christian faith, as lived by oppressed black people in particular, and oppressed people in the world in general, has been and, more important, can be an instrument of political and economic freedom. It is out of this historical context of the black church, identification of the Christian gospel with the political liberation of the poor, that I would like to say a word about faith and work, theology and the practice of political justice.

In this lecture, I will try state what faith demands of praxis, and what praxis demands of faith. The discussion will proceed with a description of faith in the context of black theology and then to an examination of the praxis inherent in that faith. We look first [to] faith in Christ the liberator.

Faith is a religious term that expresses a person's commitment to the ultimate. According to Paul Tillich, faith is a total and centered act of the personal sect, the act of unconditional, infinite, and ultimate concern. In its broadest theological sense, then, faith may refer to one's commitment to the things of this world, and more narrowly be limited to the god in organized religion. The distinctive characteristic of faith is its total commitment to that which functions as the ultimate in one's life, giving it order and meaning. Faith, then, is that total commitment that gives a people their identity and thus determines what they must do in order to actualize in society what they believe necessary for the attainment of their peoplehood.

When faith is understood as commitment to an ultimate concern, then it is obvious that there can be no separation between faith and obedience, because obedience determines faith. I know what your faith is, not by what you confess but only by what you do. [*All right!*] I will say more about this particular point in our discussion of praxis. At this juncture, I merely want to emphasize that the very nature of faith demands a practical activity, commensurate with its confession. Within the general definition of faith, I am dealing with the Christian faith, which may be defined as that total commitment arising from Jesus of Nazareth: his life, death, and resurrection. Faith as defined in the Christian context is not the leap in propositional truths designated as important by organized churches. Rather it is an ultimate commitment to a particular god who revealed the fullness of divinity in the human presence of Jesus Christ.

In order to clarify the sociological content of my theological affirmation, it is necessary to state the source of my faith perspective. My view of the Christian faith is derived from the biblical method, as interpreted in the liberation struggle of an oppressed, black, North American community and reinforced by similar interpretations among oppressed people fighting for freedom throughout the world. From the dialectical relationship of these historical contexts arises the theological conviction that the Bible is the story of God's liberation of victims from economic and political oppression.

Historically, the story begins with the liberation of Israelite slaves from Egypt and the establishment of the Covenant at Sinai. "You have seen what I did to the Egyptians, and how I bore you on eagle's wings and brought you to myself. Now, therefore, if you obey my voice and keep my covenant, you shall be my own possession among people. For all the Earth is mine, and you shall be to me a kingdom of priests and a holy nation."

In the Old Testament, faith in God is based upon a historical event of rescue, wherein Israelite slaves become God's free people with the responsibility of spreading freedom throughout the land. Faith is accepting the gift of freedom and putting one's absolute trust in the promise of God to be with the little ones in time of trouble. When Israel lapses from this faith in God's righteousness and forgets her slave heritage by treating the poor unjustly, divine love is transformed into wrath. The God of the Old Testament is a god of justice, whose revelation is identical with the liberation of the oppressed. For the basic human sin is the attempt to be God, to take God's place by ordering the societal and political structures according to one's social interest. Sin is not primarily a religious impurity but rather social, political, and economic oppression of the poor. It is the denial of the humanity of the neighbor through unjust political and economic arrangements.

When the prophets laid their demand before the kings and the priests of Israel, the demand is identical with justice for the poor and the weak. A faith that expresses itself in ritual is not enough.

> I hate, I despise your feast and I take no delight in your solemn assemblies. Even though you offer me your burnt offering and cereal offering, I will not accept them, [*All right!*] and the peace offering of your fetid beast I will not look upon. Take away from me the noise of your songs. To the melody of your harp I will not listen. But let justice roll down like waters, and righteousness like an ever-flowing stream.

Amos and other prophets contend that Israel will be sent back into servitude. Not because the people failed to attend religious services [laughter], but because of their economic oppression of the poor.

The same theme of God's solidarity with the victim is found in the New

Testament, where it receives a universal expression in the particularity of Jesus's life, death, and resurrection. The appearance of Jesus as the oppressed one prevents any easy identification with his ministry. Jesus was not a successful person by North American standards. Neither was he morally good and religiously respected. He identified with the prostitutes and drunkards, the unemployed and the poor, not because he felt sorry for them, but in order to reveal God's judgment against social and religious structures that oppress the weak. Jesus was born like the poor, he lived with them, and on the cross he died like them. If Jesus is the divine revelation of God's intention for humanity, then faith is nothing but trust in the one who came in Christ for the liberation of the poor. To place one's trust in this god means that one's value system is no longer derived from the established structures of the world, but from one's struggle against those unjust structures.

Now, it is significant that this biblical theme of God's solidarity with the historical liberation of the oppressed is notably absent in the songs and the sermons of white missionaries when they introduced their version of Christianity to African slaves in North America. Like all oppressors who interpret the Gospel in the light of their right to dominate others, white preachers contended that God willed Africans to be slaves. And they cited the biblical reference to Noah's curse upon Ham and to the Apostle Paul's "Slaves, be obedient to your masters" as the theological justification of their claim. But slaves rejected the white distortions of the Gospel and insisted that God willed their freedom and not their slavery. As evidence, they pointed to the Exodus, the prophets, and Jesus's preaching of the Gospel to the poor and not the rich.

Through sermons, prayers, songs, and testimonies, black slaves created a qualitatively different version of Christianity when compared with the religion of their masters. The distinctiveness of this black faith was its focus upon God's will to liberate the oppressed. That was why the independent black churches were created in the North and the so-called invisible, secret institution was formed in the South. Black people were determined to fashion a faith that was identical with their political fight for justice. In the ecstasy of their church services was born their encounter with the god of Moses and of Jesus. And he bestowed upon them the power to articulate in their present history the freedom they experienced in their worship and read about in the scriptures. That's why they sang, "Oh freedom, oh freedom, oh freedom, I love thee. And before I be a slave, I be buried in my grave. And go home to my Lord and be free."

The historical [em]bodiment of black faith is found not only in the creation of separate, institutional black churches, with songs, prayers, and liberation; also important is the presence of black faith outside of the confessionals and organizational framework of black churches. Black faith is found in secular songs and stories, slave insurrections, and protest assemblies. This faith cannot be imprisoned in church structures and prayers of black preachers. When I speak of black faith, I am referring only secondarily to organized religion, and primarily to black people's collected acknowledgment of the spirit of liberation in their midst—a spirit who empowers them to struggle for freedom, even though the odds might be against them. This is the historical matrix out of which my hermeneutical perspective has been formed.

Since other oppressed peoples in and outside of North America are making similar claims regarding God's solidarity with the poor, the North American black perspective is reinforced and enlarged. Indeed, the universal dimensions of the biblical faith so central in the New Testament is found in God's will to make liberation not simply the property of one people but of all humankind. Wherever people are being dehumanized, divine righteousness is disclosed in that historical struggle to be other than what is intended by their oppressors.

Faith, then, is a human response to the liberating presence of the divine spirit in an oppressed community. God's spirit is liberating because God gives people the courage and power to resist dehumanization and slavery. So through faith, oppressed people receive the gift of a new humanity that can only be realized in the historical struggle of liberation. But since faith does not have included in its confession the social analyses needed to implement its eschatological vision of freedom, it—faith, that is—must relate itself to a social theory in order to actualize in society what it confesses in its worship. This leads us to an analysis of praxis. Faith and praxis.

In philosophical and theological circles, "praxis" is a term closely related to the philosophy of Karl Marx. It is perhaps best summarized in Marx's often quoted "Eleven Theses on Feuerbach": "The philosophers have only interpreted the world in various ways. The point, however, is to change it." Praxis, then, is that directive activity toward freedom wherein people recognize that truth is not primarily a question of theory but is a practical question. In practice, people must prove the truth by destroying the existing relations of untruth. As it has been said, the question of the essence of freedom is not only a question; it wants participation in the production of freedom. It is an activity through which freedom frees itself. In its broadest sense, praxis is connected with the Christian idea of obedience and is identical with the horizontical implementation of the vertical dimensions of faith.

According to the New Testament, Jesus says, "Not everyone who says to me, 'Lord, Lord' shall enter the Kingdom of Heaven; but he that does the will of my Father who is in heaven." A similar point is made in First John: "He who does right is righteous. If one says, 'I love God,' and hates his brother or sister, he is a liar, for he who does not love his brother or sister, whom he has seen, cannot love God, whom he has not seen." For inherent in the biblical faith, then, he finds it. In contemporary theology, no one made this point any clearer than Dietrich Bonhoeffer when he said, "Only he who believes is obedient. And only he who is obedient, believes." Bonhoeffer continues, "It is quite unbiblical to hold the first proposition without the second. Faith is only real when there is obedience, never without it. And faith only becomes faith in an act of obedience. Therefore," Bonhoeffer says, "only the obedient believe. Without this preliminary step of obedience," he says, "our faith is only a pious humbug, [laughter] and leads to grace that is not costly."

In North America, black slaves' perception of this biblical insight enabled them to make the distinction between the confession of faith and the obedience that validated it. They knew that their slavery invalidated white religion. That's why they sang, "Everybody talkin' 'bout heaven ain't goin' there." [laughter] Some slaves even contended that no white people went to heaven. On one occasion, a white minister's sermon was interrupted by an elderly slave with the question, "Is us slaves gonna be free in heaven?" The white preacher paused with surprise and with anger, but Uncle Silas was persistent. "Is God gonna free us slaves when we get to heaven?" The remainder of this incident was described by a slave who was present: "The old white preacher pulled out his handkerchief and wiped the sweat from his face. 'Jesus says, "Come unto me, ye that are free from sin, and I will give you salvation,"' preached the preacher. 'Gonna give us freedom along with salvation?' asked Uncle Silas. 'The Lord gives and the Lord takes away. He that is without sin is gonna have life everlasting,' preached the preacher. Then he went ahead preaching fast-like, without paying any attention to Uncle Silas."

Uncle Silas was insisting upon a practical implication of faith, which the white preacher had no intentions of granting—especially in view of the economic and the political consequences. Now, because oppressors do not reorder the structures of society on the basis of, and appeal to, the practical implications of faith, praxis is more than the biblical understanding of obedience. It is this "more" that gives it its distinctive identity. Praxis is a specific kind of obedience that organizes itself around a social theory of reality in order to implement in society the freedom that is inherent in faith. If faith is the belief that God created all for freedom, then praxis is the social theory used to analyze the structures of injustice so that we will know what must be done for the historical realization of freedom. To sing about freedom and to pray for its coming is not enough. Freedom must be actualized in history by oppressed people who accept the intellectual challenge to analyze the world for the purpose of changing it.

The focus on praxis for the purpose of societal change is what distinguishes Marx from Hegel, liberation theology from other theologies of freedom. That is why Marx studied the economic forces in society and why liberation theologians in Latin America find his social theory so basic in the development of their theological enterprise. For the same reason, black liberation theologians also connect their theological program to social theories about racism. Feminist theologians do the same in their analyses of sexism. While there are different emphases among liberation theologians regarding the major historical contradiction in society, they all agree with the need to relate theology to our social theory of reality. Because they share the conviction that truth is found in the active transformation of unjust societal structures.

For liberation theologians, then, faith and praxis belong together, because faith can only be expressed in a political commitment to the humanization of society. We believe that inherent in faith is the love of God. And the latter can only be manifested in the love of one's neighbor. Therefore Gutierrez writes, "To know God is to do justice." He continues, "It is not enough to say that the love of God is inseparable from the love of one's neighbor. It must be added that the love of God is unavoidably expressed through the love of one's neighbor."

But in order to protect love from sentimentality, we must analyze it in the fabric of social relationship, where people are situated in economic, cultural, and racial coordinates. What does it mean to love the exploited social classes, the dominated people or modulated race? That's the question. It is in the attempt to answer this question that we must also realize that praxis is inseparably connected with faith that expresses itself in the love of one's neighbor. If the masses are our neighbor, then we will find it impossible to tolerate economic structures that are destructive to their humanity. Love demands justice—that is, the creation of space in the world so that love can realize itself in human relations. To love the neighbor requires more than a pious feeling in my heart; it requires social and political analysis so that piety will not become a substitute for justice.

The truth of the Gospel, then, is a truth that must be done and not simply spoken. To speak the truth without doing the truth is to contradict the truth that we claim to affirm. The church is good at writing resolutions and preaching sermons about this or that idea, but the denunciation of injustice is not only a spoken word or a written text; it is an action. It's a stand. The word is only a gesture of commitment. This gesture must be concretized by social analysis so that the oppressed will be empowered to change the unjust social arrangement.

The concretization of faith, actualized through love, can only be done by connecting faith with the praxis of justice. The theological assumption that necessitates the connection of faith with praxis is found in Jesus Christ. The incarnation connects faith with life and work. By becoming human in Jesus, God connects faith with social, political, and economic conditions of people and establishes the theological conclusion that we cannot be faithful to the creator without receiving the political command to structure creation according to freedom.

The best way to understand the relation between faith and praxis is to reverse the order, as seen in Bonhoeffer's contention that only the obedient believe. To be sure, ontologically, faith is prior to obedience and thus is its foundation. But practically speaking, obedience comes before faith. We do not first receive faith from God or the church and then seek to live that faith in the world. It is the other way around. One meets God in the process of historical liberation. In the historical context of the struggle for freedom, one receives the gift of divine freedom, wherein the realization occurs that the eternal structures of creation are empowering the oppressed in their fight for justice. This realization is the gift of faith.

Faith, then, is not a datum, but rather a commitment that arises out of one's struggle for freedom, and not before. The power that throws us in the struggle for freedom before we consciously see its connection with faith may be called the prevenient grace of God. This grace is ontologically prior to justification and sanctification because it is grounded in the creative will of God. Therefore, when we are justified and sanctified by the grace of God, the recognition of both experiences occurs in the struggle of freedom, and they are a gift of God.

By putting obedience prior to faith on the sociological plane, we protect ourselves from the heresy of substituting faith for action. We must never allow a prayer for justice to become a replacement for an act against injustice. But if our act against oppression is to have meaning and not be purposeless, then obedience must connect itself with a social theory of change. Why are people poor? And who benefits from their poverty? In an attempt to answer this question, theology must actualize its Christian identity through social analyses and political participation on behalf of the victims of economic injustice.

When theology defines the meaning of the Christian obedience in turn structured in sociology and politics, it becomes global in its outlook by analyzing international capitalism and multinational corporations. For what oppressors do to the people in North America, they also do in poor countries. The world becomes their domain of economic exploitation. Thus, Holiday Inn, Gulf Oil, and multinational corporations are present in South America, South Africa, and other third-world countries, exploiting the victims. Anyone who would be Christian by taking their stand with the victims must connect their obedience with praxis. That is, a social theory of change that would disclose both the causes of injustice and what must be done to eliminate it.

However, persons who would cast their lot with the victim must not forget that the existing structures are powerful and complex. Their creators intended it that way so that any action that challenges their existence will appear both immoral and useless. Oppressors want people to think that change is impossible. That is the function of the military and the police. They want to scare the victims so that any social and political analysis will lead to despair. That is what Martin King called "the paralysis of analysis." But truth is otherwise. If analysis does not elicit hope for change, then it is incorrect. For the constituent definition of humanity is that people are agents of history, capable of change in the world.

Because hope is the foundation of praxis, praxis can never be separated from faith. The Christian faith is grounded in the promise of God and is actualized in the process of liberation in history. Praxis without faith leads to despair. Despair is the logical consequence of a praxis that does not know the eschatological hope derived from historical struggle. Without hope, there is no struggle.

It was this eschatological knowledge, derived from Jesus's cross and resurrection, that enabled black North American slaves to struggle in history, but not to be defeated by their historical limitation. To be sure, they sang about the fear of "sinking down." And the dread of being a "motherless child."

They experienced the trouble and the agony of being alone, where "couldn't hear nobody pray." They encountered death and expressed that encounter with a song: "Soon one mornin', death comes creeping in my room. Oh my Lord, oh my Lord, what shall I do?" In these songs are expressed the harsh realities of history and a deep sense of dread at the very thought of death. But because the slaves believed that death had been conquered in Jesus's resurrection, they could also transcend death by interpreting salvation as a heavenly eschatological reality. That's why they sang, "You needn't mind my dyin'. Jesus gonna make up my dyin' bed. In my room, I know somebody's going to cry. All I ask you to do for me: just close my dyin' eyes." This is not passive resignation but rather an eschatological expression of an historical commitment that refuses to adjust itself to the power of oppressors. This is what the praxis of faith in the Christian context is all about. Thank you.

15.

TONI MORRISON
(1931–)

Nobel Prize Lecture

Stockholm, Sweden—December 7, 1993

Toni Morrison is a prolific and celebrated writer whose fictional accounts of African American life are part of the canon of great American literature. In 1993, Morrison became the first African American to win the Nobel Prize in literature. The Nobel committee said, "Toni Morrison is a literary artist of the first rank. She delves into the language itself, a language she wants to liberate from the fetters of race. And she addresses us with the luster of poetry."[1]

Morrison's mission has been to tell the stories of "the people who in all literature were always peripheral—little black girls who were props, background." As Morrison says, "those people were never center stage and those people were me."[2] She published her first novel, *The Bluest Eye*, in 1970. The book's main character, Pecola Breedlove, longs for blue eyes, believing they would make her beautiful. The story is a haunting exploration of racism's deep wounds. Tragedy, neglect, and abuse drive Pecola to become psychotic. Morrison says that as she began the book, "There was just one thing that I wanted to write about, which was the true devastation of racism on the most vulnerable, the most helpless unit in the society—a black female and a child. I wanted to write about what it was like to be the subject of racism. It had a specificity that was damaging."[3]

By the time Morrison became a Nobel laureate, she had already won other prestigious awards for her fiction, including a Pulitzer Prize in 1988 for the novel *Beloved*. The story centers on an escaped slave who kills her baby daughter to spare the child from slavery. In *Beloved*, Morrison was again intent on depicting the visceral experience of racial oppression. In a 1994 interview, she explained, "I wanted to say 'Let's get rid of these words like "the slave woman" and "the slave child," and talk about people with names like you and like me, who were there.' "[4] In another interview, she said, "I wanted to show the reader what slavery felt like, rather than how it looked."[5]

Since 1970, Morrison has published nine novels, a series of children's stories with her son Slade, and numerous works of nonfiction that explore literature, politics, the arts, and censorship. Morrison has also spent decades teaching, editing, and lecturing. She held an endowed chair in the Humanities at Princeton University from 1989 to 2006.

Toni Morrison was born Chloe Anthony Wofford in 1931. She was raised in Lorain, Ohio, a small steel town near Cleveland. Her father, George, worked at various jobs, including as a ship welder. Her mother, Ramah, was a homemaker. Morrison grew up in a racially and ethnically mixed community that she describes as "tight and . . . unhostile."[6] But her father grew up in the Jim Crow South and hated white people. As a child, Morrison says, "I knew he was wrong." Morrison went to school with white children and, mostly, they were her friends. "There was no awe, no fear" of whites, she says.[7] Even so, Morrison still experienced racism in Ohio. As she told one interviewer, "I remember in the fifth grade, a smart little boy who had just arrived and didn't speak any English. He sat next to me. I read well, and I taught him to read just by doing it. I remember the moment he found out that I was black—a nigger." Morrison says it took the boy six months to learn the town's racial caste system. Once he learned it, he could feel a sense of belonging by looking down at the one group below his: black people. "Every immigrant knew he would not come as [a member of] the very bottom [stratum]. He had to come above at least one group—and that was us."[8]

Within the Morrison family, as she remembers it, there was no sense of belonging to a lower caste. "My parents made all of us feel as though there were these rather extraordinary deserving people within us," she says. "I felt like an aristocrat—or what I think an aristocrat is. I always knew we were very poor. But that was never degrading."[9] Morrison grew up in a family rich with music, books, and storytelling. Her parents spun exhilarating ghost stories at night; her grandmother interpreted dreams. As Morrison says, "We were intimate with the supernatural."[10] The music, the ghosts, and the folk tales are all powerful elements that run through Morrison's fiction.

Morrison graduated with honors from high school and in 1953 earned her BA in English from Howard University. She adopted the nickname "Toni" in college. Her professors included poet Sterling Brown and philosopher Alain Locke. Morrison received an MA in American literature from Cornell University and launched her academic career at Texas Southern University in Houston. In 1957, Morrison returned to Howard to teach. She married a Jamaican architect, Harold Morrison, and the couple had two sons, Harold Ford and Slade Kevin. The Morrisons divorced in 1964.

Toni Morrison supported her young family by working as a textbook editor in Syracuse. In 1968, Random House hired Morrison as a senior editor at its headquarters in New York City. Over the next sixteen years, she made her mark in publishing by nurturing the careers of an array of popular black writers. They included Angela Davis, Lucille Clifton, and Toni Cade Bambara. One of the authors whose work she edited, former U.S. ambassador Andrew Young, said, "Toni has done more to encourage and publish other black writers than anyone I know."[11]

While working full time and raising her two boys alone, Morrison began to squeeze in time to write when the children were asleep. After *The Bluest Eye* in 1970, she produced several more critically acclaimed books. Morrison had been writing for a solid decade before she began to really think of herself as a writer. She recalls that after her 1977 publication of *Song of Solomon*, which won the National Book Critics Circle Award, someone said to her, "This is probably what you do." Morrison said, "You mean, this is what I'm going to be when I grow up?" And the person replied, "Yeah."[12] Morrison resigned from Random House in 1984 to focus on writing.

Morrison delivered the Nobel lecture in the Grand Hall of the Swedish Academy in Stockholm. The audience gave her a standing ovation as she entered the eighteenth-century room. Her close friend the theologian and writer Cornel West was there. "You talk about grace, dignity, class, elegance—when Toni walked down that aisle on the arm of King Gustav of Sweden!" he recalled. "But what I could really see was these millions and millions of black folk who had come and gone. I could see it in her walk, I could see it in her face. All kinds of humiliation and cruelty coming their way. And they just kept comin' on!"[13]

Morrison's lecture takes the form of a parable that illuminates the power of language as both a force of life and a tool of destruction. As Morrison says, "Oppressive language does more than represent violence: it is violence; does more than represent the limits of knowledge; it limits knowledge." Morrison returns to this idea in her 2009 edited volume, *Burn This Book*, a collection of essays on writing and censorship by a variety of influential authors. Morrison writes, "Certain kinds of trauma visited on peoples are so deep, so cruel, that unlike money, unlike vengeance, even unlike justice, or rights, or the goodwill of others, only writers can translate such trauma and turn sorrow into meaning, sharpening the moral imagination." Morrison continues, "A writer's life and work are not a gift to mankind; they are its necessity."[14]

THANK YOU. My sincere thanks to the Swedish Academy. And thank you all for this very warm welcome.

Fiction has never been entertainment for me. It has been the work I have done for most of my adult life. I believe that one of the principal ways in which we acquire, hold, and digest information is via narrative. So I hope you will understand when the remarks I make begin with what I believe to be the first sentence of our childhood that we all remember—the phrase "Once upon a time . . ."

Once upon a time there was an old woman, blind but wise. Or was it an old man? A guru, perhaps. Or a griot soothing restless children. I've heard this story, or one exactly like it, in the lore of several cultures. "Once upon a time there was an old woman, blind . . . wise . . ."

In the version I know, the woman is the daughter of slaves, black, American, and lives alone in a small house outside of town. Her reputation for wisdom is without peer and without question. Among her people, she is both the law and its transgression. The honor she is paid and the awe in which she is held reach beyond her neighborhood to places far away, to the city, where the intelligence of rural prophets is the source of much amusement. One day the woman is visited by some young people who seem bent on disproving her clairvoyance and showing her up for the fraud they believe she is. Their plan is simple. They enter her house and ask the one question the answer to which rides solely on her difference from them, a difference they regard as a profound disability—her blindness. They stand before her and one of them says, "Old woman, I hold in my hand a bird. Tell me whether it is living or dead."

She doesn't answer, and the question is repeated. "Is the bird I am holding living or dead?" She still doesn't answer. She's blind. She can't see her visitors, let alone what is in their hands. She doesn't know their color, their gender, or their homeland. She only knows their motive. The old woman's silence is so long, the young people have trouble holding their laughter. Finally she speaks and her voice is soft but stern. "I don't know," she says. "I don't know whether the bird you are holding is dead or alive, but what I do know is that it is in your hands. It is in your hands." Her answer can be taken to mean: if it's dead, you have either found it that way or you have killed it. If it is alive, you can still kill it. Whether it is to stay alive, it's your decision. Whatever the case, it's your responsibility.

For parading their power and her helplessness, the young visitors are reprimanded, told they are responsible not only for the act of mockery but also for the small bundle of life sacrificed to achieve its aims. The blind woman shifts attention away from assertions of power to the instrument through which that power is exercised.

Speculation on what (other than its own frail body) that bird-in-the-hand might signify has always been attractive to me, but especially so now—thinking, as I have been, about the work I do that has brought me to this company. So I choose to read the bird as language and the woman as a practiced writer. She's worried about how the language she dreams in, given to her at birth, is handled, put into service, even withheld from her for certain nefarious purposes. Being a writer, she thinks of language partly as a system, partly as a living thing over which one has control, but mostly as agency—as an act with consequences.

So the question the children put to her: "Is it living or dead?" is not unreal because she thinks of language as susceptible to death, erasure, certainly imperiled and salvageable only by an effort of the will. She believes that if the bird in the hands of her visitors is dead, the custodians are responsible for the corpse. For her a dead language is not only one no longer spoken or written, it is unyielding language content to admire its own paralysis. Like statist language, censored and censoring. Ruthless in its policing duties, it has no desire or purpose other than maintaining the free range of its own narcotic narcissism, its own exclusivity and dominance. However moribund, it is not without effect, for it actively thwarts the intellect, stalls conscience, suppresses human potential. Unreceptive to interrogation, it cannot form or tolerate new ideas, shape other thoughts, tell another story, fill baffling silences. Official language smitheried to sanction ignorance and preserve privilege is a suit of armor polished to shocking glitter, a husk from which the knight departed long ago. Yet there it is: dumb, predatory, sentimental— exciting reverence in schoolchildren, providing shelter for despots, summoning false memories of stability, harmony among the public.

She is convinced that when language dies, out of carelessness, disuse, an absence of esteem, indifference, or killed by fiat, not only she herself but all users and makers are accountable for its demise. In her country, children have bitten their tongues off and use bullets instead to iterate the voice of speechlessness, of disabled and disabling language, of language adults have abandoned altogether as a device for grappling with meaning, providing guidance, or expressing love. But she knows tongue suicide is not only the choice of children. It's common among the infantile heads of state and power merchants whose evacuated language leaves them with no access to what is left of their human instincts, for they speak only to those who obey, or in order to force obedience.

The systematic looting of language can be recognized by the tendency of its users to forgo its nuanced, complex, midwifery properties for menace and subjugation. Oppressive language does more than represent violence: it *is* violence; does more than represent the limits of knowledge: it limits knowledge. Whether it is obscuring state language or the faux language of mindless media, whether it is the proud but calcified language of the academy or the commodity-driven language of science, whether it is the malign language of law-without-ethics or language designed for the estrangement of minorities, hiding its racist plunder in its literary cheek, it must be rejected, altered, and exposed. It is the language that drinks blood, laps vulnerabilities, tucks its fascist boots under crinolines of respectability and patriotism as it moves relentlessly toward the bottom line and the bottomed-out mind. Sexist language, racist language, theistic language—all are typical of the policing languages of mastery and cannot, do not permit new knowledge or encourage the mutual exchange of ideas.

The old woman is keenly aware that no intellectual mercenary, nor insatiable dictator, no paid-for politician or demagogue, no counterfeit journalist would be persuaded by her thoughts. There is and will be rousing language to keep citizens armed and arming, slaughtered and slaughtering in the malls, courthouses, post offices, playgrounds, bedrooms, and boulevards; stirring, memorializing language to mask the pity and waste of needless death. There will be more diplomatic language to countenance rape, torture, assassination. There is and will be more seductive, mutant language designed to throttle women, to pack their throats like pâté-producing geese with their own unsayable, transgressive words; there will be more of the language of surveillance disguised as research; of politics and history calculated to render the suffering of millions mute; language glamorized to thrill the dissatisfied and bereft into assaulting their neighbors; arrogant pseudo-empirical language crafted to lock creative people into cages of inferiority and hopelessness.

Underneath the eloquence, the glamour, the scholarly associations, however stirring or seductive, the heart of such language is languishing, or perhaps not beating at all—if the bird is already dead. She has thought about what could have been the intellectual history of any discipline if it had not insisted upon, or been forced into, the waste of time and life that rationalizations for and representations of dominance required—lethal discourses of exclusion blocking access to cognition for both the excluder and the excluded.

The conventional wisdom of the Tower of Babel story is that the collapse was a misfortune—that it was the distraction or the weight of many languages that precipitated the tower's failed architecture, that one monolithic language would have expedited the building and heaven would've been reached. Whose heaven, she wonders? And what kind? Perhaps the achievement of Paradise was premature, a little hasty if no one could take the time to understand other languages, other views, other narratives. Had they, the heaven they imagined might have been found at their feet. Complicated, demanding, yes, but a view of heaven as life, not heaven as post-life.

She wouldn't want to leave her young visitors with the impression that language should be forced to stay alive merely to be. The vitality of language lies in its ability to limn the actual, imagined, and possible lives of its speakers, readers, and writers. Although its poise is sometimes in displacing experience, it's not a substitute for it. It arcs toward the place where meaning may lie. When a president of the United States thought about the graveyard his country had become and said, "The world will little note nor long remember what we say here; but it will never forget what they did here," his simple words are exhilarating in their life-sustaining properties, because they refused to encapsulate the reality of six hundred thousand dead men in a cataclysmic race war. Refusing to monumentalize, disdaining the "final word," the precise "summing up," acknowledging their poor power to add or detract, his words signal deference to the uncapturability of the life it mourns. It is the deference that moves her, the recognition that language can never live up to life once and for all—nor should it. Language can never "pin down" slavery, genocide, war. Nor should it yearn for the arrogance to be able to do so. Its force, its felicity is in its reach toward the ineffable. Be it grand or slender, burrowing, blasting, or refusing to sanctify, whether it laughs out loud or is a cry without an alphabet, the choice word, the chosen silence, unmolested language surges toward knowledge, not its destruction. But who doesn't know of literature banned because it is interrogative, discredited because it is critical, erased because alternate? And how many are outraged by the thought of a self-ravaged tongue? Word-work is sublime, she thinks, because it's generative; it makes meaning that secures our difference, our human difference—the way in which we are like no other life. We die. That may be the meaning of life. But we do language. That may be the measure of our lives.

"Once upon a time" visitors ask an old woman a question. Who are they, these children? And what did they make of that encounter? What did they hear in those final words: "The bird is in your hands"? A sentence that gestures toward possibility or one that drops a latch? Perhaps what the children heard was "It's not my problem. I'm old, female, black, blind. What wisdom I have now is in knowing I cannot help you. The future of language is yours." They stand there. Suppose nothing was in their hands? Suppose the visit was only a ruse, a trick to get to be spoken to, taken seriously as they have not been before? A chance to interrupt, to violate the adult world, its miasma of discourse about them, for them, but never to them? Urgent questions are at stake, including the one they have asked: "Is the bird we hold living or dead?" Perhaps the question meant: "Could someone tell us what is life? What is death?" No trick at all; no silliness. A straightforward question worthy of the attention of a wise one, an old one. And if the old and the wise who have lived life and faced death cannot describe either, who can?

But she doesn't. She keeps her secret, her good opinion of herself, her gnomic pronouncements, her art without commitment. She keeps her distance, reinforces it, and retreats into the singularity of isolation, in sophisticated, privileged space. Nothing, no word follows her declarations of transfer. That silence is deep, deeper than the meaning available in the words she has spoken. It shivers, this silence, and the children, annoyed, fill it with language invented on the spot.

"Is there no speech," they ask her, "no words you can give us that help us break through your dossier of failures? Through the education you have just given us that is no education at all, because we are paying close attention to what you have done as well as to what you have said, to the barrier you have erected between generosity and wisdom. We have no bird in our hands, living or dead. We have only you and our important question. Is the nothing in our hands something you couldn't bear to contemplate, to even guess? Don't you remember being young, when language was magic without meaning? When what you could say could not mean? When the invisible was what imagination strove to see? When questions and demands for answers burned so brightly you trembled with fury at not knowing? Do we have to begin our consciousness with a battle, heroines and heroes, like you have already fought and lost, leaving us with nothing in our hands except what you imagined is there? Your answer is artful, but its artfulness embarrasses us and ought to embarrass you. Your answer is indecent in its self-congratulation, a made-for-television script that makes no sense if there is nothing in our hands. Why didn't you reach out, touch us with your soft fingers, delay the sound bite, the lesson, until you knew who we were? Did you so despise our trick, our modus operandi, you could not see that we were baffled about how to get your attention? We are young, unripe. We've heard all our short lives that we have to be responsible. What could that possibly mean in the catastrophe this world has become, where, as a poet said, 'nothing needs to be exposed since it's already barefaced.' Our inheritance is an affront. You want us to have your old, blank eyes and see only cruelty and mediocrity. Do you think we are stupid enough to perjure ourselves again and again with the fiction of nationhood? How dare you talk to us of duty when we stand waist deep in the toxin of your past?

"You trivialize us, and you trivialize the bird that is not in our hands. Is there no context for our lives, no song, no literature, no poem full of vitamins, no history connected to experience that you can pass along to help us start strong? You are an adult—the old one, the wise one. Stop thinking about saving your face. Think of our lives and tell us your particularized world. Make up a story. Narrative is radical, creating us at the very moment it is being created. We will not blame you if your reach exceeds your grasp, if love so ignites your words they go down in flames and nothing is left but their scald. Or if, with the reticence of a surgeon's hands, your words suture only the places where blood might flow. We know you can never do it properly—once and for all. Passion is never enough; neither is skill. But try. For our sake and yours, forget your name in the street; tell us what the world has been to you in the dark places and the light. Don't tell us what to believe, what to fear. Show us belief's wide skirt and the stitch that unravels fear's caul. You, old woman, blessed with blindness, can speak the language that tells us what only language can: how to see without pictures. Language alone protects us from the scariness of things with no names. Language alone is meditation.

"Tell us what it is to be a woman, so that we may know what it is to be a man; what moves at the margin; what it is to have no home in this place; to be set adrift from the one you knew; what it is to live at the edge of towns that cannot bear your company.

"Tell us about ships turned away from shorelines at Easter, placenta in a field. Tell us about a wagonload of slaves, how they sang so softly their breath was indistinguishable from the falling snow; how they knew from the hunch of the nearest shoulder that the next stop would be their last; how, with hands prayered in their sex, they thought of heat, then suns; lifting their faces as though it was there for the taking, turning as though there for the taking. They stop at an inn. The driver and his mate go in with the lamp, leaving them humming in the dark. The horse's void steams into the snow beneath its hooves, and its hiss and melt is the envy of the freezing slaves.

"The inn door opens. A girl and a boy step away from its light. They climb into the wagon bed. The boy will have a gun in three years, but now he carries a lamp and a jug of warm cider. They pass it from mouth to mouth. The girl offers bread, pieces of meat, and something more: a glance into the eyes of the one she serves. One helping for each man, two for each woman. And a look. They look back. The next stop will be their last. But not this one. This one is warmed."

It's quiet again when the children finish speaking, until the woman breaks into the silence. "Finally," she says, "I trust you now. I trust you with the bird that is not in your hands, because you have truly caught it. How lovely it is, this thing we have done—together."

Thank you.

16.

COLIN POWELL
(1937–)

Commencement Address at Howard University

Washington, D.C.—May 14, 1994

When retired general Colin Powell stepped to the podium to address the 1994 graduating class of Howard University, the Washington, D.C., campus was reeling from racial turmoil. That winter, Khalid Abdul Muhammad, a member of the black nationalist Nation of Islam, had delivered two speeches at Howard making racist and anti-Semitic statements. The second speech drew loud applause as Muhammad interwove messages of black empowerment with hate-filled rhetoric.[1]

Critics berated Howard for tolerating Muhammad's diatribes, and debates raged on campus about the limits of free speech. A CBS news show hosted by Connie Chung featured a small campus rally in which a few students and some outsiders blamed Jews for aiding in the death of Martin Luther King Jr.[2]

Colin Powell, a lifelong soldier, took on the role of peacemaker. In his speech, Powell strongly defended Howard's decision to allow Muhammad to speak on campus. At the same time, he warned, "for this freedom to hear all views, you bear a burden to sort out wisdom from foolishness." Racial hatred, he said, is foolish. For Powell—a man shaped by his career in the United States Army—this was obvious.

In his 1995 biography, *My American Journey*, Powell says the military was "living the democratic ideal ahead of the rest of America." It's a fact he says gets lost in public memory. On July 26, 1948, President Harry Truman signed an executive order banning segregation in the armed services. Powell believes he and many others benefited profoundly from "less discrimination, a truer merit system, and a leveler playing field" in the military. The army, Powell says, is what enabled him to "love my country, with all its flaws, and to serve her with all my heart."

Colin Powell was born in New York City in 1937 and grew up in the Bronx. His parents were from Jamaica. Powell was raised in a large extended family and a neighborhood filled with Jews, Italians, Hispanics, African Americans, and other West Indians. "A certain rough-edged racial tolerance prevailed," Powell wrote in his biography.[3] To Powell, the South Bronx of his childhood was a vibrant, exciting place to be.

Powell's parents held stable, working-class jobs in the garment district of Manhattan. His mother was a seamstress, his father a shipping supervisor. They had a comfortable life, but expected their children to do better by going to college. "Education meant the difference between wrapping packages or sewing buttons all day and having a real profession," Powell wrote.[4] Powell had no idea what that profession might be, and no particular ambition, but in 1954 he entered the City College of New York.

Powell was quickly drawn to the Reserve Officers Training Corps (ROTC) and discovered his calling. He was wooed by several of ROTC's military fraternities and chose the Pershing Rifles (PRs). He loved every aspect of ROTC and especially life with the PRs. "The discipline, the structure, the camaraderie, the sense of belonging were what I craved," Powell wrote. "Race, color, background, income meant nothing. The PRs would go the limit for each other and for the group. If this was what soldiering was all about, then maybe I wanted to be a soldier."[5]

Over the course of a thirty-five-year career, Powell rose from second lieutenant in 1958 to the rank of four-star general, which he was awarded in 1989. Powell capped his career by serving as chairman of the Joint Chiefs of Staff—the highest post in the U.S. military—from 1989 to 1993. He oversaw the first Persian Gulf War in 1991 and emerged an immensely popular national figure.

When Powell retired from the military in 1993, politicians on both sides of the aisle urged him to "think big about his future."[6] As he toured the country promoting his autobiography, there was widespread speculation that Powell might become the nation's first black president, as a Republican or a Democrat.[7] Powell had yet to declare a party allegiance.

After agonizing about the decision, in the fall of 1995 Powell announced he would not run. Powell realized he didn't have the stomach for what would surely be a brutal campaign. He said he just didn't want to be president badly enough.[8] Nevertheless, Powell remained a powerful Washington insider, and in 2001 President George W. Bush tapped him to serve as secretary of state. Powell held the post until he retired in 2005.

Though he'd become an active Republican, in 2008 Powell endorsed Democratic candidate Barack Obama for president, calling him a "transformational figure." Speaking on NBC's *Meet the Press*, Powell said Obama "has given us a more inclusive, broader reach into the needs and aspirations of our people." Powell praised Obama for "crossing lines—ethnic lines, racial lines, generational lines."[9]

Powell criticized the Republican Party for doing the opposite. Some Republicans circulated rumors that Obama was secretly a Muslim with possible ties to Islamic terrorists. "The correct answer is, he is not a Muslim," Powell said. "He's a Christian. He's always been a Christian. But the really right answer is, what if he is? Is there something wrong with being a Muslim in this country? The answer's no. That's not America. Is something wrong with some seven-year-old, Muslim-American kid believing that he or she could be president?"[10] For the son of Jamaican immigrants who had once had a chance at the presidency himself, the answer is no.

THE REAL CHALLENGE, of course, in being a commencement speaker at any college is trying to figure out how long you're going to talk. [*Yeah!* laughter]

If you ask the students, the answer is very, very simple: talk for about four minutes and then sit down. [laughter, applause] Polls have been taken that show that ten years after the event, eighty percent of all graduating students don't have a clue who their commencement speaker was. [laughter] Well you ain't going to do that to me, the name is Powell: P-O-W-E-L-L.

Now the parents who are here today, the parents and family members behind you, they have a different view of this matter. They are arrayed in all their finery. They have waited a long time for this day—some of them not sure it would ever come. [laughter] And they want it to last, so their advice to me is, "Go on, talk for about two to three hours. We brought lunch and we want our money's worth."

The faculty member sitting up here, over there somewhere, who suggested me in the first place is nervous. He or she is hoping that the speech will be long enough to be respectable, but not so long that he has to take leave on Monday morning for a few weeks to escape the posse.

So the poor commencement speaker is left with the original problem of how long to speak. And I have a simple rule: I respond to audience reaction. If you are appreciative and applaud loudly very early on, you get a nice, short speech. [applause, cheers, chatter]

[Laughing] All right, let's get serious, huh? I want to say a few words about the controversy that your campus has been embroiled in in recent weeks. You know, this controversy has a positive side as well: it has caused this university family to go through a process of self-examination, and that is always a healthy thing to do.

And since so many people have been giving advice to the Howard family about how to handle this matter, I thought I would give you a little advice as well. I'm good at giving advice to people.

And the first piece of advice is that I believe with all my heart that Howard must continue to serve as an institution of learning excellence where freedom of speech is strongly encouraged and rigorously protected. [applause]

That is at the very essence and heart of a great university and there is no doubt that Howard is a great university.

And freedom of speech means permitting the widest range of views to be presented, however controversial those views may be. The First Amendment right of free speech is intended to protect the controversial and even the outrageous word, and not just comforting platitudes, too mundane to need protection.

Some say that by hosting controversial speakers who shock our sensibilities, Howard is in some way promoting or endorsing that message. Not at all. Howard has helped put that message in perspective while protecting their right to be heard, so the message can be exposed to the full light of day for comment and criticism.

I, for one, have every confidence in the ability of the administration and the faculty and the students of Howard University to determine who should speak on this campus—no outside help needed, thank you very much. [applause]

I also have complete confidence in the students of Howard to make informed, educated judgments about what you hear. But for this freedom to hear all views, you bear a burden to sort out wisdom from foolishness.

There is great wisdom in the message of self-reliance, of education, of hard work, and of the need to raise strong families. But there is utter foolishness, there is evil, and there is danger in the message of hatred, or of condoning violence, however cleverly the message is packaged or entertainingly it is presented. [applause] We must, we must find nothing to stand up and cheer about or applaud in a message of racial or ethnic hatred. [*Woo!*]

I was at the inauguration of President Nelson Mandela in South Africa earlier this week. [applause, cheers] You were there, too, by the magic of television, and together we experienced that remarkable event. Together, we saw what can happen when people stop hating and begin reconciling. DeKlerk the jailer became DeKlerk the liberator, and Mandela the prisoner became Mandela the president. [applause]

Twenty-seven years of imprisonment did not embitter Nelson Mandela. He invited his three jail keepers to the ceremony. He used his liberation to work with his former tormentors to create a new South Africa and to eliminate the curse of apartheid once and for all from the face of the earth. What a glorious example he is to us, what a glorious day it was.

Last week you also saw Prime Minister Rabin of Israel and PLO Chairman Arafat sign another agreement on their still difficult, long road to peace, trying to end hundreds of years of hatred and two generations of violence. And over the last two or three days, you have seen Palestinian authorities move back into the Gaza Strip and into the town of Jericho.

In these two historic events in South Africa and the Middle East, intractable enemies have shown how you can join hands and create a force of moral authority more powerful than any army—moral authority that can change the world. And although there are still places of darkness in the world where the light of reconciliation has not yet penetrated, these two beacons of hope show what can be done when men and women of goodwill work together for peace and for progress.

There is a message in those two historic events for those of us assembled here today. As the world goes forward, we cannot start going backwards. African Americans have come too far and we have too far yet to go to take a detour into the swamp of hatred. We, as a people who have suffered so much from the hatred of others, must not now show tolerance for any movement or any philosophy that has as its core the hatred of Jews or the hatred of any other group. Our future [applause], our future lies in the philosophy of love and understanding and caring and building, not of hating and tearing down. We know that—each and every one of us knows that to the depth of our heart, and we must be prepared to stand up for it and speak up for it. We must not be silenced, if we would live up to the legacy of those who have gone before us from this campus.

I have no doubt, my friends, that this controversy will pass and Howard University will emerge even stronger, even more than ever a symbol of hope, of promise, and of excellence. That is your destiny, I am sure!

Ambassador Annenberg, one of your honorees today, is a dear friend of mine, and as you have heard, he is one of America's leading businessmen and greatest philanthropists. You have heard of his contributions to education and of his contributions to this school.

A few years ago I told Mr. Annenberg about a project I was involved in to build a memorial to the Buffalo Soldiers, those brave black cavalrymen of the West. [Cheers, applause] Their valor had long gone unrecognized, and I was anxious to do something to create a memorial in their honor. And I called my friend Walter, and he immediately responded and gave us the resources we needed to help build that memorial, which stands proudly at Fort Leavenworth, Kansas, this very day. [applause]

Those Buffalo Soldiers were formed in 1867, at the same time as Howard University. It is even said that your mascot, the bison, comes from the nickname for those soldiers, the Buffalo Soldiers.

Both Howard and the Buffalo Soldiers owe their early success to the dedication and to the faith of white military officers of the Union army who served in the Civil War. In Howard's case, of course, it was your namesake, Major General Oliver Howard. For the Tenth Cavalry Buffalo Soldiers, it was Colonel Benjamin Grierson who formed and commanded that regiment for almost twenty-five years. And he fought for that entire time to achieve equal status for his black comrades.

Together, for the last one hundred twenty-seven years, Howard University and the Buffalo Soldiers have tried to show what black Americans were capable of when given education and given the opportunity, and when shown respect and when accorded dignity.

I stand here today as a direct descendant of those Buffalo Soldiers, and of the Tuskegee Airmen, and all the black men and women who have served the nation in uniform. [applause] All of whom, all of whom served in their time and in their way, and with whatever opportunity existed at that time, to break down the walls of discrimination and racism, to make the path easier for those of us who came after them. I climbed on their backs and I stood on their shoulders. I took advantage of the sacrifice they made to reach the top of my chosen profession and become chairman of the American Joint Chiefs of Staff.

And I will never forget my debt to them. I didn't just show up; I climbed on the backs of those who *never* had the opportunity that I had. [applause]

I will never forget, and you must never forget, the debt we owe to those who came before us, and to the white Colonel Griersons and the white General Howards and the distinguished Ambassador Annenbergs of the year, who helped me over the thirty-five years of my life as a soldier.

And so, my friends, never forget the debt that you owe to the people who came before you. And those who came before me in the military would say to me now if they were here, "Well done. And now let others climb on your shoulders."

Howard's Buffalo Soldiers did the same thing, and on the shoulders of those who came before you now stand governors and mayors and congressmen and ROTC generals and doctors and artists, writers and teachers and leaders in every segment of American society.

And they did it all for the class of 1994. So that you can continue climbing to reach the top of the mountain, while always remembering to reach back and down to help those less fortunate. [applause]

You face great expectations. Much has been given to you and much is expected from you. You have been given a quality education presented by a distinguished faculty who sit here today in pride of you. You have inquiring minds and strong bodies given to you by God and by your parents, who sit behind you today and pass on to you all of their still unrealized dreams and ambitions. You have been given citizenship in a country like none other on earth, with opportunities available to you like nowhere else on earth, beyond anything that was available to me when I sat in a place similar to you thirty-six years ago.

What will be asked of you is hard work. Nothing will be handed to you. You are entering a life of continuous study and struggle to achieve your goals, a life of searching to find that which you do well and which you love doing. Never stop seeking.

I want you to have faith in yourselves. I want you to believe to the depth of your soul that you can accomplish any task that you set your mind and your energy and your heart to. I want you to be proud of your heritage.

Study your origins. Teach your children racial pride and draw strength and inspiration from the culture of our forebears. [applause] Not, not as a way of drawing back from American society and its European roots, but as a way of showing that there are other roots as well—African and Caribbean roots that are also a source of nourishment for the American family tree.

To show, to show that African Americans are more than a product of our slave experience. To show that our varied backgrounds are as rich as that of any other American—not better or greater, but every bit as equal. Our black heritage must be a foundation stone we can build on, and not a place to withdraw into.

I want you to fight racism. But remember, as Dr. King and President Mandela have taught us, racism is a disease of the racist. Never let it become yours. Racism is a disease that you can help cure by standing up for your rights and by your commitment to excellence and to performance. By being ready to take advantage of your rights and the opportunities that will come from those rights.

Never, never let the dying hand of racism rest on your shoulder, weighing you down. Always let racism always be someone else's burden to carry in their heart. [applause]

And as you seek your way in the world, never fail to find a way to serve your community. Use your education and your success in life to help those still trapped in cycles of poverty and violence.

Above all, never lose faith in America. Its faults are yours to fix, not to curse. America is a family: there may be differences and disputes within the family, but we must not allow the family to be broken into warring factions. From the diversity of our people, let us draw strength and not seek weakness.

Believe in America with all your heart and soul, with all of your mind. Remember that it remains the "last, best hope of Earth." You are its inheritors, and its future is today placed in your hands.

And so, my young friends, go forth from this place today inspired by those who went before you. Go forth with the love of your families and the blessings of your teachers. Go forth to make this a better country, a better society. Prosper, raise strong families, remembering that all you will leave behind at the end are your good works and your children.

Go forth with my most humble but sincere congratulations. And always let your dreams be your only limitations, now and forever.

Thank you, God bless you, and have a great life!

17.

MARY FRANCES BERRY
(1938–)

"One Hundredth Anniversary of *Plessy v. Ferguson*"

Howard University, Washington, D.C.—November 14, 1996

Mary Frances Berry is a scholar and civil rights activist who rose from a childhood of stark poverty in the segregated South to become a high-ranking federal official and a professor at an Ivy League university. She served on the U.S. Commission on Civil Rights for nearly a quarter century. Berry is the author of nine books on constitutional law and American history. She has a reputation as a tough opponent and as an unsparing critic of racial inequities in American society. As conservatives gained ascendency in American politics at the end of the twentieth century, a newspaper profile of Berry said she "stands firmly—and restlessly—on the left and makes no apologies for it."[1]

Berry was born in 1938 in Nashville, Tennessee. She was the second of three children in a family that experienced intense hardship. When her father deserted the family, Berry's mother was so poor she had to place young Mary Frances and her older brother in an orphanage for a time. The children were often hungry because the orphanage fed them inadequately. Berry told an interviewer that the experience taught her "early on that you have to fight, that you have to really stick to it, that you have to be persistent."[2]

Berry was a determined student. She earned her BA and MA in history from Howard University, then a PhD and law degree from the University of Michigan. Berry taught at several universities and served as assistant secretary of education in the administration of President Jimmy Carter from 1977 to 1980. In 1980, Carter appointed her to the U.S. Commission on Civil Rights, a bipartisan agency that monitors the enforcement of civil rights laws. She served until 2004 and was the commission's chair for nine years. Since 1987, Berry has had an endowed chair in American social thought and history at the University of Pennsylvania.

Historian Darlene Clark Hine praised Berry's scholarship for making "truly unique and powerful contributions to African American and U.S. political and constitutional history, and especially to Black Women's Studies."[3] But Berry's service on the civil rights panel was controversial. The head of the Leadership Conference on Civil Rights, Wade Henderson, praised Berry's tenure, calling her "a tireless advocate for not only blacks, but Latinos, Asians, women and anyone considered outside of the mainstream."[4] But Berry's liberal views and sharp-elbowed style infuriated conservatives for much of her time on the commission. She fended off a move by President Ronald Reagan to unseat her and later challenged President George W. Bush, as one writer said, on "everything from his election in 2000 to the impact of his civil rights policies."[5] Berry left the civil rights commission when Bush replaced her as chair with a conservative. "I decided to go on about my life," Berry told an interviewer. "I had served the commission well and will be remembered as doing such."[6]

Berry gave this speech at a conference on constitutional history at Howard University. A number of distinguished civil rights lawyers attended the speech. They included Washington attorney Dovey Roundtree, a pioneering black woman who fought for civil rights at a time when few women of any race were practicing law. Also attending were Oliver Hill and Jack Greenberg, members of the NAACP legal team that won the landmark 1954 Supreme Court case outlawing school segregation, *Brown v. Board of Education*.

The subject of Berry's speech is the historic Supreme Court decision in 1896 *Plessy v. Ferguson*, which *Brown* sought to reverse. The *Plessy* decision upheld the constitutionality of racial segregation in public accommodations under the doctrine of "separate but equal." The case involved a Louisiana law requiring separate railway cars for blacks and whites. In 1892, Homer Plessy took a seat in a "whites only" car of a Louisiana train. Though Plessy was seven-eighths Caucasian, he was considered black by Louisiana standards. To challenge the segregation law, Plessy refused to move to a car reserved for blacks. He was arrested. The Supreme Court decided 8–1 that Louisiana's law did not violate the Fourteenth Amendment's promise of equal protection because Plessy had been offered a separate and (supposedly) equal accommodation on the train. Justice John Harlan dissented, writing, "Our Constitution is colorblind and neither knows nor tolerates classes among citizens."[7]

Harlan's dissent became the main theme of the unanimous decision of the Court in *Brown v. Board of Education.* The Court found that separate schools are "inherently unequal" because the act of segregating black children creates "a feeling of inferiority as to their status in the community that may affect their hearts and minds in a way unlikely ever to be undone."[8]

In recent decades, opponents of affirmative action and other government policies meant to redress racial inequality have argued that a truly color-blind society should not tolerate racial preferences in any form. In her speech, Berry takes on those who she says invoke color blindness for "nefarious purposes." She also proposes an unusual, alternate reading of Harlan's dissent in *Plessy.* Berry says there is a sentence in the dissent that few people pay attention to that throws an entirely different light on the idea of America as a color-blind society. It's a light, Berry says, that bodes trouble for African Americans.

COURTS, LIKE THE COURT in which *Plessy* was decided, are venues in which people tell stories. Judges and lawyers bring stories into the court, and they talk about rules and stories based on thousands of years of common law. But there are other people who have stories, too, who come into the court. There are the litigants, the plaintiffs, the defendants, the jury, the people who are the witnesses; they all have their stories. And out of that complex of stories, and the rules, all mixed up together, you get decisions of courts. We have to keep that in mind so we understand the impact of people's life experiences in courts, and that we are not simply talking about black-letter rules that are unchanging over time. And so when we look at *Plessy Against Ferguson,* we must keep this point about stories in mind.

Houston Baker, who was another alumnus of this institution, and who teaches with me at the University of Pennsylvania, says that a war is in progress against black America. A war is in progress against black America. I think he's probably right, in a sense. Houston is, of course, in English literature, and he may phrase things differently than I would, but there is a kind of war, and need I remind you of the symbols in that war, whether we're talking about the issues concerning Texaco, the riot in St. Petersburg and the police killing there, and the acquittal yesterday of the police involved in that incident, the police brutality around the country in the fallout from the O.J. Simpson case, and then the second case, all of these issues about race which are polarizing in this country.

And in this climate, the case in which the Supreme Court endorsed separate-but-equal may seem to some people like a relic tossed on the trash bin of history. But Homer Plessy had a story and he was as much a part of the black protest tradition as Rosa Parks, who sat down on the bus in Montgomery. And people forget that. Homer Plessy was part of an African American citizens' committee that chose him deliberately to challenge the segregation law. After he lost, the Fourteenth Amendment, of course, became a refuge for corporations instead of African Americans, until a brief period in the years after *Brown*.

Today, the Fourteenth Amendment is the refuge of whites who accuse African Americans of discrimination against them. The strange odyssey, the story of Plessy, underscores the African American predicament. Our history is mostly survival in defiance of law, and not because of law.

And the case that bears Homer Plessy's name still illuminates the path of our struggle, our victories, and our defeats. John Blassingame and I, in *Long Memory*, called the Supreme Court's *Plessy* decision one of the killers of the postemancipation dreams of African Americans. That was one killer.

The second killer was the Republican Party, which turned its back on African Americans and decided to build up a lily-white wing in the South, and then in Washington did nothing to stop the oppression of blacks in the South. The third killer we talk about in the book was scientists who used Darwin's theory of evolution to rationalize scientific racism, which was consistent with majority opinion in *Plessy*.

In 1996, we have some new killers of the dream. One in three African American men are ensnared in the criminal justice system. Over half of black children live in poverty, and drugs are infused into our community to spread death by AIDS or violence, from somewhere else, because they don't grow in our community. Police violence occurs everywhere, and the offspring of Jim Crow Jr. works to confine opportunity for African Americans. The Supreme

Court and the Congress and many state governments are as hostile as they were in 1896. The Republican Party, need I mention it, the Republican Party's Southern strategy to attract white racists to the party to win in the South has burgeoned nationally. Hereditarian racists such as Charles Murray reword the same old theories into best sellers, insisting we are too inferior genetically to benefit from opportunity when it is presented.

In 1996, African Americans are certainly better prepared for the struggle than we were in 1896. Much of that progress is due to the 1950s and 1960s civil rights movement. We have greater literacy, more assets, stronger black colleges and universities, and the right to vote and run for office. In 1896, we were blamed for our subordination. We were defined as ignorant, lazy, or unfit. Today we are still defined as less intelligent, hardworking, and able than we are. And we are also blamed for our own predicament, and for problems that exist elsewhere in society. African Americans are among the convenient scapegoats for America's social and economic problems.

After the turn of the century, African Americans had white corporate supporters of black colleges, who gave money and built buildings and served on boards. And we also had progressive supporters who organized the NAACP. In today's consensus, many white liberals and black and white conservatives blame a lack of values among African Americans for whatever social problems we have. My belief is that, even with ever larger percentages of immigrants coming into this country, and even immigrants of color—be they undocumented or legal—the race problem in America still centers on African Americans. Because of our history and present predicament, we remain the issue. Other immigrant groups try to distance themselves from us.

Everywhere in the world, everyone knows that African Americans are the American other—the largest indigestible mass in the American intestinal system, that doesn't go away no matter how much Pepto-Bismol you take, or Tums for your tummy, or whatever. You can travel anywhere in the world, as many of you have and I have, and you find people distancing themselves from African Americans. I spent a lot of time in Japan, and I have people tell me, "Well, we know that in America, the Negroes, the African Americans, you colored people, are inferior. We don't want to have anything to do with you. We see it on TV, we see it everywhere. You have all these problems." And when immigrants come to this country, the first thing they're taught, even if they don't know it when they come, is that you don't want to identify with African Americans. Even people from the Caribbean, you know, who are blacker than I, feel the same way, and not because they're racist but because they know that we are "the other." So some people get accents overnight, sometimes, that they didn't have before.

In the one hundred years since *Plessy*, Justice Henry Brown's majority opinion, and Justice John Marshall Harlan's dissenting opinion, have both been implicated in the African American struggle. Most of us have never been integrated. And we were not desegregated after slavery or when the successive waves of new immigrants began assimilating into American society. Neither were we really desegregated during the civil rights movement. If you look at our history, we have tried everything: coalitions with whites, we tried the NAACP and LDF and CORE and SNCC, we've tried Charles Hamilton Houston and Thurgood Marshall and Jack Greenberg and Roy Wilkins and Martin Luther King, and we tried to gain reparations and Garveyism, and the Black Muslims and Malcolm X and the Panthers, and Karenga's US [Organization] and the Republic of New Africa and Farrakhan. And yet empowerment remains elusive for us. We've tried migration up North and then later out West and then back South again, and still we are harmfully affected by the persistence of racism. And our quest for empowerment through community solidarity remains problematic.

Justice Brown's opinion in *Plessy* merely expressed conventional legal wisdom in 1896. There was nothing extraordinary about his opinion. Jim Crow prevailed well before the legislation passed after *Plessy*. Also, judges and lawyers had already decided that the Fourteenth Amendment did not afford blacks social equality, which could only be had by consent and not through law.

For years, Brown's majority opinion denying Plessy's plea has been easy to denounce. It has been one of the most denounced opinions in American history. And it's easy to denounce. Brown criticized Plessy for thinking that enforced separation of the two races stamps the colored race with a badge of inferiority. "If this be so," he said, "it is not by reason of anything found in the Act, but solely because the colored race chooses to put that construction upon it. If the two races are to meet upon terms of social equality including in theaters, trains, cars, and having business relationships, it must be the result of natural affinities, in mutual appreciation of each other's merits and a voluntary consent of individuals." The law could not touch these.

Now it's easy to denounce that. All of us could gather together, as people have over time, and say, "Ridiculous, outrageous, terrible." However, what we don't often say is that Brown's views are consistent with Booker T. Washington's 1895 Atlanta exposition speech, in which he denounced agitation and said to whites that "In all things that are purely social we can be as separate as the five fingers, yet one as the hand in all things essential to mutual progress."

The first time I heard that, Rayford Logan did that in class, said that—he was the professor here at Howard who taught me years ago. Furthermore, some African Americans today believe what Mr. Justice Brown said—that voluntary separate development offers a promising avenue for empowering African Americans, and that that's what we should have. I'll give you an example: Robert Woodson, who was at the Neighborhood Enterprise Institute, asserts that he participated in the civil rights movement to gain choice, not integration. He insists that African Americans should be able to choose a good black public school rather than trying to desegregate. Now who would be opposed to that?

Legally, this position seems remarkably similar to that of Justice Brown's opinion. Blacks, if this is correct, could sue for equal facilities, salary equalization, and even equal per-pupil expenditures in public schools. We could also sue for access to public employment, public housing, transportation, and parks, if you use this analysis. Now Justice Clarence Thomas, about which I will say nothing evil this morning [laughter], although I spent almost every day denouncing him for months, and then I just got tired of denouncing Justice Thomas. In any case—and I will do it now whenever it makes me feel better [laughter]—but Justice Thomas expressed a similar view to that of Mr. Justice Brown, and that of the one I've just described in the 1995 case of *Missouri Against Jenkins*. He joined in allowing Kansas City to end desegregation and a funding plan for racially isolated black schools. Racially isolated, of course, just means mostly segregated. That's what it means—it's a polite way of saying that.

Thomas announced that before the—get this—that before the 1954 school desegregation decision in *Brown*, and I'm quoting, "Of course, segregation additionally harmed black students by relegating them to schools with substandard facilities and resources, but neutral policies such as local school assignments do not offend the Constitution when individual private choices concerning work or residence produce schools with high black populations."

Therefore, racial separation in public education, he said, is not inherently unequal. That the *Brown* case was wrong. It's not inherently unequal. However, when separate-but-equal as a legal principle prevailed in the years after *Plessy* was decided, African Americans discovered something very interesting: that the *Plessy* decision by Mr. Justice Brown was never meant to make us equal or to afford equality of opportunity for a quality education, or anything else. And frustration with all those years of trying to enforce the equal part of the separate, led Charles Hamilton Houston, Marshall, Greenberg, and others to attack separation. That's why they did it—because, you know, it didn't work.

Choosing separate schools as a possible way of gaining quality education in 1996, right here in 1996, is as fraught with difficulties as earlier. The record in the Kansas City case showed that the black children's schools were in dismal shape, that that is what the desegregation order was for. And also, if you don't believe that the schools are in dismal shape, you should go visit some of them. And if you don't feel like visiting them, then go read Jonathan Kozol's *Savage Inequalities*, which is a good book. Which shows that along with crime and discipline and substandard facilities and buildings crumbling and water coming from the roof and a lack of good textbooks—or even *some* textbooks—and inadequate funding and a lack of leadership by people who are not committed and who are worried about their own perks—all of these things uniformly plague all-black or racially isolated schools, all of them taken together.

Now separate and equal, separate and equal, some people argue that what we have got to go back to is separate and equal—in 1996, that is what we ought to do. To go back to *Plessy*, say we want separate and equal, and try to get the equal part. Well, I don't think that's an achievable option. Why do I think that? It is undermined by the 1992 Mississippi higher education desegregation case, *Fordice Against Ayers*. The Supreme Court acknowledged inadequate resources for black public colleges in Mississippi, but then Mr. Justice White said that, you know, the state doesn't have to fund these schools adequately or even equally. He said, "Because the former de jure segregated system of public universities in Mississippi impeded the free choice of prospective students, the State, in dismantling that system, must take the necessary steps to ensure that this choice now is truly free."

Then he went on to say this does not mean black choice, and then I quote: "If we understand private petitioners to press us to order the upgrading of Jackson State, Alcorn State, and Mississippi Valley, so that they may be publicly financed, exclusively black enclaves, we reject that request." What he said was that you could have neutrality, the schools could stay, but they didn't have to be funded adequately. They could still be separate and unequal. Justice Thomas concurred in this unanimous decision in the Court.

Now in 1996, beating up on Justice Brown, as I said, is very easy. But what I'm about to do is something that isn't easy and that most people don't understand why I'm doing it. In 1996, Mr. Justice Harlan's dissent in *Plessy*, I think, presents just as many problems for African Americans as Brown's majority opinion. It is just as problematic. Not because Mr. Harlan intended it to be; that's not the point. But the point is, using his opinion is pernicious and insidious and is problematic for African Americans. Remember, he said, "In view of the Constitution, in the eye of the law, there is in this country no superior dominant ruling class of citizens, there is no caste here. Our Constitution is color-blind and neither knows nor tolerates classes among citizens. In respect to civil rights, all citizens are equal before the law," and so on.

However, right before this quote is something that people never read, or almost never read. I can't get students to read it. Right before this quote he assures white America that nothing he says is threatening their power or their status. He says, "The white race deems itself to be the dominant race in this country, and so it is in prestige and achievements and education and wealth and in power, so I doubt not it will continue to be for all time. Given range true to its great heritage it holds fast to the principles of Constitutional liberty."

In other words, if white America enforced the principle of color blindness, it need not fear African American progress, equality, or power. That is very important. That color blindness didn't mean that white Americans should fear that they would lose their power, or that African Americans would become equal. All they had to do was use the principle and move on.

Now, when Harlan died, African Americans were in despair. The historical record shows that black people cried, they went to the funeral; they were crying and they wept because they said that color blindness was most likely to lead us to the promised land. And in 1911, when Harlan died, that seemed to be the case. African Americans and their friends who sought equality in the courts argued color blindness and had been arguing it since the earliest abolitionist days. And they argued it because it seemed to be a weapon that they could use to win. After the NAACP was founded, civil rights lawyers, including the whole panoply of them I've described, used Harlan's opinion to assail segregation. They used color blindness because they wanted remedies.

One of the things you have to remember is that while the law consists of stories and their impact on rules, lawyers are in the business of finding remedies. I mean, lawyers aren't just trying to find something to do or an argument that sounds intellectually stimulating. What they're trying to do is win—persuade, interpret to persuade. Civil rights lawyers used color blindness because it seemed like an argument they could use, and it did work, to win opportunity for African Americans, which is what they were trying to do. But soon after *Brown* was decided in '54, the limitations emphasized by Harlan in his arguments on color blindness became very apparent. The civil rights movement didn't do the job, equal opportunity for many African Americans remained out of their reach, and the window of opportunity briefly opened by the civil rights movement and the color-blind principles slammed shut. Many schools remained segregated and unequal, and employment and business opportunities remained limited.

Civil rights lawyers began to differentiate between arguments against discrimination against us, and affirmative remedies which might take race into account. In other words, they started looking for more remedies. And the Civil Rights Act of 1964 responds to this distinction. And so civil rights activists said, "We want color blindness, that's the goal. But we have to use remedies for discrimination which will use race to get beyond the effect of racism against African Americans." Or for that matter use sex to get beyond sex discrimination against women. And what happened? When they start making those arguments, from then until today, civil rights proponents have been assailed by people who said it was all right to desegregate lunch counters, but what are you people talking about? You're talking about getting the best jobs and educational opportunities. And you're being inconsistent and should stay within the limits of Mr. Justice Harlan's color blindness. We thought you guys liked Mr. Justice Harlan's opinion. Why were you crying if you didn't like it? So you should stick with it, because after all, it's black-letter law, and you got to stick with it.

And, so, civil rights advocates made the argument that they needed to make. People who had never met a merit standard themselves got up in court making arguments about merit. They never met one themselves. No one would know what it looks like if they saw one. Blacks who were trying to desegregate schools were confronted with white flight and the complaints that the problem was not desegregation but busing, by people who sent their children to school every day on buses to mediocre, white private academies established to avoid desegregation. With a sign on the side of the bus:

"Moderately Mediocre Private White School." Try and get on the bus to go there to avoid black people.

This opposition, and the insistence on overbusing African American children, killed any attempt to desegregate schools. And since 1965, color-blind jurisprudence has been increasingly a stalking horse for black exclusion. We saw that in the Proposition 209 debate out in California, with this rather benign language, which is a stalking horse for black exclusion. And civil rights lawyers were not being consistent. What they were doing was seeking remedies.

The other thing that's used against us is Martin Luther King and the lawyers. Martin Luther King believed in a color-blind society. They had this ad out there in the 209 debate showing Martin Luther King—in the context, it made it look like he was against affirmative action. Coretta [King] had to write a letter to the *New York Times*, or something, explaining what everybody who can read, and who has ever read *Why We Can't Wait*, ought to know—which came out after the March on Washington—that Martin Luther King supported both affirmative action based on race and affirmative action based on poverty. Because he understood that the problem was, we needed remedies for the exclusion of people, and not that we should worry about whether we were being true to Mr. Justice Harlan's whatever. And that he had said in the March on Washington that the goal was color blindness, not that everything was color-blind in the first place.

Now today, some of the most important people who use color blindness for nefarious purposes are sitting there on the U.S. Supreme Court. And we would hope that something would be done about that fairly soon if the opportunity to make some new appointments ever comes to pass. And it is, again, Mr. Thomas and the rest of the people there. When they explain things like, why we don't need black majority districts, Sandra Day O'Connor said, in *Shaw v. Reno*, "Racial classifications of any sort pose the risk of lasting harm to our society. They reinforce the belief held by too many for too much of our history that individuals should be judged by the color of their skin." Well, everybody would agree with that. But the point is, remedy. And what do you do to remedy what has happened, in order to create a context in which you can reach for color blindness?

So the practical result of the use of color blindness as a cudgel is to perpetuate the advantages of those who have been prospering from the use of everybody's tax dollars—getting all the contracts and everything else. Similarly, those who have suffered from underemployment and unemployment, glass ceilings, and sticky floors, and no government contracts, remain disadvantaged. Lawyers on both sides have made clear to the court that their formulation of color blindness means that government can never make a policy that takes race into account, even to remedy its own invidious discrimination on the basis of race. That that's what the jurisprudence amounts to.

Mr. Justice Bradley asked in the civil rights cases when African Americans will stop being a particular favorite of the law? The answer is, his question is ridiculous. We have not been a favorite of the law, ever. And so long as we use color blindness in an invidious way—and its brothers and sisters, the "level playing field" and "not by the color of their skins and only the content of their characters"—in the law, we will never be.

The overall lesson of *Plessy* today is the example as given to me as, "Look, in the elections we just had, Cynthia McKinney won her seat, and Sanford Bishop won, so that means you didn't really need black majority districts anyway." The issue is not whether you elect people who have black faces. The issue is whether you elect African Americans who are independent actors in black interests—that's what the issue is. And we don't have [an] answer to that in the jurisprudence that is there today.

During the civil rights movement, SCLC's motto was, "To redeem the soul of America." But if America still refuses redemption, I guess we'll just have to figure out some way to save ourselves. And we hope that it will. But at this hour, it is more important that we remain more than one-step thinkers, able to consider more than one approach to problems at the same time, and therefore we ought to understand the uses of the law, and the uses of *Plessy*. And what we really ought to do is to follow the example of Homer Plessy and his co-conspirators in 1896 and join and support our organizations, and each other, as if our lives depended on it—because they do.

Thank you very much.

18.

WARD CONNERLY
(1939–)

"America: A Nation of Equals"

Harvard University, Cambridge, Massachusetts—April 6, 1998

Ward Connerly is the most prominent leader of the drive to eliminate affirmative action policies in the United States. A Republican businessman of mixed-race heritage, Connerly gave little attention to the issue of racial preferences until 1993, when he was appointed to the Board of Regents of California's public university system. Connerly was approached by the parents of a young white man who was rejected by one of the state's medical schools. Connerly investigated and decided that California's practice of affirmative action in education amounted to "reverse racism."

On matters of race, Connerly's libertarian views have made him a controversial figure. His opponents have labeled him an Uncle Tom and "the most hated black man in America." His supporters regard him as "a principled hero."[1]

Connerly helped lead an effort in California to pass Proposition 209, a ballot initiative approved in 1996 banning the consideration of race, ethnicity, or gender in hiring, contracting, college admissions, and state programs. He also co-founded the American Civil Rights Institute, an organization devoted to ending affirmative action across the country. Connerly's campaign succeeded in a few states. Voters passed measures similar to Proposition 209 in Michigan, Washington, and Nebraska, while in Florida the legislature rolled back racial preference policies.

Affirmative action is the practice of considering personal character- istics such as race, ethnicity, or gender when making decisions about applicants for a job, a contract, or enrollment in school. Supporters of the policy say the disadvantages caused by historic discrimination justify these attempts to increase the representation of women and minorities in education and the workplace. As President Lyndon Johnson said in a speech at Howard University in 1965, "You do not take a man who for years has been hobbled by chains, liberate him, bring him to the starting line of a race, saying, 'You are free to compete with all the others,' and still justly believe you have been completely fair."[2]

Ward Connerly opposes affirmative action out of what he calls a "passion for fairness." He believes race-based remedies only prolong America's racial divisions and inequities.[3] In his memoir, *Creating Equal*, Connerly says race is "a scar" in America that he first saw as a toddler in the segregated South. He yearns for race consciousness to dissolve in America's melting pot, but without government turning up the heat. "Left to their own devices, I believe Americans will merge and melt into each other. This is as it should be," he writes.[4]

Ward Connerly was born in the western Louisiana town of Leesville. His father left the family when Ward was two years old; the boy's mother died when he was four. Connerly was raised by relatives in California. He first lived with a working-class aunt and uncle in a primarily black sec- tion of Sacramento. Connerly credits them with teaching him the values of hard work and self-respect. At twelve, he moved in with his maternal grandmother, who struggled to make ends meet. Some of Connerly's relatives have said that, in later life, Connerly exaggerated the depth of his childhood poverty in Sacramento for political effect. It is a charge Con- nerly vehemently disputes.

Connerly's ethnic heritage is a mix of Irish, black, French, and Choctaw Indian, but he identifies himself as black "because blackness is an experi- ence and others have forced that experience upon me."[5] He attended American River Junior College and then Sacramento State College, gradu- ating with a BA in political science in 1962. A year later, he married a white classmate, Ilene Crews. It was a time when mixed-race couples were still a relative rarity in the United States. The couple had two children.

In 1964, Connerly was drawn to Republican politics by GOP presidential candidate Barry Goldwater's devotion to free markets and free-enterprise views. Connerly worked as a housing consultant to State Senator Pete Wilson, then started his own consulting and public housing development company. He ran it for more than two decades and became a millionaire. When Wilson was elected governor of California, he appointed Connerly to the Board of Regents.

Connerly's crusade against affirmative action has made him an icon to the conservative right. William F. Buckley Jr. called him "the high priest of equal treatment, and the targeted enemy of the preference brigade."[6] Connerly has been accused, as a black businessman, of benefiting from the very minority-contracting policies that he attacks. But *Time* magazine journalist Eric Pooley reports that "these charges don't hold up under scrutiny."[7]

In a front-page profile, *New York Times* writer Barry Bearak described Connerly as an activist driven by principle, an "extravagantly patriotic" man who says he silently recites the Pledge of Allegiance and parts of the Declaration of Independence every day. Connerly says the harsh battles he's endured over affirmative action have only made him more dedicated to his country. "My fight against race preferences has sharpened my appreciation for the principles that are at the core of the American ex-periment," Connerly writes in his memoir. "I feel more fully a citizen now—more part of this nation—than ever before in my life."[8]

Connerly gave this speech at Harvard University's Kennedy School of Government before a standing-room-only crowd. The forum's moderator instructed the audience to respect Connerly, a controversial conservative speaking on a predominantly liberal campus. According to the Harvard campus newspaper, many students were more offended by remarks made introducing Connerly than by the speaker himself. Government professor Harvey C. Mansfield described Connerly as belonging in the company of "the greatest black thinkers" and noted that such thinkers, including Martin Luther King Jr. and Malcolm X, often disagreed. When Connerly took the podium, he politely reproached Mansfield for suggest-ing that his skin color should be a factor in a public policy debate. "It should not be relevant," Connerly said.[9]

IT IS A GREAT HONOR to be here in one of the nation's intellectual capitals— one of the two intellectual capitals, the other being my alma mater, American

River Junior College. [laughter] I never thought that I would be able to over-come the obstacles of being born in Leesville, Louisana—orphaned at four, and growing up in the Heights, Del Paso Heights, and being able to come here and visit with some of the best minds in the world to share a perspec-tive. W. C. Fields often said, "Start each day with a laugh, and get it over with."

And it prompts me to remember the story of Gretchen Alexander as I talk about overcoming obstacles. And Gretchen Alexander was sightless, but she never let that stand in her way of enjoying life's experiences. She could play golf, swim, softball. Great at archery. And she was lecturing one of her high school classes and a student asked, "Is there anything that you won't do?" And she said, "Yes, I won't sky dive; it would scare the hell out of my dog." So I'm not going to let any obstacles stand in my way.

I want to get right to the introduction because, candidly, I have a prob-lem with the introduction, with all due respect, professor. And my problem with the introduction goes to the heart of what my reason for being in this whole movement is. And that is the presumption that my skin color should be relevant in a public policy debate. It should not be relevant.

And I mean no disrespect to him. He is positioning the issue the way the public seems to portray it. And that is that somehow I am out of step from the black establishment because of the views that I hold. I would submit to you that if you find fifty black people you will probably find fifty variations of opinions. It just seems that on some issues there is more coalescing around certain points of view than others. But I dare say, you would not find any greater differences between us than you would find among others on issues as well.

And I really hope, I really hope with every fiber of my being that I will live to see the day when that kind of introduction would be totally unnecessary. That no one would have to invoke the question of my race, whatever the hell that is, or my skin color in relation to a position that I am espousing.

That, my friends, is why I have taken upon myself to say to my nation, "Let's confront this, folks!" Let's confront it, because you're putting me and others like me—and I don't mean fifty-eight and bald—into a little box. You're herding us into a box, and the expectation is that we're going to stay within that box with respect to how we conduct ourselves. And all my life I have defied operating within the box.

The question arises over and over again: Why is this black man leading this effort to eliminate affirmative action in a state like California? Let me kind of try to respond to this—throw away the script—and respond to you as candidly as I can, why I, as a fellow American, have taken upon myself to converse with you, my fellow Americans, about an issue that I think goes to the core of who we are as a people. Why we're here in this place and time, in this great nation, trying to perfect this experiment that we call democracy.

People who have come here from different parts of the globe, some born here, different experiences, different cultures, different sexual orientation, disabilities, different races—however we define that—different ethnic backgrounds. How do we forge this, all these differences, into one nation, without the divisible parts? Without any presumptions about our abilities or the things to which we can aspire? How do we do this?

I was sentenced to an unpaid twelve-year term on the Board of Regents in 1993. And all my life prior to that time, I had grown up believing in this American experiment that I just described to you. I believed as a political science student in those great thirty-six words in the Declaration of Independence—and you know them: about holding these truths to be self-evident, that all men are created equal, endowed by their creator with certain inalienable rights, that among these are life, liberty, and the pursuit of happiness. I grew up believing that.

I believed in Lincoln when he talked about our founders bringing forth on this nation—I'm not giving you the actual words; you know them. Conceived in liberty and dedicated to the proposition that all men are created equal. I honestly believed that stuff! And as a young student of the sixties, when the man after whom this great facility is named said on June 11, 1963, "Race has no place in American life and law," I believed that stuff! To the core of my being I came away from that period and time believing, as Dr. King said, that this nation would live out the true meaning of its creed and treat me as an individual—not judge me by what I am, but judge me by who I am. If I'm a rotten scoundrel, judge me accordingly. But at least let me prove to you that I'm a rotten scoundrel rather than your presuming that on the basis of some immutable traits.

And so it was that, as a regent, when I discovered that the University of California was really using different standards to admit people. We were classifying them on the basis of whether they're African American, or Chicano, or Latino, or American Indian, or Asian, or white. We're making people fill out these silly little boxes and saying if you fill out this one, these are the number of points that you get; if you fill out this one, these are the number of points that you get. Based on the system of values that I brought to the university as a regent, I thought, "This is wrong. This is not what the experiment is."

So you may disagree with me, but I felt that I had no choice but, as a fiduciary of the board of regents, to act according to my beliefs, that this is wrong. And so I proposed that the regents abolish the consideration of race.

Now this was not a precipitous move. I had looked at the evidence and I saw that, in 1989, the number of black students who had applied to the University of California was 2,191. In 1995, the number was about 2,191. The number of Asians that had applied in 1989 was about 8,000. The number for a corresponding period was about 12,000. And so, I thought, something here is wrong. If the number of black students is flat over that period of time, with affirmative action, and the number of Asian students is going up, with all of our efforts basically to suppress their numbers, because we didn't want Berkeley to become all Asians, something is wrong.

And so it just seemed to me that if we as a university really want to do what's right, maybe we should think about a different way of doing this. Maybe we should really commit ourselves to finding out what's going on. Examine whether race is, in fact, "one of many factors." And as I began to expose the reality of what was happening, I say to you that race was not one of many factors. That was a big lie. Race was *the* factor. So the choice at that point was, do I go back into my shell as a regent and pretend that I never knew those facts? Or do I proceed with what I think is right? The rest is history.

Having done that, there was an immediate response. People saying we were going to resegregate the university. I knew differently, because anyone who was admitted to the University of California was guaranteed then, and is guaranteed now, a seat at the University of California. It may not be Berkeley; it may be San Diego or Davis or whatever, but no one is denied an opportunity on the basis of race, if you're eligible for admission to the University of California.

But there was a continuing outpouring from students and others, who really were more intent upon stirring up trouble than they were dealing with problems, to rescind the vote. Every meeting, there were students protesting, "Rescind the vote! Rescind the vote!" And so the only way that it seemed to me that I could guarantee that this principle of treating all of our students equally would manifest itself throughout history in the state of California would be to put it into the constitution. And those thirty-seven words are now in fact in the constitution of the state of California: "The state shall not discriminate against or grant preferential treatment to any individual or group on the basis of race, sex, color, ethnicity or national origin in the operation of public employment, public education or public contracting." Simple. Direct. Clear. No hidden mysteries about those words. They're in the constitution of California.

Now, this is not just about eliminating preferences, however. It's about dealing with the issue of race, still the unfinished business, social and legal, of America. It's about race. It's about diversity, as we call it. Students on campuses—and I've been to, like, twenty-five in the last three months. We have the diversity on campuses, but we don't have integration. Black students at Emory University are just as isolated as if they weren't at Emory University.

It's about people who are marrying. You know, Dr. King said he looked for the day when little black boys and little white girls would be holding hands. They're doing more than holding hands. They're getting married and raising families. But in too many parts of this nation, there are interracial couples who are still subjected to the hostility, the stares. It's about confronting this. Leave them alone! Let them enjoy their lives without the intrusions of a society that is passing judgment.

It's about people who happen to be gay, wanting to live their lives alone, without people bothering them. And that's a sensitive subject, but I believe in equality! And if you believe in equality, you do not diminish the dignity of another human being.

It's about dealing with those subjects of how we interact with our fellow man. And whether we're big enough to accept doing away with preferences, extending dignity to every person, without passing judgment ourselves on the value of that person.

And so I want to allow as much time as I can tonight for questions because I think that really is where we can move this dialogue forward and move it up the field.

But I want to leave you, as I provide my opening comments, with the essence of what this movement really is about: it's getting the American people, you among them, to accept the proposition that if this experiment is going to work, none of us, none of us can expect any different treatment than anybody else. And none of us should tolerate any different treatment of another human being. Because people who are not equal are not free. When your society forces you to check the box and decides whether you win or lose in the competitions of life on the basis of the box that you check, your freedom is diminished. Because today it might be you, tomorrow it might be you—that doesn't quite match up with the matrix.

And if that's the kind of government we want, if that's the kind of society that we want, the experiment has failed. Let's call the game right now, because it's failed. It doesn't work. It will not work if any of our citizens are allowed to be treated differently by their government on the basis of traits with which they are born.

19.

CONDOLEEZZA RICE
(1954–)

Speech to National Council of Negro Women

Washington, D.C.—December 8, 2001

When she was U.S. secretary of state, Condoleezza Rice was the highest ranking and most powerful African American woman in history. Rice served as national security adviser (2001–05) and then secretary of state (2005–09) for President George W. Bush. She was an exceptionally close adviser to the president. One of her biographers described Bush and Rice as "virtual soul mates."[1] Rice was also a star of the Republican Party and was mentioned as a possible candidate for the presidency in 2008. Rice chose to return to Stanford University as a professor in the political science department and to join the Hoover Institution as a senior fellow.

Condoleezza Rice was born in Birmingham, Alabama. Her father was a Presbyterian minister and school guidance counselor, her mother a schoolteacher. Birmingham was regarded as the South's "most segregated city."[2] In 1963, when Rice was nine, Martin Luther King Jr. teamed up with local ministers and civil rights activists to launch a major assault on Jim Crow discrimination in Birmingham. He organized marches by African American schoolchildren as well as adults. White resistance was fierce. Blacks had nicknamed the city Bombingham because of its long history of violent white vigilantism.³ The head of the Birmingham police, Eugene "Bull" Connor, set police dogs and fire hoses on the peaceful marchers—including children. Pictures and television footage of the violence caused outrage around the world.

Rice's father and his church stayed largely out of the fray. He objected to King's use of children in the demonstrations. One of Rice's schoolmates was among the four black girls killed in the infamous 1963 bombing of a Birmingham church, but Rice lived in a middle-class black enclave where her family kept their distance from the civil rights movement. "Rather than agitating for the overthrow of the system," journalist and Rice biographer Marcus Mabry writes, "middle and upper-class [black] leaders continued the tradition of carving out what freedom they could under segregation."⁴ When whites threatened their neighborhood, Rice's father would stand watch with his shotgun. Otherwise, he focused on ways to make life better for his family and community.

Over the years, Rice would give varying accounts of how keenly she felt the sting of white racism as a little girl in Birmingham. Journalist and biographer Elizabeth Bumiller says Rice's assessment of the civil rights movement reflects the self-help philosophy of her parents. "What I always disliked was the notion that blacks were somehow saved by people who came down from the North to march," Rice told Bumiller. "Black Americans in Birmingham and in Atlanta and places like that were thriving and educating their children and being self-reliant and producing the right values in those families, and in those communities. And when segregation did lift they were more than prepared because of what blacks had done on their own."⁵

When Rice was eleven, the family moved to Tuscaloosa, Alabama, where her father became a college administrator. Two years later, they moved to Colorado so her father could assume the post of vice chancellor at the University of Denver. There, Rice attended her first integrated school.

John and Angelina Rice raised their only daughter to be a high achiever. She did so well in school that she skipped the first and seventh grades. She also took lessons in piano, violin, ballet, French, and figure skating. Rice's mother gave her the unusual name Condoleezza, a variation on the Italian musical term *con dolcezza,* meaning "with sweetness." She graduated from high school at age fifteen and entered the University of Denver to train as a concert pianist.

Although she was a talented musician, Rice realized she could not make it a profession. She was drawn to international relations in an introductory course taught by Professor Josef Korbel, a specialist on the Soviet Union and, coincidentally, the father of future secretary of state Madeleine Albright. Rice earned her PhD from the University of Denver in 1981 and won a fellowship at Stanford University's Center for International Security and Arms Control. A year later she was on the Stanford faculty. In quick succession, Rice served as a Soviet expert on the National Security Council under President George H.W. Bush, then returned to Stanford as provost—the university's second in command. She was thirty-eight years old.

As provost, Rice was effective and controversial. In a *New Yorker* magazine profile of Rice, journalist Nicholas Lemann observes that Rice's appointment to such a powerful position at such a distinguished school was regarded as a milestone for women and minorities. And while Rice was thought by some "to be the classic beneficiary of affirmative action," Lemann writes that she did not show evidence of concern over gender or race issues as she cut millions of dollars from Stanford's overdrawn budget. Lemann adds, "Rice, rather than agonize over her role as Stanford's bad cop, gave the appearance of being completely untroubled by it." Rice was there to do a job, not redress social ills.[6]

Rice's position on affirmative action has been described as "centrist" or "lukewarm," though she has freely acknowledged benefiting from race and gender preferences in her own academic career.[7] In 2003, Rice distanced herself from the Bush administration's support of a lawsuit against the University of Michigan that challenged the use of race as a factor in admissions. "I believe that while race-neutral means are preferable, it is appropriate to use race as one factor among others in achieving a diverse student body," Rice said in a statement.[8] In a 1998 faculty meeting at Stanford, when Rice was provost, she said, "I myself am a beneficiary of a Stanford strategy that took affirmative action seriously."[9] But Rice did not believe in considering race, ethnicity, or gender in making faculty tenure decisions, a position that produced bitter controversy in her time as provost.

In the summer of 1999, Rice took a leave of absence from Stanford to become foreign policy adviser to the presidential campaign of Texas governor George W. Bush. After he won, Bush appointed Rice as his national security adviser. She was the first woman ever to fill that post. Shortly before she left California for Washington, Rice's father died. Her mother had passed away in 1985. "Rice was keenly aware that she was experiencing one of the most important events of her life without the two most important people in her life," writes biographer Elisabeth Bumiller, "but she was comforted by her belief that somehow her parents knew."[10] Once in Washington, Rice devoted herself to her job and her president with a singularity of focus that was exceptional even by the workaholic standards of the nation's capital. Rice became close with George and Laura Bush, spending off-hours with the president watching football games or exercising. She also shared Bush's devout Christianity.

By virtue of her position and her relationship with Bush, Rice played a key role in shaping the U.S. response to the September 11, 2001, terrorist attacks, especially the decision to invade Iraq in search of weapons of mass destruction that turned out not to be there. When Secretary of State Colin Powell retired at the beginning of Bush's second term, Rice got the post in January 2005.

As secretary of state, Rice was twice ranked by *Forbes* magazine as the most powerful woman in the world. *Glamour* magazine honored her in 2008 for her ability to mix style and power on behalf of women. "Here's how we're used to seeing Condoleezza Rice," *Glamour* declared, "clicking down a cool marble hallway in her Ferragamo heels and tailored suit, the only female in a phalanx of men." The magazine celebrated Rice as "the warrior princess" who helped direct hundreds of millions of dollars in government money to programs for women's health and political development and to a campaign against sex trafficking.[11]

Rice gave this speech in 2001 as she accepted the Mary McLeod Bethune Award from the National Council of Negro Women. The NCNW is an advocacy and development organization founded in 1935 by Mary McLeod Bethune, a legendary black educator and civil rights leader. Although she was speaking to a room filled with other African American women, Rice's comments are characteristically muted on the issue of discrimination. When bias got in her way, Rice's lifetime response was to overpower her foes "by sheer force of her excellence."[12] Rice has been described as "an unabashed believer in the American experiment, in the United States as a model for good in the world."[13] Rice is a passionate advocate of education as a primary solution to inequality in America. Given how much her family believed and invested in her education, Rice says in this speech, she should have accomplished much.

• • •

I COULD NOT BE MORE honored than to receive the Bethune Award, because I feel a great kinship with Mary McLeod Bethune, and I think we all do. I was reading a little bit of her biography in recent days, and it's extraordinary. It's extraordinary to think that at the time that Dr. Bethune lived, she was asked by a president of the United States to go to Liberia, in 1952, on a diplomatic mission. It's extraordinary that she was invited to the White House in 1928. It's extraordinary that a young black woman from South Carolina could found a college and be its president for almost four decades. It's extraordinary, not because she wasn't talented enough to do it, but because she lived and toiled at a time when to do that as an African American woman was extraordinary. [applause]

I also feel a kinship with her because I've learned that she collected miniature elephants. She must have been a Republican. [laughter]

I also feel, of course, a great, great kinship with this wonderful organization. It's been a part of our lives and a part of our histories from the time that any of us could remember. It is an organization that stands for the best in America because it stands for opportunity, and it stands for hope, and it stands for belief. It stands for everything that it really means to be American. It also stands for the tremendous gains that we as African Americans, and African American women, have made in these many years. But those gains would not have been possible without organizations like this in our lives. And so let me ask you to join me in thanking you, this great organization, for the long years of service to African Americans, and African American women in particular. Thank you. [applause]

I also feel a great kinship to Dr. Bethune and to this organization because we share a passion for education. There is no more important element for the United States of America than the promise of education. I'm a living example of what education can mean, because it goes back a long way in my family. I very often tell people that I *should* have been able to accomplish what I accomplished, because I had grandparents and parents who understood the value of education.

Maybe some of you've heard me tell the story of Granddaddy Rice, a poor sharecropper's son in Ewtah—that's E-W-T-A-H—Alabama, who somehow in about 1919 decided he was going to get book learning. And so he asked people who came through how a colored man could get to college. And they said to him, "Well, you see, there's this college not too far away from here called Stillman College, and if you could get there, they take colored men into college." And so he saved up his cotton and he went off to Tuscaloosa, Alabama, to go to college. He made it through his first year having paid for it with his cotton, but the second year he didn't have any more cotton, and they came and they asked him for tuition. And he said, "Well you see the problem is, I don't have any money." And they said, "Well, you'll have to leave." So he thought rather quickly and he said, "Well, how are those boys going to college?" And they said, "Well, you see, they have what's called a scholarship, and if you wanted to be a Presbyterian minister then you could have a scholarship too." And Granddaddy Rice said, "You know, that's exactly what I had in mind." [laughter] And my family has been Presbyterian, and it has been college-educated ever since. [laughter]

My grandfather understood something, and so did my grandmother and my mother's parents, and that is that higher education, if you can attain it, is transforming. You may come from a poor family, you may come from a rural family, you may be first-generation college educated, but once you are college educated, the most important thing about you, in many ways, is that you're a college graduate and you are transformed. And I have to tell you that if I have a concern at all today in America, it is that we have got to find a way to pass on that promise to children, no matter what their circumstances, because it's just got to be the case in America that it does not matter where you came from, it only matters where you're going. [applause]

I used to love to stand in front of a class at Stanford University, because at Stanford University, one of the finest universities in America, there was always some kid who, of course, was a fourth-generation Stanford legatee. But you know what? He or she was sitting right next to a kid who was an itinerant farmworker's son, or a daughter of a migrant, or maybe a kid from the inner city. Because, somehow, these kids were getting a good enough education to come and study side-by-side at Stanford University and be transformed together. But we have a hard job ahead of us if that promise is going to continue to be fulfilled. We've got an educational system that is, frankly, not living up to the demands of today to educate our children.

I know that this conference talks about leaving no one behind. President Bush has talked about leaving no child behind. America has got to recommit to precisely that sentiment because we will not be who we are if it is not true that you are able to do whatever your talents can allow you to do—that you are not somehow constrained and hemmed in by where you started.

Now, there's another message that we need to deliver to our kids. It's that educational excellence is key, but so are limitless educational horizons. You know, I didn't start out to be a Russian specialist. I'm not Russian, in case you haven't noticed. [laughter] And so I went to college to be a concert pianist. I could read music before I could read. But, about my sophomore year in college, I started to encounter those kids who could play from sight everything that it had taken me all year to learn. And I thought, I'm in trouble. I'm not going to end up playing at Carnegie Hall; I'm going to end up playing in a piano bar, or teaching thirteen-year-olds to murder Beethoven, or maybe playing at Nordstrom, but I'm not going to play Carnegie Hall. And so I went home and had that conversation with my parents.

"Mom and Dad, I'm changing my major."

"To what are you changing your major?"

"I don't know."

"You are going to wind up a waitress at Howard Johnson's because you don't know what you want to do with your life."

"Well, after all, it is my life."

"Well, after all, it is our money." [laughter]

AND AFTER THIS LITTLE conversation, my parents and I decided that I only had two years to finish college. I was already now a junior in college. And so I wandered the wilderness looking for a major. And fortunately, in the spring quarter of my junior year, I wandered into a course in international politics taught by a Soviet specialist—taught by a man named Joseph Korbel, Madeleine Albright's father. And suddenly, I'd found love. People say, "Why are you interested in Russia?" It's like love. I'd suddenly found my passion. And it never occurred to me to ask why a black woman from Birmingham, Alabama, might want to do that.

And so I studied Russia. And I studied Russian. And I became proficient at what I did, and I went off to teach. And President Bush, the first, asked me to come and be his specialist for Soviet affairs. And, in June 1990, I found myself in a helicopter taking off with Mikhail Gorbachev, Raisa Gorbachyova, me, and the Secret Service, and I thought to myself, "I'm really glad I changed my major." [laughter]

For me, the passion came in something quite unusual. We have to tell our kids, too, that it's OK for your passion to come in something that's not expected of you. If you can be excellent at something, if you love something, go and do it. And then provide them the education to do so. That, in many ways, is our most important value as Americans, but you know what? It's actually a universal value.

We're seeing it today in Afghanistan, where women are throwing off their burqas. But that's not really what they're talking about. They're talking about re-entering colleges, and going back to work as doctors, and educating their daughters for the first time since the Taliban came to power. That's the power of this value—that people ought to be able to attain whatever they can attain.

Ladies and gentlemen, it was the way that Mary McLeod Bethune believed, it has been the way that this great organization has believed, it is what we, as Americans, believe.

I want to thank you for the honor of being with you, of now carrying an award that carries the name of one of the great pioneers of our people and of our country. I want to thank you again, Dr. Height, for being here with me. May God bless you, and God bless America. [applause]

20.

MAXINE WATERS
(1938–)

"Youth and the Political Process"

The Catholic University, Washington, D.C.—August 9, 2003

Maxine Waters is a forceful and outspoken congresswoman from California known for her passionate commitment to the poor and minority residents of her Los Angeles district. She came to national attention in the wake of the 1992 Los Angeles riots. Poor sections of the city erupted after four police officers were acquitted of the videotaped beating of black motorist Rodney King. Waters appeared in numerous news accounts arguing that chronic poverty and discrimination were root causes of the violence. She was assailed by some critics for calling the event an "uprising" and for appearing to sympathize with looters. Waters shrugged off the criticism, saying her life experience gave her a unique understanding of the problems of the disenfranchised.

Maxine Moore was born in St. Louis, Missouri, in 1938, the fifth of thirteen children reared by a single mother, Velma Lee Moore. The family lived in public housing and often relied on welfare to get by. Maxine was a conscientious student and a hard worker. She got her first job at age thirteen in a segregated restaurant. As a teenager, she also found work in factories. After graduating from high school, Maxine Moore married Edward Waters. They had two children. The couple moved to Los Angeles in 1961, where

Maxine Waters worked at a garment factory and as a telephone operator. Following the 1965 riots in the black neighborhood of Watts, Waters signed on as an assistant teacher in a newly created Head Start program—a federal initiative to help poor children prepare for school by providing nutrition, education, health care, and other social services. While working at Head Start, Waters earned a bachelor's degree in sociology at California State University–Los Angeles.

Waters inherited an interest in local politics from her mother, who had worked at the polls and was involved in community organizing. In her job at the Head Start program, Waters began to help organize parents who wanted to get better government services for their children. From there, Waters got involved in local elections, and her political career accelerated. In 1976, Waters won election to the California State Assembly. She served there for fourteen years, becoming a powerful legislator who challenged the state's male-dominated political hierarchy. Waters championed a change in state law to prohibit police strip searches for nonviolent misdemeanors. She pushed for the divestment of state pension funds from apartheid South Africa and sponsored the nation's first law requiring employers to give workers notice before closing a plant.

Waters was elected to the U.S. House of Representatives in 1990. According to *Ebony* magazine, she arrived in Washington with a "national reputation for being ferociously outspoken on issues close to her heart."[1] Waters has advocated for job training programs for unemployed youth, business expansion in struggling city neighborhoods, health care for African Americans stricken by HIV/AIDS, debt relief for Africa, and pro-democracy programs for Haiti. She has been active in national Democratic politics, supporting the presidential campaigns of Jesse Jackson and Bill Clinton and chairing the Congressional Black Caucus in 1997–98. When she encounters obstacles that can't be overcome by gentle persuasion, she turns up the volume. "I think she sees injustice and gets outraged," said Democratic U.S. senator Barbara Boxer of California. "She puts that outrage into action."[2]

When the 1992 Los Angeles riots broke out, the *New York Times* reported that Waters was "all over the airwaves, acting as a voice of the disenfranchised." When Waters was criticized for seeming to justify the rioting and looting, she shot back that she had condemned the violence in "101 different ways." She added, "What I didn't do is use the airwaves to call people hoodlums and thugs for burning down their own communities.

It only makes them madder when you call them hoodlums and thugs, as [President George H. W. Bush] did." In the wake of the riots, Waters learned that the president had invited congressional leaders to the White House to talk about what to do next. But he hadn't invited her. Waters showed up at the White House and elbowed her way into the meeting. "I don't intend to be excluded or dismissed," she said.[3]

In the summer of 2003, Waters gave this speech at a national African American youth leadership conference in Washington, D.C., sponsored by the Tavis Smiley Foundation. She talks about a trial in Los Angeles that had ended the previous week in a hung jury and a mistrial. The case involved a black teenager who alleged that a white police officer had used excessive force in arresting him in the Los Angeles suburb of Inglewood. The arrest was captured on videotape and showed the handcuffed teenager being slammed onto a car and beaten in the face. Inglewood is a predominantly low-income, minority neighborhood just east of Los Angeles International Airport. It is part of Waters's congressional district.

In the speech, Waters also makes reference to the USA Patriot Act, legislation Congress passed in the weeks following the September 11, 2001, terrorist attacks. The act granted federal agencies sweeping new powers, at home and abroad, to gather intelligence and evidence in terrorism investigations. Although the Patriot Act was approved by wide margins in Congress, it has been assailed by civil liberties advocates as a violation of basic American rights and freedoms. Waters voted against the measure.

In speaking to a group of young African Americans, Congresswoman Waters was addressing a constituency she cared deeply about. From her days as a Head Start teacher through the decades she has spent in state and national government, Waters has been an ardent champion of inner-city children. She has directed federal dollars and corporate support to programs that help young people break free from poverty. Waters told a reporter, "When you come from the kind of background that I've come from, you just have to fight to make things better."[4]

IN LOS ANGELES RECENTLY, there was a trial. This was a trial about police officers in the city of Inglewood. Many of you saw on television a young man being picked up, looked almost like a rag doll, and his head was slammed against a police car. His name was Donovan Jackson. And he'd been stopped by Inglewood police. Something had taken place in a service station with his father. And this incident was videotaped by a man named Mitchell Crooks. And they had an opportunity to use the information from the videotape to bring these police before the bar of justice and have a trial to determine whether or not they had violated this young man's rights, whether or not he had, in fact, been abused by the police.

The trial took place, I think, about a week ago, and it was a split decision, seven-to-five. And so people were saying, "How could that happen? It was so obvious what happened to Donovan Jackson." Well, if you followed the case, you know that they bring in the expert witnesses, they analyze the tape, they make the arguments, they have a jury, and the jury decides whether or not the police officers were guilty of having violated their oath of office and abused this young man in a way that was unacceptable. Some people say, "Well, how could they not have seen what happened on that videotape?" The arguments are made and the jury decides.

Who makes up this jury? A lot of people were very, very concerned because there was only one black person on the jury. The city of Inglewood is majority minority, and majority African American. How could this have happened? How could you get a jury with only one black, in a case where the defendants are African American, in a city where it is majority minority and mostly black? How could this happen?

Well, most people don't know enough about the criminal justice system, and how juries are picked, to be able to understand that. First of all, you have to realize that they can pick people within a twenty-mile radius of the court-house that decided this case, and that courthouse serves not only Inglewood, but many of the cities around Inglewood in this twenty-mile radius. So that many of these citizens are predominantly white, they are beach cities, and they, too, are asked to serve as jurors on this panel. Why did so many of them get picked to serve? First of all, what's the first qualification you must have to serve on the jury? [unintelligible audience response] I can't hear you.

Sorry, I didn't hear you. You should be, you must be a registered voter. Is that right? [Yes] Why are we begging folks in the year 2003 to get registered to vote? Now, we hear a lot of rhetoric about the fact, "Oh yes, our forefathers, our ancestors, died for the right to vote." We hear it over and over again. But we also learn that when young people turn eighteen years old, they don't register to vote. Some of them say, "I don't wanna be bothered with politics. That doesn't have anything to do with me. I don't believe in any of those political parties. I just haven't had time. I've got to go to school. I've got to work." But the fact of the matter is, in this society if you don't vote, you don't count.

If you don't vote, you don't count in many, many different ways. The first thing is, you're not going to be selected to serve on anybody's jury, and so, when the cases come up about young Donovan Jackson, or anybody else where you think there could be a miscarriage of justice, when you're outraged, when you see that kind of abuse, if you're simply talking about it, not willing to register to vote, not willing to be a part of the efforts to get other people to register to vote, then you may as well shut up, because you don't count.

So when we say, "Young people, fourteen, fifteen, sixteen, seventeen, eighteen years old, you should be raring . . . I can't wait until I get to be eighteen so that I can register to vote, because when I register to vote, not only am I going to be willing to serve on a jury panel, I am going to be willing to exercise this right in certain ways that will help to elect people to office who will represent me, who will represent my community."

And so, on this panel, not only are we picking from a twenty-mile radius of people who are registered to vote, they receive a questionnaire. And I asked the district attorney, "Why were so many blacks maybe excluded from the jury?" He said, "Well, I want you to know, Miss Waters, the way that they filled out the questionnaire, they were not able to answer the questions in a way that showed that they could be objective, that they could be fair, that they could sit on this panel, listen to all of the information, and make a good decision."

What's that all about? Ladies and gentlemen, it's simply about education. It's simply about being able to read, to understand, to reason, to answer a question, and to fill out forms. The day is over when folks can say, "Well, I'm smart. I don't need to be educated, I don't need to go to college, I don't need to get a master's, I don't need to get a PhD." The world operates for and about educated people.

Folks who don't get educated, who cannot reason, who cannot think, who cannot fill out forms, are out of it. You cannot negotiate your environment. And the smarter you are, the better it is. Not everyone has a three-plus, a four-plus [grade point average]. We understand that. But if you cannot fill out the forms that are required today in every aspect of our life, you gonna get left behind. How many folks have sat down and filled out a package just for the Pell Grant? Know what the Pell Grant is? Student aid. How do you get some money to help supplement the money that your parents may have?

How do you fill out the forms for a Stafford loan? The packets are like this [she demonstrates by holding hands far apart]. How many folks have asked their parents, what did they have to fill out in order to buy a house? The packet is like this [demonstrates by holding hands far apart].

Whether it's a Section Eight program, student loans, purchase of a house—in this society you've got to be prepared to not only read the forms, [but to] understand the forms, answer the forms intelligently, and not be dismissed because you could not do that. Well, I believe that we can teach people the importance of being able to do all of these things. But this district attorney told me that many of the African Americans who were required to fill out the form to see if they could be fair and impartial simply filled them out in ways that said that they could not be. That's because they didn't understand some of the questions on the form. We've got to get beyond this.

Now, I see a lot of young people who really can fill out a lot of forms, who should be able to, who are in school every day. They don't like to take the time, they don't like to have to focus, but if I ask them every song that Ludacris has made or 50 Cent, they can tell you. If I ask them everything that's been produced by P. Diddy, they can tell you. The difference between wanting to know, wanting to be involved, understanding the power of education and being involved, and not really caring, is monumental. And that's what makes the difference in whether or not we are successful in our lives and in our communities.

You're here this morning, and you are going to talk about rights and responsibilities. You're gonna to talk about police profiling. Everybody gets upset about that, but what are your rights? How many people now, at your age, have studied the Constitution of the United States? Raise your hands. [Hands go up in the audience] That document is something. Not only should you know and study, but it should be the reference for your life, for the rest of your life. In that document there are guarantees in this society, in a democracy, that you must know and understand and be willing to stand up for and willing to fight for, to ensure that we have justice and equality in our society. This is not simply an exercise in school that you have to go through with. It's not simply an exercise about the three branches of government. You have the Bill of Rights there. You have the first ten amendments to the Constitution, that talks about freedom of speech, freedom to organize, freedom to assembly, freedom to be free of search and seizure. These things are extremely important and they're always relevant.

Today, in the Congress of the United States, we are fighting hard about this Patriot Act. The Patriot Act came about as a result of terrorism. After the attacks of 9/11 on the Twin Towers in New York and on the Pentagon here in Washington, and that plane that went down in the fields of Pennsylvania, there's been this great war on terrorism led by the president of the United States. And, of course, we were all horrified by these attacks. We were not only horrified, we were traumatized. Never did we think, in this great country, we would have anyone who would plot and plan in ways that would create the kind of death and destruction that was created that day.

Having said that, and we all understand that, then we have to talk about how do we deal with terrorism? How do we deal with these threats? [The] president of the United States and some others are saying, "We gotta be tough. We gotta be strong. We've got to let the world know that we will not tolerate these kinds of attacks." And they came up with laws. Out of the laws, you see such things as the Patriot Act. In the Patriot Act they tread on the rights and freedoms and the liberties of every American citizen. And some folks just walk around every day, not knowing, not thinking, just thinking, "Oh, they've got to go fight terrorism."

Are you willing to give up civil liberties in the name of fighting terrorism? Are you willing to give up some of the gains that your ancestors have died for? Are you willing to give up some of the changes that were made in the Constitution to cover all of the people of this nation in this fight on terrorism? I don't know what your answer is, but you should not be willing to do that. In this Patriot Act, where they expand the ability to place people under surveillance, where they expand the ability to do wiretapping, where they expand the ability to invade your privacy. How many people know that if you check out books at the library that you could be targeted? And that the books that you read could, somehow, trigger the FBI and the Justice Department to start to investigate you, because you're reading books that they think are the kind of books that may lead you to commit an act, or join a group, or to do something that wouldn't be in the best interests of this country? How many people knew or know that you could be targeted for checking out a book in a library?

How many people know that your e-mail could be under surveillance? How many people understand that the Patriot Act that I'm referring to was organized, legislated, and signed off on in the name of fighting terrorism, but it goes very, very close to crossing that line. In some instances it does cross the line, and I maintain that it is in conflict with the United States

Constitution, and if you know that, how many of you people are willing to fight to change the Patriot Act? [applause]

I would like to thank you all for being here. Some of these sessions are going to be a little long. Not all of them will be entertaining. Not all of them will be as interesting. But this opportunity that you're being afforded is a once-in-a-lifetime opportunity. They didn't have this when I was a young person coming along, wondering about how the world really worked, wondering about who made the decisions and how can I get to make some of those decisions? There were no leadership conferences; there were no Tavis Smileys, per se. At different times, in the history of this country, we've had leadership exercised in different ways. But to organize young people and bring them from all over this nation to talk about these issues is extremely important.

And you don't get to come here and go home and do nothing. Somebody has said that you've got some leadership qualities. Who, in this conference, is going to be the next president of United States? [applause] All right! Who, in this conference, is going to be the next United States senator from their state? [applause] Who, in this conference, is going to serve in the House of Representatives? [applause] Who, in this conference, is going to do what Tavis Smiley is doing and be on the cutting edge of the issues in journalism and leadership? [applause] Who, in this conference, will be willing to take on the issues at the university that you will attend? Who will be able to be the next Cornel West? Who will be willing to take what you are learning here, take the precious talent that you have, and do something that will further the aims and goals of our people, and help us to achieve justice and equality in this country? Who is willing to do that? Who is willing to put themselves on the line? [applause]

Thank you, ladies and gentlemen. I came here this morning because I believe in you. I came here this morning because I do believe that you're special, that you're smart, that you're intelligent, and that you understand what your responsibilities are. I really believe that. And no matter how difficult it gets in the Congress of the United States, no matter what battle we are fighting, whether it is trying to get peacekeepers into Liberia, whether it is dealing with the Patriot Act, whether it's trying to stop the consolidation in the media industry, whether it's preserving the civil rights laws and the Voting Rights Act that our ancestors fought for—sometimes those fights are very difficult. And sometimes you go to bed rather disheartened that you were not able to win a battle that day. But after a good night's sleep and an opportunity to interact the way that I am doing here with you today, I am optimistic about our future.

I'm very optimistic about your future. I do expect you to do better than the last generation. I want you to be the leaders that I know that you can be. I want you to have all of these positions of leadership. I want you to have a good quality of life. I want you to earn good money, have a great career. I want you to live well. I want your children's children to live well. Some people say, "Well can we have all of that?" Ladies and gentlemen, we can have all of that. We deserve that, and you must have it. [applause]

21.

HENRY LOUIS GATES JR. (1950–)

"America Beyond the Color Line"

The Commonwealth Club of California,
San Francisco, California—January 28, 2004

Henry Louis Gates Jr. is one of the most prominent African American intellectuals of his time. He is a renowned scholar of black studies and the director of the W.E.B. Du Bois Institute for African and African American Research at Harvard University. Gates is a prolific writer, an engaging speaker, and a public television star. His accomplishments read more like a course catalog than one man's résumé. Gates has defined a new critical approach to black literature. He has unearthed lost artifacts of African American history, including rediscovering the first novel by a black writer, *Our Nig*. He helped produce a vast new collection of reference works on black history and culture. He elevated the place of African American Studies in higher education. He has drawn wide attention to the complicated stew of America's genetic lineage, with television programs that reveal the mixed ancestry of celebrities such as Oprah Winfrey, Yo Yo Ma, Chris Rock, and Meryl Streep. Finally, Gates's 2009 arrest, as he tried to enter his own home, made headlines and provoked a national dialogue on race.

Gates was born in northern West Virginia and grew up in the town of Piedmont, a small community in the foothills of the Allegheny Mountains. "Skip," as Gates is known to friends, is the younger of two boys.

His mother worked as a housekeeper. His father held down two jobs, loading trucks during the day at a paper mill and working as a janitor at the local telephone company in the evenings. In a memoir titled *Colored People*, Gates describes Piedmont as a segregated town where blacks and whites lived largely separate lives, where there was little open friction between the races, and where the civil rights movement played out as a relatively muted drama compared to elsewhere in the nation. There were no big protest marches or lunch counter sit-ins in Piedmont. "Civil rights took us all by surprise," he recalls in *Colored People*. It was a conflict his family watched on the TV news. "Whatever tumult our small screen revealed . . . the dawn of the civil rights era could be no more than a spectator sport in Piedmont. It was almost like a war being fought overseas."[1]

The Piedmont public schools responded to the 1954 U.S. Supreme Court ruling banning school segregation by promptly and rather quietly opening the doors of white schools to black children. Young Skip's parents encouraged their boys to excel in the newly integrated schools. Gates remembers being recognized and nurtured as a gifted child by the white faculty. He also developed an early sense of ease and friendship with white children. "We were pioneers, people my age, in cross-race relations, able to get to know each other across cultures and classes in a way that was unthinkable in our parents' generation," Gates says. "To speak to white people was just to speak. No artificial tones, no hypercorrectness."[2]

Gates grew up in an African American community—in terms of both geography and his extended family—that was rich in culture and characters. He tells their tales with the affection and relish of a natural storyteller, a trait he credits to his father's love of a good yarn. He also describes an early "avidity for information on the Negro," anticipating his life calling as a student and exponent of African and African American heritages.[3] As a teenager in the 1960s, Gates and his cohort experimented with the ideologies of Black Power and Afrocentrism they increasingly saw on TV and read about in the newspapers. Gates fondly remembers developing elaborate soul-brother handshakes, spouting the few phrases of Swahili he managed to master, and growing the tallest afro in town. He also chuckles at his father's sardonic reaction: "KKK hair, Daddy called it: Knotty, Kinky, and Kan't-comby."[4]

In 1968, Gates left home for college. He majored in history at Yale University, then won a fellowship to Cambridge University, where he earned a PhD in English literature in 1979. Gates taught at Yale, Cornell, and Duke, establishing himself as a powerful new figure in English literary criticism and the interpretation of African American literature. He has published prolifically, branching out from literary studies to co-produce extensive reference works on African American history and culture. These include a massive encyclopedia called *Africana*, first imagined a century earlier by scholar W.E.B. Du Bois as a Negro equivalent to the *Encyclopedia Britannica*.

In 1991, Harvard recruited Gates to revive and lead its struggling Afro-American Studies department. Gates lured eminent scholars from other leading universities to his program, including Cornel West, William Julius Wilson, and Evelyn Brooks Higginbotham. Gates and his dream team resuscitated the program at Harvard. They are also widely credited with lifting the academic status of black studies as a whole. Gates's mission was to free black studies from the grip of Afrocentrism and to welcome interested students and scholars of all racial and ethnic backgrounds. "We stand as a rebuttal to the idea that Afro-American studies is primarily about building the self-esteem of other African Americans, or that only African Americans can understand, interpret and therefore teach black studies," Gates told an interviewer.[5] Harvard sociologist William Julius Wilson says he has never met Gates's match for intellectual leadership and interpersonal skills. "He's probably done more to create a positive image for African American studies than any other scholar in the world," Wilson told the *Boston Globe*.[6]

As his academic reputation soared, Gates also established himself as one of America's leading public intellectuals. He has published widely in the nonacademic press—from *Newsweek* to *Jet* and *Art in America* to *Sports Illustrated*. He has appeared in seven major PBS television series on race and African American culture. In 1997, *Time* declared Gates one of the twenty-five most influential Americans, saying he combines "the braininess of the legendary black scholar W.E.B. Du Bois and the chutzpah of P.T. Barnum."[7] The British magazine *The Economist* describes Gates as a "silver-tongued intellectual imp" who has emerged as the "chief interpreter" of the black experience for the white, American establishment.[8]

While Gates is certainly a high-profile figure compared to most academics, he is perhaps best known to some Americans as the Harvard professor who got into a scuffle with a cop and then made peace over a beer on the White House patio. On July 16, 2009, Gates was returning home to Cambridge, Massachusetts, after an overseas trip. His front door was stuck, so Gates and his taxi driver tried to push it open. A neighbor called the police to report a suspected burglary. Gates and a white officer got into a verbal confrontation and Gates was arrested for disorderly conduct. The charges were dropped, but the incident sparked a vociferous national conversation over the persistence of racial discrimination in the United States. Commentators found reason to blame both parties for the fracas. The story culminated with a White House "beer summit" between Gates and the officer, James Crowley, hosted by President Barack Obama.

Gates gave this speech at the Commonwealth Club of California, in San Francisco, the nation's oldest and largest public affairs forum. He was speaking in advance of the premiere of his 2004 PBS project, *America Beyond the Color Line*. The program was a kind of State of the Union report on black America at the dawn of the twenty-first century. Gates describes what he learned traveling the country to interview a cross section of African Americans for the show and concludes with his own declaration of the most pressing obstacles in the nation's long struggle for racial equality.

I'M GOING TO SHOW YOU a clip from my new film series, and I'm going to tell you about it. In 1900, W.E.B. Du Bois, of course, the greatest black intellectual of all time . . . You know, they talk about our generation of black intellectuals and writers, they talk about my main man, Cornel West, and they talk about Kwame Anthony Appiah, and Manning Marable and Claude Steele up at Stanford. You could add us all up together and put us in a Cuisinart and pour us out and we would not be worthy of tying W.E.B. Du Bois's shoelaces. W.E.B. Du Bois was the man. And he woke up in 1900 and he predicted, famously, that the problem of the twentieth century would be the problem of the color line. And that turned out to be true; certainly no one could dispute that.

So at the beginning of the twenty-first century, I wanted to ask, and attempt to answer, the same question: What will the problem of the twenty-first century be? But unlike the lordly Du Bois, who sat at his desk up in Harlem and just pronounced the answer, I wanted to travel all throughout the United States, interviewing a cross section of the African American community and address the question the following way: Where are we, as a people, thirty-five years after the brutal assassination of the Reverend Dr. Martin Luther King? Where are we as a people? Have we progressed? Have we gone far enough? How much further do we have to go?

And the result is, as you heard in the marvelous introduction, I interviewed dozens of people. From the rich and powerful and famous, to the homeless, the not-so-powerful, the impoverished, the infamous, the imprisoned. I interviewed Colin Powell, I interviewed Vernon Jordan, I interviewed Russell Simmons, I interviewed Alicia Keys, Maya Angelou. I went and did a segment on black Hollywood; I interviewed Chris Tucker and Bernie Mac. I mean, it was hilarious, I could barely ask the questions for laughing for the whole time. But I also interviewed single heads of households on the South Side of Chicago. I went to Cook County Jail and interviewed prisoners. I interviewed people who formerly were drug dealers, who were now reformed drug dealers and most probably will fall off the wagon and be drug dealers again. I wanted to ask black America, in every possible shape and size and even color, "Where are we as a people?" The result is a four-hour series. Fortunately I was lucky enough to have PBS and BBC give me a film crew and let me travel around the country, interviewing people, and the result's a four-hour film series that will air on PBS on February 3 and February 4. It's called *America Beyond the Color Line*. Now part one is called "Ebony Towers," and it's about the new black middle class that's emerged since Dr. King was killed in 1968.

Part two is about the amazing phenomenon of black people from the North reverse-migrating to the South. You could look through all of the annals of African American literature, and you'll find tens of thousands of references to black people in the South following the North Star, or following the Drinking Gourd—which was a metaphor for the Big Dipper, which, of course, involves the North Star—but you will not find one, not one, that says, "Black man or black woman, find your freedom by heading back to Mississippi." Or as my dad says, Missibama or any of them other Misses. But in the 1990s, the most incredible thing happened, which was far more black people from the North started migrating back to the South. And I wanted to ask why? Because for me, when I was growing up in the fifties, the South was a litter of crosses and the corpses of black men. And why would these people—and these are upper-middle-class black people—moving back to Atlanta, moving into all-black neighborhoods, all million-dollar homes, all-black country clubs, all-black swimming pools? And I wanted to ask them, "Is this what Dr. King died for? If Dr. King came back, would he like this? Or would he not like this?" I wanted to ironize it and put them on camera and see how they felt.

Part three is called "Black Hollywood." And I shot this in the wake of Denzel [Washington] and Halle Berry getting the Academy Awards and Sidney [Poitier], of course, getting a lifetime achievement award from the Academy. So I wanted to go to Hollywood and ask, "Has racism disappeared in Hollywood because we have so many black actors on the A-list?" Chris Tucker takes me to church. Bishop Noel Jones's church, he's Grace Jones's brother, in South Central. And we went, I mean rocking. And so we're sitting there, and I look up, and Stevie Wonder walks in, with his new baby, and I guess his new wife. And Stevie Wonder performs a duet with Ali Wilson from the old Temptations. You know, if Bishop Jones's sermon didn't make me get the Holy Ghost, Stevie Wonder almost did. It was fantastic. And the answer to that question is: No, racism has not disappeared in Hollywood, in case anyone's holding their breath to wonder if there's a news flash that I had received that you hadn't.

And finally, I wanted to go to the inner city. And so I chose the Robert Taylor Homes on the South Side of Chicago. The Robert Taylor Homes, set up in the early 1960s, symbolized all that was possible, all that was supposed to be good about public housing. And my film crew was the last, or one of the last, film crews in the Robert Taylor Homes, because the problems had become so severe that the city of Chicago had decided that they couldn't be fixed, that they had to tear them down. And I wanted to record that history, that movement, over a forty-year period—from the time the Robert Taylor Homes represented optimism and hope to the time that the Robert Taylor Homes became synonymous with poverty and the self-perpetuation of poverty, by a significant segment of the African American community.

Now, I went to Yale University in September 1969. I was one of ninety-six black men and women to go up to Yale in September of 1969. By contrast, the class of '66 at Yale had six black men to graduate. What, was there a genetic blip in the race? And all of a sudden there were ninety smart black men and women who existed in 1969 who hadn't existed in 1966? Of course not. We got in because of affirmative action. We were the affirmative action crossover generation. It doesn't mean that we weren't qualified to get into Yale. It's just that we couldn't have gotten into Yale before because there were strict racist quotas on the number of black boys—Yale didn't go co-ed until 1969—the number of black boys who were allowed to be entered into

Yale. And I wouldn't have gotten into Yale, definitely, without affirmative action, no matter what my scores were. Why is that?

Well, my daddy, who is ninety years old, my dad, God bless him, my dad turned ninety on June 8th of this past year. My dad is so funny. My dad makes Redd Foxx look like an undertaker. We asked my father, we had this big party, right? [laughter] We asked my father, "Daddy what do you want for your ninetieth birthday party? What's your fondest ambition, your greatest wish, your dream?" He thought about it for a nanosecond and then he said, "Boy . . ." that's his term of endearment for me, for the last fifty-three years—"boy." He said, "Boy, all I want is to bump Bob Dole off that Viagra commercial." [laughter] I said, "I don't want to think about that, Daddy, I don't want to go there." Anyway, my dad, for thirty-seven years, worked two jobs to put me and my brother through college. I have one brother, no sisters. My brother's five years older; he's a very successful oral surgeon, chief oral surgeon at Bronx Lebanon Hospital in New York. Then there's little old me bringing up the rear. My daddy would go to work at six-thirty in the morning, at a paper mill, and we lived in a company town basically, an Irish and Italian company town.

In 1950, the year I was born, there were 2,100 people in Piedmont, West Virginia, 386 of whom were black. Most of them were my relatives, which made it very rough about dating time, you know what I mean? People say, "Vice is nice but incest is best," especially in West Virginia, but I don't want to play that! [laughter] So the mill—daddy would go to work at six-thirty in the morning, and at three-thirty in the afternoon, the mill whistle would blow and we would get out of school, because basically it was a company town. He'd come home and wash up. We'd have our evening meal at four o'clock, and at four-thirty he'd go to his second job as a janitor at the Chesapeake and Potomac Telephone Company. He'd get home about seven-thirty, eight. We'd do our homework, then we'd watch TV, and then we'd go to bed.

So he worked two jobs for thirty-seven years. Now, no matter how intelligent I may or may not be, I would not have had the class profile, within the African American community, to be one of those six black boys who went to Yale. What am I talking about? All the black people in here know what I'm talking about. If you look at the biographies of the fathers of those black boys—one's father was a doctor, one was a lawyer, one was an undertaker, one worked at the postal office, and one was a numbers runner. [laughter]

That put you in the black upper class in the old days. I was stone working class, so it means I wouldn't have been allowed, I wouldn't have been allowed to make it through the filters within the race behind closed doors—behind what Du Bois called "the veil," in order to show up for Yale. Affirmative action was a class escalator when it started, as well as a race integrator.

So, ladies and gentlemen, all that's happened to me in my fortunate life has been enabled by affirmative action. And for me, who's benefited so much from affirmative action, to stand at the gate—no matter how small my gate— it would be disingenuous for me to say I'm not a gatekeeper. Of course I'm a gatekeeper. For me to stand at that gate and then to oppose other people of color . . . or women, because no one has benefited from affirmative action more than white women in American society. Everybody leaves that out of the discussions of affirmative action, but that's the truth. For me to be a gatekeeper, standing at the gate, to keep out women or other people of color would be for me to be a hypocrite as big as Mr. Justice Clarence Thomas. And I am not going to be that kind of person. [applause]

So we all were the affirmative action babies. And you have to imagine what I looked like: I had a two-foot-high afro. You've got to imagine this head with a two-foot-high afro. My daughter Maggie just graduated from Wesleyan University in Connecticut. She looked at my yearbook a couple of years ago, and she said, "Daddy you're not on the page." And I said, "Yes I am, baby. There I am." And she said, "That's you, Daddy?" And I said, "Yeah." She said, "You look just like a Klingon!" [laughs] I said, "I was a good-looking Klingon." I had a closet full of dashikis. I looked like a ball of black cotton candy walking down the street. You know Cornel West; Cornel West's afro looked like a crew cut next to my afro.

And we were going to be the revolutionary vanguard for our people. We were going to reclaim W.E.B. Du Bois's notion of the talented tenth. You all know what that is, what he called the "college-bred Negro." At the time Du Bois wrote that essay, in 1900, it was probably the talented "oneth," in terms of black people with a four-year college degree. In fact, we only . . . our people only hit double digits with a four-year college degree in the 1990s, and today, only seventeen percent of us have a bachelor's degree, among the African American people. But we were going to be the vanguard. And we were going to show Du Bois that he had been wrong, that you could produce a talented tenth that would be socially responsible. We were going to reach back in the ghetto and pull all the brothers and sisters—whether kicking and screaming or not—we were going to drag them into historically white, elite institutions, symbolized by places like Mother Yale. We called Yale the Yale "plantation." [laughs] And we were the nouveau black people, coming to change the shape of the plantation.

Well, at the end of my first year at Yale—this great year when we had all these black people there—we shut Yale down. In April of 1970, we had a big strike. Remember on May Day of 1970 the whole country went on strike? Remember? Because Nixon and Kissinger invaded Cambodia. Then after that was Kent State, then Jackson State. Everybody forgets about Jackson State, but more kids were killed at Kent State than there were killed at Jackson State. Two weeks before, at Yale, we went on strike.

The strike was led by Kurt Schmoke. Black man, used to be mayor of Baltimore. Was a Rhodes scholar, became my hero. In fact I went to Cambridge largely because Kurt had become a Rhodes scholar two years before. And we persuaded all of our colleagues to go on strike, because the Black Panther Party—which started out here in Oakland, of course—the Black Panthers were being persecuted by the police. Bobby Seale was on trial in New Haven. And we persuaded Kingman Brewster, the president of Yale, to issue a statement saying that he was skeptical of the ability of a black revolutionary to get a fair trial in any court in the United States. Of course, it cost him his job, but it led to the strike at Yale. And so all these revolutionaries came to Yale. And their lawyers, like Garry, who defended the Panthers, and William Kunstler. David Hilliard got out of jail, and he came. Huey Newton was in jail, Eldridge Cleaver was in exile, but everybody else was there, right? And so we had this huge rally.

Now you have to imagine this: five thousand people—most of them, they were white—and then the ninety-six black kids at Yale. So we waited till they were seated, and we all walked in, march step. You know, we were bad. Man, we had our dashikis, our 'fros were all teased out—we knew we were the vanguard, we were the revolutionaries! Fists on your chests and all that stuff. Remember the soul handshake? We had that elaborate soul handshake?— we would change, you know, like your security code for your computer that changes every month? We would change the soul handshake every month just to make sure you were still black, you know, to make sure you were up to blackness. [laughter] You had to do the dap; the Vietnam guys would teach you all that. It was great, so we were smoking, man. Some of us had berets on, like the Panthers; some of us had those long black leather jackets on, most of us had dashikis on. So we walked in lockstep, sat down. Jean Genet, the French playwright and revolutionary, had been flown over from Paris to address us. Man, this was the revolution. It was happening! Right before our very eyes! And he had this beautiful woman—I'll never forget—he had this beautiful woman who was translating, because he spoke no English. And so amidst . . . you know, officially we were supposed to be learning Swahili and stuff, but I made a mental note: Learn French. [laughter]

So Jean Genet gives us this great stirring speech: this was the end of capitalism, corporate capitalism was in its final days! Sure as shootin', as Marx had predicted, Western capitalism was being brought down. Marx predicted it would collapse; it was collapsing. And the revolution was being led not only by the great American Negro people, as he said at that time, but by the lumpenproletariat from the inner cities, the natural leaders of whom were the Black Panther Party for Self Defense, being unjustly imprisoned, persecuted by that fascist J. Edgar Hoover, et cetera, et cetera, et cetera. So we were jumping up and cheering. This was our moment. Then he said he wanted to make a final address, a direct comment to us, the new black students at Yale. And he looked at us, and he said if there was a revolution—and he was convinced there was a revolution—if there was a revolution, it would occur in spite of the fact that we had accepted admission into Yale University. [laughter] And we all looked at each other and said, "That woman musta got that translation wrong."

We were nouveau race traitors. We were the new Uncle Toms. The system was smart enough to adapt just enough to save itself. And it was adapting through the creation of this new concept called affirmative action, and the ninety-six black people sitting there, in spite of their afros, their dashikis, their berets, and their black leather jackets, were tools or pawns of the system, diffusing the genuine revolutionary fervor of the lumpenproletariat, represented by its true leaders, Bobby Seale, Huey Newton, and Eldridge Cleaver. Man, we were flabbergasted, man! [laughter] Everybody, five thousand white people are looking at us, you know? [laughter] And we'd been jumping up and down with our fists and stuff. Then he quoted Herbert Marcuse, how many of you remember Herbert Marcuse?—the great Marxist philosopher. Who was Herbert Marcuse's greatest student? Come on, anybody. Angela Davis, professor of philosophy at Brandeis. Angela Davis, he said, was his most brilliant student. He then, Genet, cites an essay Herbert Marcuse had written in 1958, in which Marcuse predicted that the principal outcome of a successful civil rights movement would be the creation of a new black middle class. And that would be it. And things, then, would go back to normal. OK? How cynical! We thought, *What did this Frenchman know?*

Let him go back to Paris. So, you know, we got up and tried to save the day [laughs] and moved on with our business. But that thought haunted us.

Putney Swope. How many of you saw the film *Putney Swope*? Who were our heroes? Paul Robeson, W.E.B. Du Bois, Frederick Douglass, Nat Turner, Thurgood Marshall. Not so much Dr. King, to be honest. Dr. King had fallen out of favor with the young, with the revolutionary. We were Stokely Carmichaelites. You know, Martin Luther King was old. His day had passed. No. We wanted the revolution. And Stokely was going to lead us. But *Putney Swope*? *Putney Swope*, the first blaxploitation film. Robert Downey Sr., even a young Mel Brooks is in this film. It opens: the board of directors' room at a Madison Avenue advertising firm. One token Negro in a three-piece suit, sitting at the board meeting. Everybody else, of course, is white. Chairman of the board is giving this rousing speech about making money—very, very greedy speech—has a heart attack, falls face down on the table at the board of directors' meeting. All the white guys jump up, pick his pockets [laughs], they push his body out the way and call for the election, on the spot, of a new CEO. So you do it by secret ballot, of course. So they count the votes, and the man says, "Hmm. We have to count the votes again." They count the votes again. Then he stands up and announces the vote had been nine to two, nine votes for Putney Swope. The camera pans in on one white guy, and he says, "I thought nobody would vote for him but me." [laughs] Next scene: so you think, what's going to happen? Next scene: Putney comes in, first day at work. He got rid of his three-piece suit; he has on military fatigues, looks like a Black Panther. Has a little military hat on, fires all the white people in the advertising agency, changes the name to the Truth and Soul Advertising Agency, hires inner-city black people, and revolutionizes the advertising industry by mounting new approaches to the marketing of products, such as Victrola Cola, Ethereal Cereal, and—my favorite—Face Off Pimple Cream. [laughter]

Putney Swope amasses $156 million in the next six months. A hundred fifty-six million dollars sounds like a lot now; it was a hell of a lot in 1969. And when he's so hot, you know, he becomes famous on the cover of all the magazines. He's descended on by all the black revolutionaries—four guys representing the four major streams of the black movement: there's a Black Panther figure; there's a figure, a cultural nationalist from Karenga and Amiri Baraka; there's a Stokely Carmichael figure for Black Power; and then there's a Whitney Young figure—remember Whitney Young?—a Whitney Young figure from the National Urban League.

And they all have their stock slogans. The Panther guy says, "We need power for the people." The Stokely Carmichael guy says that "Black power is the only way." And the guy from the cultural nationalists says, "Violence is a cleansing force." And then the hapless, suited figure from the National Urban League, the Whitney Young figure, says, "Violence . . ."—he looks at them and says, "Violence will not help our people. Violence will get us nowhere. Violence will not get us a job." And one of the Panther figures looks at him and says, "Yeah, violence might not get us a job, but it will certainly eliminate the competition." [laughter] So they all then unite in one thing. Which is, they're only there to hustle Putney Swope. They want money, and Putney Swope throws them out, says they're all frauds and the real revolution will come by penetrating the system and transforming the system from the inside.

Putney Swope was our secret hero. What we wanted to do, ladies and gentlemen—our self-styled, revolutionary vanguard that integrated Yale in large numbers—was to go in the system and transform it from the inside, forever eliminating racism and fundamentally changing the class structure of the African American community. Thirty-five years later, ladies and gentlemen, where are we?

Well, since 1968, since, in fact, that day that Martin Luther King was killed, the black middle class has almost quadrupled, which is a wonderful thing. But at the same time, the percentage of black children living at or beneath the poverty line is forty percent. Four out of ten black kids live at or beneath the poverty line. You know what the figure was the day Martin Luther King died? Forty percent.

Was Herbert Marcuse right? Was the principal outcome of the civil rights movement and affirmative action the production of a new black middle class, or not? For the African American community, in other words, it's the best of times, but it is the worst of times. Do you know that in 1990, there were 2,280,000 prisoners, black men in prison, on probation or parole. You know how many black men got a college degree in that year? Twenty-three thousand. That's a ratio of ninety-nine to one. Do you know what the ratio that year was for white males in prison, on probation and parole, who got college degrees was? Six-to-one. In Chicago, right now, forty-five percent of all black males between the ages of twenty and twenty-four are both out of school and out of work. And most of them who are out of school didn't finish school, or if they finished school, they are essentially functionally illiterate, which means you can't read the front page of the *Chronicle* or the *L.A. Times* or the *New York Times* and pass an examination on it. Sixty-nine percent of all of the households in Chicago are headed by single mothers—the black households, are headed by single mothers. The average life span for a black man in Chicago is fifty-nine. And in any given week in Chicago, only forty-five percent of the members of the African American community are gainfully employed. Fifty-five percent of the African American community, of all ages, in Chicago, are unemployed.

So what did I learn when I traveled the country, interviewing this cross section of the African American community? What did I learn when we talked about "Where are we as a people?" We learned that the causes of our poverty are both structural and behavioral. Now what's that mean? Well, first of all, structural: you cannot enslave a people for three centuries, followed by a century of de jure segregation, and then cure it with thirty-five years of affirmative action and post–civil rights entitlement legislation. Institutional racism is a fundamental aspect of the American society, and our people have suffered disproportionately from that. In addition, the economic structure began to change in the 1960s. The traditional way of moving from the no-class to the working class, and the working class to the middle class, was through factories in the cities. That's why we went to the cities in the first place, and all the white immigrants did it. What happened in the sixties and the seventies? Factories moved south, shut down in the cities. First they moved south, to the southern part of the United States, then they moved south of the border. Now they're dispersed wherever people can most efficiently exploit a large labor force. So that the traditional way of moving up the economic scale in America disappeared.

How do we address these structural problems? We need a federal jobs program that will create meaningful job opportunities for those most impoverished in this society, whether they're black, white, Hispanic, or whatever. We need to give people hope in the system again. We need to make it worthwhile—make them feel worthwhile—that it's worthwhile for them to stay in school, to work hard, to take a job-training program, because they're going to get a meaningful job in a twenty-first century, highly technological, global economy. And not flipping burgers down at McDonald's. I interviewed a drug dealer who was—if we had played the tape you would have seen him. An ex–drug dealer who was making six thousand dollars a day dealing drugs. And he realized—just why he realized it, I don't know—but he realized he was headed directly to Cook County Jail. And so he decided he didn't want to spend the rest of his life in jail, even for six thousand dollars a day. So he just finished his first semester in college. But when I interviewed him, he was working at Popeye's. His name is Lyndell. I said, "Lyndell, may I ask you—how much money do you make a month working at Popeye's?" And he said, "six hundred dollars a month." And I said, "Do you ever think about that six thousand dollars a day that you used to make selling drugs?" He said, "Are you crazy? I think about it all day long while I'm flipping them burgers down at Popeye's." He is the exception. Who among us could resist the lure of six thousand dollars a day of ostensibly easy money, if you didn't feel that you had a stake in the system, if you didn't feel that you could be successful if you stayed in school?

We need school reform, ladies and gentlemen. I went to Boston English High School last Black History Month. I was waiting for all the kids to be assembled. It was an all-school assembly. I asked the teacher—I mean I was in school, right?—I raised my hand and asked the teacher if I could go to the bathroom, which I thought was the appropriate thing to do. She said, "Oh, certainly, Dr. Gates. Um. It will only take ten minutes and you can go." I said, "No ma'am, you don't understand. I have to go to the bathroom." She said, "No. You don't understand. You cannot go to the bathroom without a police escort. And it will take ten minutes for the policeman to be here." Our schools have become nightmares. How could any of us have learned what we learned when we were growing up, if we hadn't had order in our schools? We need to establish a safe learning environment for our children. We need to change the way taxes are distributed for our schools. The amount of money spent per student should be exactly the same in the poorest, blackest, most Hispanic neighborhood as is being allocated per student in the richest, whitest suburb. This is only fair. It is only fair. [applause] The Department of Education needs to look at programs that are working in our public schools. And I'll tell you briefly about three.

Many of my friends are Jewish, and they would all tell me about how horrible Hebrew school was. I'd listen to them tell me about Hebrew school. Then I'd think, horrible? Man, that Hebrew school sound like a pretty good thing. Then I'd think, how come we can't have Hebrew school? If Jewish people had to wait on the state, on the public school system, for the perpetuation of Jewish culture and the Hebrew language, there wouldn't be Jewish culture and there wouldn't be Hebrew language. Why can't we use our churches and our mosques to start after-school programs that teach African American history and culture? In other words, we go around the public school system. I got a $500,000 grant from the Markle Foundation, wired the Reverend Eugene Rivers's church in the inner city in Roxbury, and now we have an after-school program that teaches black history, African history; they learn about the black pharaohs of the Nile and learn computer skills using Encarta Africana. It is a runaway success. It has spread to the city of Baltimore, it's going to Philadelphia, and it's going to Cleveland. How come our churches can't do that, like the Jewish people did through Hebrew school? Of course they can.

We need to transform our great black sororities and fraternities—the Deltas, the Kappas, the Alphas, et cetera, et cetera—into self-esteem, black self-help factories. We need to begin to teach our people about entrepreneurial opportunities. We need to use these secular and sacred organizations to sponsor what you might think of as the new face of the civil rights movement, which will stress our traditional values of education. Ladies and gentlemen, when I was growing up in the fifties, the blackest thing you could be was Thurgood Marshall or Martin Luther King. The blackest thing you could be was a doctor or a lawyer, not a basketball player or a football player. What's happened to our people? Learning the ABCs, staying in school, getting straight A's, was firing a bullet straight into George Wallace's racist white heart. That's what we were taught in school. You know, my father must have told me a thousand times, "Get all the education you can, boy, because no white racist can take it away from you." Our people have lost that. I read the results of a poll from the *Washington Post* recently that interviewed inner-city black kids, and it said, "List things white." You know what they said? The three most prevalent answers: getting straight A's in school, speaking standard English, and visiting the Smithsonian. Had anybody said anything like this when we were growing up, they would have smacked you upside your head and checked you into an insane asylum. Somehow, we have internalized our own oppression.

Far too many members of our own community have internalized our own oppression. Which brings me—since I've been getting this sign from this woman right here, that I should get off this podium—which brings me . . . there are two other programs that I wanted to talk about, but you can see them in the film series.

But it brings me to the other reason our people are still impoverished. I said that half of the reason was for structural causes like institutional racism. The other half, ladies and gentlemen, is because we need a revolution in attitude and behavior within the African American community itself. [applause] Nobody makes you, no white racist makes you get pregnant when you're sixteen years old. I'm sorry, we do not have time for this form of behavior anymore. It is killing our people. No white racist makes you drop out of school. No white racist makes you not do your homework. No white racist makes you equate academic or intellectual success with being white. If George Wallace and Bull Connor and Orval Faubus had sat down, in their wildest drunken, bourbon fantasies, in 1960 and said, "How can we continue to control them niggras," as they would have said, one of them would have said, "You know, we could persuade them to have babies in their teens, do crack cocaine, run drugs, and equate education not with being Thurgood Marshall or Martin Luther King but with being white, then we'll have them."

Ladies and gentlemen, that's what's happened to our people. We have lost the blackest aspect of the black tradition. Frederick Douglass famously said the slave had "to steal a little learning" from the white man. We've all been stealing a little learning. We've all been embracing education as if the collective life of the African American people depended on it—until recently. And now, for far too many of our people, getting an education is something alien to our tradition. It's much easier to become a professional basketball player. Well listen to these statistics: In 1991, I did a piece for *Sports Illustrated*, and I asked them—on the black athlete—and I asked them . . . and before I tell you this, don't get me wrong, some of my best friends are athletes. I'm going to go to the Super Bowl this weekend. You know, I love watching the Final Four. I love championship sports. And I love the fact that so many black people have done well. But here's the reality: 1990 census, the number of black lawyers, black doctors, black dentists, and black professional athletes—twenty thousand black lawyers, fourteen thousand black doctors, five thousand six hundred black dentists. You know how many black professional athletes? Remember, there are thirty-five million black Americans. You know how many black professional athletes? One thousand two hundred black professional athletes in all sports. It's easier to be a black brain surgeon than to make it into the NBA, but somehow our people are like Jimmy the Greek—they think we have an extra basketball gene. [laughter] My daddy . . . when I was a professor at Duke, my house was near a black neighborhood that had a basketball court that was lit. I go to bed at midnight, I pass it, it would be packed. I wake up, go to work at nine in the morning, it would be packed. [laughs] I don't know if they played basketball all night long, because I would be asleep. My daddy said, and I will censor what he said, my daddy said, "Ain't this a damn shame." He said, "If our people studied calculus like we study basketball, we would be running MIT." And you know that that's true.

We also have to stop scapegoating other people who we should be emulating. Homophobia is rampant in the African American community. We have to stand up as leaders and fight homophobia in the black community; we have to fight sexism and misogyny in the black community; we have to fight anti-immigrant feeling in the black community. Do you know that seventy-five percent of my black students at Harvard are of West Indian descent? You know what that figure was when I was an undergrad at Yale? Ninety-nine percent of us had four African American grandparents. Now, of the black kids at Harvard, only twenty-five percent have four African American grandparents, seventy-five percent are second-generation West Indian, and that leads to a lot of scapegoating. We need to be more like black immigrants from the West Indies and stop scapegoating them. And finally, we have to stop scapegoating the Jewish people. We need to emulate the best aspects of Jewish culture. And leaders have to stand up and say, "The Jews are not our problem. The Jews did not run the slave trade. Thirteen rabbis do not rule the world and sit there and decide that black people are going to be impoverished. This is rubbish." Why should we do this? We do this for the Jewish people? No, we have to do it for ourselves. You cannot get the solutions to your problems straight until you understand the nature of the problem itself. You have to understand what the target is, and the target is not Haitians, it's not West Indians, it's not gay people, and it's certainly not the members of the Jewish community.

Our goal, ladies and gentlemen, in sum, is to change the bell curve of class within the African American community. We need the same percentage of black poor as white poor, the same percentage of black rich as white rich, the same percentage of black people in the middle class as white people, and black people in the working class as white people. And we can only do this with a two-pronged attack, addressing the structural causes of poverty on the one hand, and the individual, behavioral, attitudinal problems that we, ourselves, are causing for ourselves. We have internalized our own oppression. We are perpetuating our own poverty, and leaders—whether it is Jesse Jackson, Al Sharpton, Colin Powell, Farrakhan, whomever—have to have the courage to stand up, join together, and lead a moral revolution within the African American community. Because if we don't, the class divide within the African American community is destined to be permanent. And never the twain between those two classes shall meet. And I, for one, will not be content until we do something about that, ladies and gentlemen, because Martin Luther King did not die so that some of us would make it and most of us would be left behind in the inner city of hopelessness and despair.

22.

MICHAEL ERIC DYSON
(1958–)

"Has the Black Middle Class Lost Its Mind?"

The Commonwealth Club of California,
San Francisco, California—June 2, 2005

Michael Eric Dyson is a prolific and influential social critic whose work explores multiple dimensions of African American life. Since publishing his first set of essays in 1993, Dyson has averaged close to a book a year, many of them bestsellers. His analyses range from the meaning of hiphop culture to the legacies of Malcolm X and Martin Luther King Jr., and to the dramas and absurdities of American race relations. Meanwhile, Dyson also works as an ordained Baptist minister, has held a series of prestigious positions at major universities since 1993, and at times hosts his own daily radio talk show.

Dyson was born in 1958 and raised in Detroit. He was the second of five boys. Dyson's mother worked for the Detroit Board of Education. His father was an auto worker for thirty-three years before getting laid off. Dyson's father then took a variety of jobs, including as a landscaper. Dyson's parents struggled for money but always impressed upon their sons the virtue and necessity of hard work. Despite whatever hardships the family suffered, Dyson says he was shaped in an environment "where black achievement was taken for granted, where black excellence was expected."[1] He remembers his neighborhood as "a vibrant, vital black world teeming with possibility beyond the ballyhooed violence that stalked poor and working-class blacks."[2]

Nevertheless, Dyson was haunted by the riots that engulfed Detroit in the summer of 1967. Inner-city blacks had grown furious over police brutality, a lack of jobs, and a dearth of affordable housing. When a vice squad raided an after-hours club in a black neighborhood, a five-day riot ensued. "I vividly recall," Dyson writes, "the ominous, dirty clouds that hovered over our troubled city and the gleeful looters who reigned over this bizarre carnival of urban decay."

For Dyson, the assassination of Martin Luther King Jr. the next year sparked a disturbing racial awakening. As he writes, "King's death was my initial plunge into the tortuous meanings of racial politics, and I began to believe that the world was largely predicated upon color, its vain and violent ubiquity becoming increasingly apparent to my newly opened eyes."[3] Yet Dyson was also deeply inspired by King, whose life, he says, "served as a startlingly resilient symbol of the possibility of achieving meaningful life beyond the ruinous reach of racism."[4]

Dyson excelled as a student and won a series of public speaking contests sponsored by the Detroit Optimist Club. When he was sixteen, Dyson won a scholarship to a prestigious, all-white boarding school in the lush suburbs of Detroit. Dyson attended the school for almost two years but left before graduating. He'd never been to school with whites before and found the wealth of his new peers discomforting. He was also the target of racist pranks. Dyson's schoolwork suffered, and he started getting into trouble. Eventually he was expelled.

Dyson moved back to the city. He took a job in the factory where his father once worked and earned his diploma attending night school. In short order, Dyson got his girlfriend pregnant, married her, and entered a period of poverty that involved going on welfare and occasionally living out of his car. Dyson and his wife soon divorced, and he decamped to Tennessee, where he enrolled in college and studied philosophy and religion. In 1982, Dyson graduated with honors from Carson-Newman College and his academic career took off. He earned his doctorate from Princeton University's Department of Religion and became a successful freelance writer.

After finishing graduate school in 1993, Dyson was offered immediate tenure at both Brown University and the University of North Carolina–Chapel Hill. It was an achievement almost unheard of in academia, but Dyson had already published his first book, *Reflecting Black: African-American Cultural Criticism*, to high acclaim, and his second book was about to come out. After moving through a sequence of increasingly prestigious academic jobs, Dyson moved to Georgetown University, where in 2007 he was named a university professor, the highest possible faculty position.

Dyson is known for his fearless approach to racial controversies. As writer Erin Aubry Kaplan put it, "Far from despairing or keeping silent about black issues that feel to many of us like existential riddles, Dyson savors them. He eats them for lunch."[5] In 1997 Dyson explained to an interviewer, "I love black folk, which is why . . . I'm not afraid to disagree with mass black opinion, to call into question beliefs, habits, dispositions, traditions, and practices that I think need to be criticized."[6]

In 2004, Dyson trained his critical lens on one of the nation's most beloved entertainers, Bill Cosby. On May 17 of that year, Cosby gave a speech chastising poor African Americans for what he described as immoral and self-defeating behavior. Cosby was the keynote at an NAACP celebration of the fiftieth anniversary of *Brown v. Board of Education*, the U.S. Supreme Court decision that outlawed school segregation. Cosby had a long record of supporting civil rights causes, speaking out on behalf of poor people, and donating millions of dollars to black institutions. As journalist Juan Williams later wrote, "He was expected to be a safe choice." Instead, "Bill Cosby got mad."[7]

In his speech, Cosby praised the work of the lawyers and civil rights leaders responsible for destroying Jim Crow but then decried the high dropout rate among black teenagers, the high percentage of black men imprisoned, and rampant black teenage pregnancy. "No longer is a person embarrassed because they're pregnant without a husband," Cosby lamented. "No longer is a boy considered an embarrassment if he tries to run away from being the father of the unmarried child," he said. "Ladies and gentlemen," Cosby declared, "the lower-economic and lower-middle-economic people are not holding their end in this deal."[8]

According to Juan Williams, Bill Cosby went on a "righteous roll," criticizing everything from the way young black people wore their clothes to the unconventional names they gave their children to the way they spoke. "Everybody knows it's important to speak English except these knuckleheads," Cosby said. "You can't land a plane with 'Why you ain't . . . ' You can't be a doctor with that kind of crap coming out of your mouth. These people are fighting hard to be ignorant."[9]

Cosby's speech drew a standing ovation, but in the days that followed word spread about what he had said, and controversy erupted. Many people praised Cosby for speaking truthfully about the self-inflicted problems of poor African Americans. Others were appalled, accusing Cosby of blaming the victims of poverty for problems they did not cause. Michael Eric Dyson was one of Cosby's most vocal critics. In this speech, delivered at the Commonwealth Club of California, Dyson lays out his case against Cosby and accuses him of "a ghastly, almost conscience-less assault" on poor black people. At the time, Dyson's book *Is Bill Cosby Right? Or Has the Black Middle Class Lost its Mind?* was beginning to sell in bookstores.

Just as Cosby's 2004 speech drew praise and condemnation, so did Dyson's book. One critic wrote, "Parents, particularly black parents, should read this material with the greatest caution. This book is wrong about everything."[10] Another wrote that Dyson had paid Cosby the "ultimate compliment one social critic can pay another. He has taken Cosby seriously and mounted a closely reasoned rebuttal."[11] Cosby himself dismissed Dyson's critique. He told one audience, "Dyson means nothing to me. I am not afraid of any Mr. Dyson."[12]

Civil rights veteran Jesse Jackson, who sat near Cosby as he delivered his 2004 remarks, eventually came to Cosby's defense. In an open letter published in the *New Pittsburgh Courier*, Jackson noted his friendship with Dyson but declared the professor's criticism of Cosby "too harsh." Jackson wrote, "We should respect Dr. Cosby's cumulative record of service [in support of civil rights] and appreciate the context of his pain and challenge. We cannot justifiably make Bill Cosby the 'poster child' for cultural insensitivity."[13]

Dyson has been widely lauded as a public intellectual. Writers, scholars, and critics have described him as "an academic who is unafraid to speak accessibly to a mass audience," a scholar whose genius lies in his ability to "flow freely from the profound to the profane, from popular culture to classical literature," and a "radical thinker who refuses to say anything other than the truth."[14] Dyson sees his work as a "calling to help hurting humanity." He describes an intellectual as "a person with a great passion to think and study and to distribute the fruits of his labor in useful form." One of the reasons he became an intellectual, Dyson writes, "was to talk back to suffering—and if possible, relieve it."[15]

Dyson believes that, however painful it might be, black intellectuals must take part in tough conversations about African American life. As he writes, "The will to clarify our aims and examine our identity is, in its own way, just as important to our freedom as the blows struck in our defense by revolutionary stalwarts." Dyson says that he learned from Malcolm X, in particular, "that the black freedom struggle is no good without self-criticism and holding each other morally accountable."[16]

THANK YOU SO VERY KINDLY, Ms. Davis, for that warm introduction and for the opportunity to address such an august and distinguished audience about topics that are central not only to African American culture but indeed to the American mainstream. I'm honored to be here today to engage you in discussion and dialogue and perhaps open debate about the issues of race and class and culture and generation.

I wrote my book on Bill Cosby, rather more directly his remarks, now infamous as Ms. Davis has indicated, precisely because those remarks did not appear out of or get driven into a vacuum. The remarks Mr. Cosby made on May 17, 2004, to an equally distinguished audience gathered together at the Constitution Hall in Washington, D.C., sponsored by Howard University— Howard University a major sponsor, along with the NAACP Legal Defense Fund and the NAACP at large—where Mr. Cosby was to receive an award on behalf of his extraordinary philanthropy and generosity and that of his wife, Dr. Camille Cosby.

Instead of giving the usual "thank you very kindly" speech, Mr. Cosby lapsed into one of the most remarkable rants of recent times—remarkable for its vigor, remarkable for its rancor, even more remarkable for the acrimony and the bitterness that it poured upon the heads of the black poor. Mr. Cosby began a rhetorical rampage against the vulnerable by indicting them for failing to live up to the great promise of the civil rights movement. He looked around that august crowd and called the great cloud of witnesses who had gathered either symbolically or literally, calling upon Dorothy Height and others who were similarly distinguished for their extraordinary sacrifice in contributing to the civil rights movement and wondered aloud what they must think in the face of the degrading disappearance of dignity marked by the infamous and scandalous and even dangerous rise of the black poor, and the way in which their habits so vehemently denied the incredible uplift that was delivered by the civil rights movement.

He said, among other things, that poor black people, in letting down the civil rights movement, didn't speak the right way. In fact, Mr. Cosby offered that he was scarcely capable of speaking the way "these people speak," end of quote. He went on to suggest that they didn't speak English. Everybody knew to speak English except "these knuckleheads." Mr. Cosby went on to suggest that black poor people were especially licentious, having two and three children with four and five different men in the house at any particular time, and that as a result of that licentiousness, they had communicated and transmitted a virulent virus of immorality to their children.

In fact, he suggested that perhaps one would have to have a DNA card in the ghetto pretty soon to determine if they were making love to their grandmothers. He said that your grandmother is a woman who had a baby at twelve, her child has a baby at about thirteen or fourteen, do the math, they're about twenty-six years old, he said, and they could be a grandmother, and therefore he was trying to prevent the kind of incestuous relations that might result from people being incapable of determining genetically that one was related to a woman that one was pursuing because she was so young. He went on to suggest that people who give their children names like Shaliqua and Taliqua and Mohammad and "all that crap," that's a direct quote—and "they're all in jail," another direct quote—are the very ones who are tearing away the fabric of conscience in the community.

Mr. Cosby, among many other things, suggested that this poor black community was especially, especially anti-intellectual, uninterested in investing in education while they spent $500 on gym shoes as opposed to $250 on Hooked on Phonics. On and on he went, in a kind of improvisational rant, kind of Charlie Parker meets Dennis Miller, [laughter] and he remonstrated extravagantly against the poor. And when he made his initial comments, the *New York Times* called me. I responded to them. Mr. Cosby got me on the phone, we spoke. He told me that perhaps I hadn't heard the entire balance of his comments. I didn't understand the context within which they were delivered. And as a result, he offered to send me both the audio and the transcript of his speech.

And when I received that audio and transcript, I was mortified, dumbfounded, bewildered, befuddled to a certain degree, but incensed at another level. He incensed me to action, to reaction to be sure, and to bleed my pathos on the page, the results of which are contained in, *Is Bill Cosby Right? Or Has the Black Middle Class Lost Its Mind?*

So for me, such an incendiary title, of course, evokes an equally incendiary response. To be sure, I expect that, and yet one remarks upon and observes with not this mythological objectivity but with, not even bemused interest, but with a kind of shudder that people might be offended by such a subtitle who were not offended by the initial assault on the poor. A drive-by by a prominent figure within the community, a ghastly, almost conscienceless assault upon them in the name of their betterment: that kind of tough love was mostly tough, not love.

And so I began to think about these issues in the broader social and political and moral context within which they inevitably resonate. And when I began to think about it, I tried to put Mr. Cosby's career in context. I began in my first chapter speaking about the interesting irony of Mr. Cosby delivering such a broadside against the vulnerable and disadvantaged, himself having emerged from the Richard Allen projects in Philadelphia. Of course back then, the Richard Allen projects were probably like new condominiums. The folk who were poor . . . and the landscape was quite different forty and fifty years ago than it is now, as poverty itself has undergone radical transmutation as a different animal. The DNA of impoverishment is quite different. It adapts to different circumstances now than even when I was poor, say twenty-five to thirty years ago.

And so out of this tremendous groundswell of anxiety that Mr. Cosby spoke from, we remember his childhood of poverty after being middle class. We also remember his remarkable rise, going to school, and in the sixth grade his teacher recounting that Bill would rather clown than study. How good that is, since he's a comedic genius.

And then in the tenth grade, he flunked, not once, not twice, but three times. After flunking out of school and dropping out, he went to the navy. And after going to the navy, received a GED, then enrolled in Temple University. And after two years, he dropped out to pursue his legendary comedic career. Later on, he was given the BA from Temple University based upon life experience, then invited to study for the master's and doctor of education degree at University of Massachusetts at Amherst, where he wrote a dissertation on Fat Albert and the Cosby kids. Then one of his dissertation advisers lamented the degree, saying it was an empty credential. I think that lamentation is far too harsh, and yet it does underscore the ironic pedigree of Mr. Cosby's educational attainment, in light especially of his vigorous assault upon those who have not been equally vigorous about pursuing education.

But when we see the backdrop, we see a great inspiration like Dr. Cosby having himself overcome impediments and obstacles that were in the way to achieve at the height of the terminal degree in America, and yet when we began to peel back the layers with the forceps provided by critical analysis, we began to see beneath the skin, subcutaneously, some of the contradictions, like folk done helped you out along the way, giving you stuff in acknowledgment of your genius. That's fine, but in terms of the same patterns that other people have to pursue, it's a good thing that Bill Cosby wasn't around when Bill Cosby was a child, or else he might not have become Bill Cosby.

The interesting irony as well is in one sense exacerbated, or compounded at least, when one recalls that Mr. Cosby for most of his career has demurred upon his representative faculty as a black icon. He has resolutely refused to represent the race, saying that his fame and celebrity meant that he was a great comedian, not a leader. Time after time, Mr. Cosby demurred in sometimes colorful fashion saying that, "I am not a leader. I'm a comedian. That's all. Why do people insist that I make statements about the race? Why must I make all of the statements about the race? Why must I carry this burden, this burden of what James Baldwin called the 'burden of representation'? Why must I," Mr. Cosby said on one occasion, "represent the race in that fashion?" In 1985 when he appeared on the Phil Donohue show, Mr. Cosby said in answer to a question: "I am not an expert on blackness. Why are you asking me this question? Why don't you let me be an H-U-M-A-N B-E-I-N-G."

Mr. Cosby said, "In my comedy, I will not depend upon color." Initially, of course, he was in the mode of a Dick Gregory, acerbic witty comments upon the acid realities of race in America, but then he chose a different path. He said, "I want to be a race transcender. I want to speak universally to all Americans, and therefore I don't think you can speak about the things that divide us. We must speak about the things that bring us together." Fine. And yet in that path that he has pursued rather diligently and conscientiously, Mr. Cosby has reneged upon the necessity thrust upon others in similar positions to speak for or on behalf of the race. He has given extraordinary amounts of money. His philanthropy is unquestionable. The genius of his giving has inspired remarkable response just in recognition of what he has done; and yet that philanthropy must never cause us to be silent in our dissent. Otherwise—elsewhere sprinkled out in his rant was the notion that young black people were pimping their parents—otherwise the "pimp/ho" metaphor would be applied with vicious particularity to us and Mr. Cosby.

Giving money can never be the litmus test for great black leadership. Otherwise Bill Gates would be the greatest black leader we've ever had.

Mr. Cosby's background, to be sure, is relevant but I spend most of my time not on him but on the issues, lest people think that I have devolved into an ad hominem attack full of animus against a great icon. No, I want to deal with the issues he raised, and they're quite interesting. He says that he doesn't know how to talk like these people "be talkin'." Oh, I be disagreein' with that. I think if one examines the speech that night, it was full of ebonicisms, witty articulations predicated upon pigmented linguistic and verbal invention. "Standin' on the corner."

When one thinks about the speech that night and listens to it, it is full of the bristling integrity of street speech. It fairly glimmers with the possibility of the faint recognition, no even more than faint, a powerful recognition of the power of speech: black speech, black Ebonics, black articulation, black English. And so full was that speech of these ebonicisms and witticisms drawn from black culture that one must remark that Mr. Cosby is unconscious of his facility. But let's be honest. He's made a whole bunch of money off of black English too. I mean, Fat Albert didn't exactly speak the king's English to the queen's taste. He didn't go around spouting Tennyson,

> *Though much is taken, much abides; and though*
> *We are not now that strength which in old days*
> *Moved earth and heaven; that which we are, we are;*
> *One equal temper of heroic hearts*
> *Made weak by time and fate, but strong in will*
> *To strive, to seek, to find, and not to yield.*

No, he said, "I'm-ba gon-ba be-ba back-ba soon-ba." [laughter] An interesting contrast to be sure, even if you're not in for, say, metaphysical poetry from Donne or even the high vernacular of Mr. Hewes, who could switch from "I Know Why the Caged Bird Sings" to "Little Brown Baby with Sparklin' Eyes."

Code switching is always in order, and of course Mr. Cosby is right. We want our children to be able to move from one vernacular to the other. After all, don't be deceived. Even standard English has its vernacular intonations. If you contrast this to, say, what's going on in Europe right now, even in England, the English we speak here is not standard to the English being spoken there. Standards are dictated by local communities and circumstances. Standards are judged by societies that have the power to reinforce one variety of a language as uniformly, universally recognized and accepted. Never misunderstand the fact that language is always implicated in notions of power. Who has the power to tell you what's right and wrong, to speak "American," or to be in California, with its nativist, xenophobic passions unleashed across the board, and yet the grand irony, perhaps God's *grande blague* and great joke— to have Schwarzenegger as the governor. Oh, the delicious irony of it all is too much not to comment upon. "Cali-fornia." And you against Ebonics.

And so, the suggestion here, of course, is to say, as James Baldwin said, "If black English isn't a language, then tell me what is?" The literal name of an essay that one of the great masters of the eloquence of the English language imbued with a sense of the King James rhetoric that his family transmitted to him, and you can hear it broiling beneath the rhetorical surface in his novels, but especially in those majestic essays, some of the best in the English language that rival the best speakers of the tongue.

And yet he said that the purpose of black English was for black folk to be able to speak in such a fashion as not to be murdered, in the face of white folk who were trying to murder them, in slavery and on plantations, in Jim Crow regions and arenas where Ameri-partheid—American apartheid— reigned. And so Mr. Baldwin suggested that the virtue of black English is the ability to facilitate a communication that will not be easily spotted in the dominant culture with the power to crush the minority. So the moral utility of the language must be examined and acknowledged as one makes dissertation upon the faults and failures of that language. Of course, Cosby is right. We don't want folk going to their job and saying, "Break me off dat application. You know what I'm shi-zayin' razight nizap? Yeeeah, 'cause I'm tryin' to get dat job." That's probably not the best thing to do, unless you're applying say at the local hip-hop establishment. And even there, Puffy might not dig that.

So the point is, we know we got to be able to code-switch. Sociolinguistics speak about it all the time; when you're with your people, Italians, Irish, Jews, Poles, African Americans, you talk the way they do. Oy vey, shlemiel, shlemazel, do your thing Yiddish. Intonations, however, through brilliant comedians have marked the linguistic landscape of American society. And so even there, the specific vernacular intonations bleed beyond their linguistic and indeed native boundaries, beyond their ethnicities to seize the American scene, and they shake them in profound ways. As has Ebonics. I mean I saw two elderly white women, or an elderly white woman and an elderly white man.

"Wha' choo doin'? Where you at?"

"Oh, just chillin' wit my peeps, trying to get my groove on."

. . .

NETWORKS, UPN, WB, making millions of dollars off of Ebonics, as has Mr. Cosby through his movie and through that Saturday morning entertainment of a cartoon where we saw the moral propriety of the ghetto brought to bear upon American society and reversed what Du Bois fathomed in 1903 as a cruel irony that black people must ever judge themselves according to the tape of another world, seeing themselves through the prism of a white world that miscomprehended them, and yet the script has been flipped, so to speak, and now America sees itself through the eyes of its minorities, through jazz and hip-hop alone. Pop culture. Entertainment. We measure ourselves, the durability of the American genius in the postmodern sense in black and brown and colored flesh.

And so Mr. Cosby is right to say we want our kids to be able to perform well, but he was miscomprehending about the complex realities of the languages we speak and hear in your neighborhood, up in Oakland, over across the bay. The reality is that when those teachers are part of the Oakland school district, they were not trying to teach Ebonics to kids. They already be knowin' it. You ain't got to do it. They be comin' there speakin' it. The point is: Can you meet them where they are to take them where they need to be, to facilitate a transition from where they are to where they need to be? If you come to school, speak it. And if you're French, somebody got to speak French to you to try to teach you to speak English. *"Ce n'est pas difficile d'apprendre français. C'est facile."* Now if you understand that, either you're advanced or you're Haitian. You're in the wrong class, or you're a refugee from France somewhere. So get in the right class, but for the rest of us, we've got to then take people where they are, what they speak. The linguistic features of these indigenous communities must be recognized so that we can teach well.

And yet there is some furious disregard and remarkable indifference— sometimes evinced by people of standing who used to speak it when they mamas prayed for dem. Now they done got their degrees and they high and mighty and they is up on the hog or, as they used to say, "Doing something in high cotton and wiping with the top leaf." Now we've forgotten. We have Afro-amnesia, a kind of black forgetfulness. Now that we've succeeded, we forgot our mama 'n' dem used to pray. Mama 'n' dem used to pray for us in that language we now look down upon. "Thank you, Lord, dat da walls of ma room was not da walls of ma grave. Ma sheet wadn't my winding sheet and

ma"—right?—"ma bed wadn't ma coolin' board. And you let the golden mo-
ments roll on a little longer. I'm like an empty pitcher before a full fountain.
Lord, have mercy." If I was in church, I know somebody might say Amen.
[*Amen!*] Commonwealth Club got the Holy Ghost. [laughter]

So the reality is that those people deployed those linguistic leftovers because folk always who are against the wall makin' it on broken pieces and
rhetorical chitlins, for all we know. Now these chitterlings are being sold as
futures markets. [laughter] And so, my brothers and sisters, the point being
simply that, yes, we must facilitate transition from where people are, status
quo, to where they need to be, the ideal. But we must do so recognizing the
integrity of their speech. America finds it difficult to think about difference
without hierarchy. They just, something is different and therefore it's better.
No, it's different. Standard in this community is not standard in that community. When you're in the hood . . . I grew up in Detroit; they say, "Watch
out for that alley, apple." Excuse me? Is that fruit that grows in an alley? No,
that was a brick in my community. So if you didn't speak the standard English of my community, you might be in the emergency ward tonight having
been hit in the head with an alley apple.

It's contingent upon circumstance. Local color adds insight and meaning
to words, and power is always at stake. Here you are in California, the power
to say we're only going to speak English. Isn't it interesting that America is
so arrogant and yet ignorant that it would be proud of the fact that we are
mono-linguistic? Cabdrivers, you look down on speaking four dialects of one
language and about six other languages, and you feel superior. Of course,
you can tell them to take you to the airport because your pockets are swole,
as the young people say; you have significant capital.

Well Mr. Cosby went on and remonstrated against the poor in so many
other ways. He said, "You give your kids these names, Shaliqua, Taliqua,
and Mohammad and all that crap, and they're all in jail." Now, Bill Cosby
ain't got no business telling you what to name your kids unless he's paying
yo' child support. And if he's doing that, you might want to consider his
linguistic choices. Well, there was a study done in 2003; it said if your name
was Shaniqua, Taliqua or Shanaynay or Kenya or Kenyata, or something
sounding black—like the beautiful young lady at the desk here whose name
is Shantel.

She's a white woman. I thought she was a sister. [laughter] Just on the
name. So we be doin' signifyin' on the name. So when you've got them kind
of black-sounding names, I said, "I bet your application got rejected a whole

bunch of times 'till they saw you were a white woman." Just joking with her. Sort of. [laughter] Right? That's what they said in 2003, a sociological study, excuse me, economic study, a study that said—two economists—that you can't even get in the door anymore. It used to be that you could get in the door to be rejected despite your Harvard degree. "Don't call us; we'll call you." Now you can't even get into the door because your name is Shantel, Shaquille. So should we therefore say, "Aha, black people should not name their kids that?" That's one approach but dag-gone, how about challenging the bigger thing in society that refuses to acknowledge your virtue despite your name?

Because Oprah ain't got no regular name. [*Go ahead!*] But when you see Oprah, what do you see? You see greatness, grand eloquence, magnificence, just, just formidable! You see something almost incomprehensibly huge, gargantuan, let's appeal to Swift, Brobdingnagian. Thank you, *Gulliver's Travels*, for your postmodern application. You see something huge in the culture, a colossus bestriding the society with such ascendency and power! And so the reality is, you learn to love Oprah; you love to learn the name. And you love to learn the name, and you learn to love the name. In fact, you appreciate what she is and who she is. You see greatness. You see billionaire. You see one of the most well-respected, if not the most well-respected woman in the country. But if somebody had told her, "Your name is Oprah, you need to change it because you just look like a ghetto queen," that would have been destructive to her. Perhaps she would do it enough as it was.

Think about Shaquille O'Neal. Would Mr. Cosby step to him and tell him to change his name? Perhaps not. "I will beat you down right now Mr. Cosby, get you on the court and treat you like a little child. [laughter] Thank you very much." That monotone would reinforce, with his muscles, his superiority. Mr. Cosby would not challenge him.

How about Condoleezza? I know she was here recently. Lord have mercy. [laughter, cheers] Condo-leezza. That ain't no regular name, y'all. [laughter] Let me see. Leasing a condo, how did, you know—what happened there? Mama was a musician inspired by the musical Italian signatures. That's like naming your kid Basso Profundo, right. Con dolcezza. Condoleezza. That's a musical signature in Italian. That's what Africans do—make up stuff based on what they like. Condoleezza? And don't tell me about the Condoleezzas and the Shaquilles and the Oprahs. These are people of extraordinary achievement who have done well. And so if we learn to create a society that is against the bigotry that denies them opportunity, we're doing better.

Otherwise if we concede the legitimacy of bigotry toward these names, we're telling King he was wrong. He should have accepted the status quo. Instead, he challenged it!

And people ought to be able to name their kids what they want. This ain't the first generation to name their kids after consumer products in African American culture. Africans have always been creative. If your name was Akua, your name was Wednesday. Black people name their kids on the days of the week, days of the month, name their kids after the months, I should say—June, July, August—name their kids after the circumstances of their birth: hard times, pleasant times, good times. Black people have always done this. In Africa . . . I have an entire chapter on this in the book. And then what they did in the thirties, forties, and fifties after consumer products: Listerine, Creamola, Hershey Bar, Cadillac, El Dorado? Oh, you thought it started with Alizé and Versace and Lexus? Black people always name their kids after stuff they want but can't have. Mercedes, Good Lovin'—whatever they want and can't get access to. [laughter]

And the point is that we don't want to sanctify the bigotry. Plus, to me, it ain't the Negroes. It ain't the Africans. It ain't the black folk named Shaniqua that are problematic. Oh, Pookie might steal your car, but he ain't gonna write no judgment against you on the Supreme Court that will affect millions of lives now and in the future, Clarence! It's those good old American-named Negroes, Africans, and black folk, who have been problematic. The high bourgeois-attaining, English-named figures who have been so subversive of the potential of democracy to be spread.

And on and on Cosby went, and on and on I respond. A couple of more points before I end.

Mr. Cosby said that black people are more licentious than others, and the black poor. Look, they're more vulnerable. They're more easily targetable. Am I arguing that black poor people ain't got no problems? No. I've been black and po'. Do you think I'm crazy? The people who are most upset by black people who are poor who do terrible things are black people who are poor. Who do the right thing. Which is most of them. The blur of stereotypes that obscured Mr. Cosby's visions, that distorted his perception of the problem, that rendered him as a comedic observer with ingenious comedic skill but real low social analysis. Given his career of denying the legitimacy of speaking about race and refusing to engage it, therefore he lacks the skill. I'm not saying he's a Johnny-come-lately and therefore he doesn't have the authentic right to engage in a race discourse, I'm saying he doesn't have the skill to parse eloquently and complexly the nuances in a sophisticated fashion of public discourse about race in America! We are not interchangeable as black people, so that any black person will do who just happens to be famous and gave a bunch of money. That don't qualify you as a social critic. "Old Cosby said nothing different than Leroy on the corner say." Leroy ain't on C-SPAN! [laughter] And your cousin Bubba in the barbershop, funny as he is—and Craig Mayberry has a beautiful new book about barbershop discourse, it's great—but he ain't on *Nightline* in a thirty-minute space to debate the serious and insidious issues of African American culture, because black folk are not interchangeable, despite the internalization of that white supremacist predicate. Folk be doin' stuff because they got skills at it. It takes time to develop it. And what other culture turns only to a comedian and claims that he is the greatest leader we've ever produced? Better than King and Garvey and Ella Baker and Fannie Lou Hamer and James Baldwin or Angela Davis, better than Ida B. Wells-Barnett and Du Bois and Frederick Douglass? This is the *greatest leader*? Wow. Where ya' been, brah?

In America now, especially the right wing, the acid conservatism in this country heaps huge praise upon Mr. Cosby's head by saying, "Finally a black leader has spoken about responsibility." Where have you been? Any black leader worth his or her salt speaks about this weekly, daily. Any intellectual worth his or her salt talks about it as a necessity for forward progress. The problem is, Mr. Cosby spoke about personal responsibility outside of the context of social responsibility. They are reciprocal and dynamic. And the point is, is that we wait. We don't wait for social responsibility to behave right. But behaving right will not solve the problems Mr. Cosby pointed to. Good behavior will never stop job flight. It can never stop capital bleeding, can't stanch the bleeding of downsizing and outsourcing. Can't stop the exploitation of indigenous marketplace in Indonesia. When you call Take-out Taxi tonight because you don't want to cook, the person answering you might be in Burma. And when you make a local call, "You know that place right around the corner from 595 on the Commonwealth? You know, that place?" "Sir, I am in India."

The international processes that have been absorbed by multinational corporations which control seventy percent of the business transfers in America—when you think about three-hundred-and-some-odd companies who control the expansion of global wealth, speaking about local responsibility is critical, it's necessary, but it's not sufficient in philosophical terms. Good behavior is its own reward, and most black people I know urge it upon their children with vigor and intensity. And yet—as I come to my close here—and yet the reality is that that taking of personal responsibility, which is critical in terms of moral character in the black community, will never solve the fundamental economic and social problems where concentration of poverty is the problem.

You see, good behavior won't keep billboards out of your neighborhoods that are black and poor or Latino, that celebrate drugs in terms of liquor and in terms of alcohol—to be redundant—and in terms of smoking. Why is it a fact that rich white kids and rich black kids have to come into the ghetto to get their "relief." [Get] their chemical transgression on? To engage in that? Why must they come there? Because zoning laws keep that stuff out' the suburbs. So the concentration of poverty is a result of political and public policy decisions, and if you are already fragile with your back against the wall, you don't have any political power. Then you don't have the power to keep this stuff out of your community! And please don't correlate morality with class status. That would mean the richest people were the best. Oh, Lord have mercy. [laughter, affirmations]

I AIN'T MAD AT HER but what about, what about your girl Ms. Hilton? Ms. Paris. I'm a be quiet here because I know I got to shut up but I got to say this 'fore I shut up. Er, uh, as my uncle used to say—er, uh, from Alabama—"Er, uh, Ms. Hilton, she had great parenting, I suppose, but maybe the parent can't be coordinated with the cash you got." Maybe people who are rich . . . I mean, she's got not one but two sex tapes. I have to watch these things. I'm a cultural critic. [laughter] It's very difficult for me to endure *One Night in Paris* and its follow-up. But alas for you, the people, I engage in that sacrifice. [laughter] Then she's got a show on TV whose ratings are through the roof, and [she's] building a multimillion-dollar empire on being what Cosby accused the black poor of being: a ho. So she done made, she done found gold in them there hills, high heels. She done found gold in being a ho. And so now being a ho ain't something that's correlated with your economic status. God bless her. Amen. Hoin' ain't easy. [laughter]

The problem is, my friends, as we interrogate and scrutinize this peculiar conundrum, that we can never correlate class status and social status and moral attainment, because in the end, we know that some of the best people in the world have no money and some of the best people have money. So we can never associate exclusively the province of impropriety with those who are poor.

As I end for real—a Baptist preacher got to end about three times—as I end for real here, we want all people to be responsible, but how can Mr. Cosby overlook himself in this alleged and ostensible self-critique? The last time I checked, you've got to critique the self in order to be self-critical. If you're rich, self-critical means criticizing the rich folk, not the po' folk; otherwise, that's criticizing other folk. Just want to hip you to that term. "He was being self-critical." Against who? I didn't hear him mention any rich black people.

See, black people want the . . . they finally defended Mr. Cosby. "Well we've got to get our dirty laundry out there and get it aired and cleaned." Let me see. Do you want everybody's dirty laundry or just the poor people's dirty laundry? I wrote a book on Dr. King, called him the greatest American who ever lived, talked about promiscuity and plagiarism. Black people went crazy on me. [Whispering] "Why you got to do that? Why you got to let that out?" First of all, because it happened. Secondly, because I'm trying to anticipate those tapes that will be released in about twenty, thirty years, and if I've already called him great and having anticipated their release and knowing what they said and still said he was great, then I'm ahead of the game. It's a strategic and intellectual choice, it's a methodological and procedural one. And it's also (un)intellectually honest. We claimed about dominant white culture, "They just choose the stuff they like, and the stuff they don't like, they don't talk about it." Thomas Jefferson. They romanticize him. Don't speak about the slaves, but you can't talk about Dr. King without talking about the foibles and the faults. But you don't want that dirty laundry out there, because we're not interested in putting black dirty laundry; we're interested in putting *poor* black dirty laundry out there. Because speaking about black men of high achievement who hate Shaliqua's name but love her sex—I know about them, see them. MBAs from Harvard diligently pursuing their careers and yet exploiting with crassness the erotic intensity of the young girls who titillate them. Hypocrites. Do we want to put black ministers who rail in their pulpits with theological certitude against being gay or lesbian, themselves closeted gay? Do we want to tell *that* truth? Do we want to out *that* story? No. When *Barbershop* came out, nobody said what Cedric the Entertainer's character said about Dr. King was wrong; we just didn't want it out there.

So the point is, if it's good for the goose, it's good for the gander. Let's love all of our people, and let's be honest and self-critical and desirous of virtue. In the postemancipation culture, black former slaves were looked down upon by the black elite because the black elite felt embarrassed. Bill Cosby said in a speech, "The white man must be laughing at us!" He still feels the gaze of a dominant white culture that he assaults to please but rarely has chosen to challenge. And now because he has spilled the *venom* and directed *anger* and hostility against his *own*, he is being uplifted as a hero, and yet we fail to challenge him with his perch high in a dominant culture. Have you borne witness yet to the truth of what you know about how other black people who are poor suffer, if you do remember? We don't want to put everybody's dirty laundry on the table. We can't even admit O.J. did what he did! Put that dirty [laundry out]. And Michael Jackson. "Bless and pray for him." Yeah. Pray for them kids, too. Praying for Michael Jackson. I love Michael Jackson. Born the same year. I'm going to shut up in a minute. Born the same year, 1958. Love that brother, but come on! A black icon exploiting poor, white people. We can't get it right. We're trying to coordinate it. "Let me see. He's black, so he must be victim at a certain level," and yet we can't coordinate the fact that these poor white crazy people with their mama out of her mind, yet these young children with cancer are being victimized by a black icon, and he gets racial cover. Back against the wall, black against the wall! Now he recovers the blackness he lost. It doesn't make a difference if you're black or white, as he gets whiter and whiter and whiter. Moonwalks back into a primal conception of African identity and he finds cover! And you want to talk about exposing black pathology? *Deal with that! [All right!]*

So my point is, as I take my seat or at least my end, that Mr. Cosby has delved deeply into pools of profound, critical issues with a shovel demanding a bulldozer. He's brought a sledgehammer to the surgeon's table, where a scalpel is necessary. And as my dear friend and his dear friend Reverend Jesse Jackson says, "When you're in a pit, do you want a shovel to dig you deeper, or do you want a rope to pull you out?" I think Mr. Cosby threw down a shovel. I'm trying to let down a rope. Thank you so very kindly. [applause]

23.

Barack Obama
(1961–)

"A More Perfect Union"

*National Constitution Center,
Philadelphia, Pennsylvania—March 18, 2008*

It may have been the most important speech of Barack Obama's 2008 presidential campaign. With just a month to go before the crucial Pennsylvania primary, Obama spoke directly and at length about one of the most politically volatile issues in America: race and racism. The occasion was forced on him by controversy over incendiary statements made by the pastor at Obama's Chicago church, the Rev. Jeremiah A. Wright Jr. The uproar had been fueled by conservative broadcasters who played excerpts of Wright's sermons and statements, accusing the pastor of being anti-American. Obama's primary opponent, Hillary Rodham Clinton, also criticized Wright. Obama confronted the problem in a speech that drew wide, but not universal, praise for its frank and nuanced recognition of the enduring divisions between blacks and whites in America. As one journalist observed, "Obama is a black candidate who can tell Americans of all races to move beyond race."[1]

Obama began attending Wright's Trinity United Church of Christ in the late 1980s when he was a community organizer in Chicago. In his memoir, *Dreams from My Father*, Obama described himself at the time as a "reluctant skeptic" of religion.[2] He sought Wright's help in his community work.

Obama was immediately intrigued by the learned and engaging pastor and impressed by the depth of Trinity United's commitment to serving poor and marginalized Chicagoans. Obama began visiting Sunday services. The *New York Times* described Wright as "a dynamic pastor who preached Afrocentric theology, dabbled in radical politics, and delivered music and profanity–spiked sermons." Trinity was no fringe congregation, however. With more than eight thousand members, it was the largest congregation within the United Church of Christ. The respected University of Chicago religious scholar Martin Marty "had often attended Wright's services and found inspiration there."[3] At Trinity United, Obama discovered a new sense of faith and connection. "At the foot of that cross, inside the thousands of churches across the city, I imagined the stories of ordinary black people merging with the stories of David and Goliath, Moses and Pharaoh, the Christians in the lion's den, Ezekiel's field of dry bones," Obama wrote. "Those stories—of survival, and freedom, and hope— became our story, my story."[4] Barack and Michelle Obama got married in Trinity United. Their two daughters were baptized in the church.

When U.S. Senator Barack Obama of Illinois set out to run for the presidency, he and his campaign knew that Wright's caustic assertions about pervasive white racism in America might be a problem. Negative press reports on Wright began to surface, and Obama canceled plans to have Wright deliver the invocation at his campaign kickoff. Then the clips of Wright's sermons and statements began to circulate rapidly on the Web. Among the most controversial were Wright declaring "God damn America" for its historic cruelties to African Americans, his invocation of the Ku Klux Klan in referring to the United States as the "U.S. of K.K.K. A.," and his claim that America's misdeeds abroad had provoked the September 11 terrorist attacks.[5] Obama said he had not heard Wright say such things either in church or privately,[6] but in March 2008, media and campaign pressures compelled Obama to denounce Wright's most divisive statements as "inflammatory and appalling." As the news story continued to boil, the Obama campaign scheduled a major speech for March 18 in hopes of cooling down the race issue.

Obama's Philadelphia speech drew heavily on his own biracial biography. Obama was born in 1961 and raised primarily in Hawaii. His mother was a white woman, originally from Kansas. His father was a black man from Kenya. Obama's father left the family when Obama was a baby to attend Harvard, then moved back to Kenya. Obama's mother married an Indonesian businessman, and Obama lived in that country for four years, returning to Hawaii when he was ten to live with his grandparents. Obama spent two years at Occidental College in Los Angeles and then transferred to Columbia University in New York. He earned his law degree from Harvard, where he was the first black person elected president of the *Harvard Law Review*. Obama worked as a community organizer on Chicago's South Side and practiced civil rights law. He taught constitutional law at the University of Chicago and was elected to the Illinois Senate in 1996. In 2004 he was elected to the U.S. Senate.

Obama made this speech at a museum in Philadelphia devoted to the U.S. Constitution. He spoke to a small audience of local supporters, clergy members, and politicians. Obama encouraged Americans of all colors to reflect on the nation's history of racial injustice and discord. He urged Americans to understand where racial resentments and bigoted attitudes originate, among blacks and whites. The *New York Times* observed that Obama had "placed himself squarely in the middle of the debate over how to address [race], a living bridge between whites and blacks still divided by the legacy of slavery and all that came after it." While Obama repudiated Wright's offensive comments, he did not disavow Wright himself, as many critics insisted Obama should. "I can no more disown him than I can disown my white grandmother," Obama said, adding that she was known to make racially insensitive remarks from time to time. It was a generational thing, Obama said, reflecting attitudes born from racial strife.

Many writers and politicians praised the speech, including Democratic challenger Hillary Clinton. Some leftists said Obama was too easy on whites and their historical responsibility for centuries of black oppression. Conservative critics doubted Obama's ability to truly bind America's racial wounds. Historian Omar H. Ali said the speech served as a kind of "blank slate upon which each of us places our own histories, experiences, and ways of working through our thoughts and feelings."[7] Political pundit Keli Goff said Obama's speech especially reflected the racial perspective of a new, multiethnic, post–civil rights generation that looks to the future more than the past. "For all the talk of our country being a melting pot, we are only now really beginning to melt—and meld—together."[8]

Obama lost the Pennsylvania primary to Clinton, though by a narrower margin than expected. When he won the November general election and became the first African American president in U.S. history, sociologist Orlando Patterson said the victory reflected Obama's "cathartic power to mine unity from difference."[9]

"WE THE PEOPLE, in order to form a more perfect union."

Two hundred and twenty-one years ago, in a hall that still stands across the street, a group of men gathered and, with these simple words, launched America's improbable experiment in democracy. Farmers and scholars, statesmen and patriots, who had traveled across an ocean to escape tyranny and persecution, finally made real their declaration of independence at a Philadelphia convention that lasted through the spring of 1787.

The document they produced was eventually signed but ultimately unfinished. It was stained by this nation's original sin of slavery—a question that divided the colonies and brought the convention to a stalemate until the founders chose to allow the slave trade to continue for at least twenty more years and to leave any final resolution to future generations.

Of course, the answer to the slavery question was already embedded within our Constitution. A Constitution that had, at its very core, the ideal of equal citizenship under the law. A Constitution that promised its people liberty, and justice, and a union that could be, and should be, perfected over time.

And yet words on a parchment would not be enough to deliver slaves from bondage or provide men and women of every color and creed their full rights and obligations as citizens of the United States. What would be needed were Americans in successive generations who were willing to do their part—through protests and struggles, on the streets and in the courts, through a civil war and civil disobedience, and always at great risk—to narrow that gap between the promise of our ideals and the reality of their time.

This was one of the tasks we set forth at the beginning of this presidential campaign—to continue the long march of those who came before us, a march for a more just, more equal, more free, more caring, and more prosperous America. I chose to run for president, at this moment in history, because I believe deeply that we cannot solve the challenges of our time unless we solve them together—unless we perfect our union by understanding that we may have different stories, but we hold common hopes. That we may not look the same and may not have come from the same place, but we all want to move in the same direction—towards a better future for our children and our grandchildren.

And this belief comes from my unyielding faith in the decency and generosity of the American people. But it also comes from my own story.

I am the son of a black man from Kenya and a white woman from Kansas. I was raised with the help of a white grandfather, who survived a Depression to serve in Patton's army during World War II, and a white grandmother who worked on a bomber assembly line at Fort Leavenworth while he was overseas. I've gone to some of the best schools in America and lived in one of the world's poorest nations. I am married to a black American who carries within her the blood of slaves and slave owners, an inheritance we pass on to our two precious daughters. I have brothers, sisters, nieces, nephews, uncles, and cousins, of every race and every hue, scattered across three continents, and for as long as I live, I will never forget that in no other country on Earth is my story even possible.

It's a story that hasn't made me the most conventional of candidates. But it is a story that has seared into my genetic makeup the idea that this nation is more than the sum of its parts—that out of many, we are truly one.

Now, throughout the first year of this campaign, against all predictions to the contrary, we saw how hungry the American people were for this message of unity. Despite the temptation to view my candidacy through a purely racial lens, we won commanding victories in states with some of the whitest populations in the country. In South Carolina, where the Confederate flag still flies, we built a powerful coalition of African Americans and white Americans.

This is not to say that race has not been an issue in this campaign. At various stages in the campaign, some commentators have deemed me either "too black" or "not black enough." We saw racial tensions bubble to the surface during the week before the South Carolina primary. The press has scoured every single exit poll for the latest evidence of racial polarization, not just in terms of white and black but black and brown as well.

And yet it's only been in the last couple of weeks that the discussion of race in this campaign has taken a particularly divisive turn. On one end of the spectrum, we've heard the implication that my candidacy is somehow an exercise in affirmative action—that it's based solely on the desire of wild, and wide-eyed, liberals to purchase racial reconciliation on the cheap. On the other end, we've heard my former pastor Jeremiah Wright use incendiary language to express views that have the potential not only to widen the racial divide, but views that denigrate both the greatness and the goodness of our nation, and that rightly offend white and black alike.

I have already condemned, in unequivocal terms, the statements of Reverend Wright that have caused such controversy, and in some cases pain. For some, nagging questions remain. Did I know him to be an occasionally fierce critic of American domestic and foreign policy? Of course. Did I ever hear him make remarks that could be considered controversial while I sat in the church? Yes. Did I strongly disagree with many of his political views? Absolutely. Just as I'm sure many of you have heard remarks from your pastors, priests, or rabbis with which you strongly disagree.

But the remarks that have caused this recent firestorm weren't simply controversial. They weren't simply a religious leader's efforts to speak out against perceived injustice. Instead, they expressed a profoundly distorted view of this country. A view that sees white racism as endemic and that elevates what is wrong with America above all that we know is right with America. A view that sees the conflicts in the Middle East as rooted primarily in the actions of stalwart allies like Israel, instead of emanating from the perverse and hateful ideologies of radical Islam.

As such, Reverend Wright's comments were not only wrong but divisive. Divisive at a time when we need unity. Racially charged at a time when we need to come together to solve a set of monumental problems: two wars, a terrorist threat, a falling economy, a chronic health care crisis, and potentially devastating climate change—problems that are neither black or white or Latino or Asian, but rather problems that confront us all.

Given my background, my politics, and my professed values and ideals, there will no doubt be those for whom my statements of condemnation are not enough. Why associate myself with Reverend Wright in the first place, they may ask? Why not join another church? And I confess that if all that I knew of Reverend Wright were the snippets of those sermons that have run in an endless loop on the television sets and YouTube, if Trinity United Church of Christ conformed to the caricatures being peddled by some commentators, there is no doubt that I would react in much the same way.

But the truth is, that isn't all that I know of the man. The man I met more than twenty years ago is a man who helped introduce me to my Christian faith. A man who spoke to me about our obligations to love one another. To care for the sick and lift up the poor. He is a man who served his country as a United States marine and who has studied and lectured at some of the finest universities and seminaries in the country. And who, over thirty years, has led a church that serves the community by doing God's work here on Earth. By housing the homeless, ministering to the needy, providing day-care services and scholarships and prison ministries, and reaching out to those suffering from HIV/AIDS.

In my first book, *Dreams from My Father*, I described the experience of my first service at Trinity. And it goes as follows:

> People began to shout, to rise from their seats and clap and cry out, a forceful wind carrying the reverend's voice up into the rafters. And in that single note—hope!—I heard something else. At the foot of that cross, inside the thousands of churches across the city, I imagined the stories of ordinary black people merging with the stories of David and Goliath, Moses and Pharaoh, the Christians in the lion's den, Ezekiel's field of dry bones. Those stories—of survival, and freedom, and hope—became our stories, my story. The blood that spilled was our blood, the tears our tears, until this black church, on this bright day, seemed once more a vessel carrying the story of a people into future generations and into a larger world. Our trials and triumphs became, at once, unique and universal, black and more-than-black. In chronicling our journey, the stories and songs gave us a meaning to reclaim memories that we didn't need to feel shame about. Memories that all people might study and cherish, and with which we could start to rebuild.

That has been my experience at Trinity. Like other predominantly black churches across the country, Trinity embodies the black community in its entirety. The doctor and the welfare mom, the model student and the former gangbanger. Like other black churches, Trinity's services are full of raucous laughter and sometimes bawdy humor. They are full of dancing, and clapping, and screaming and shouting that may seem jarring to the untrained ear. The church contains, in full, the kindness and cruelty, the fierce intelligence and the shocking ignorance, the struggles and successes, the love and, yes, the bitterness and bias that make up the black experience in America.

And this helps explain, perhaps, my relationship with Reverend Wright. As imperfect as he may be, he has been like family to me. He strengthened my faith, officiated my wedding, and baptized my children. Not once in my conversations with him have I heard him talk about any ethnic group in derogatory terms or treat whites with whom he interacted with anything but courtesy and respect. He contains within him the contradictions—the good and the bad—of the community that he has served diligently for so many years.

I can no more disown him than I can disown the black community. I can no more disown him than I can disown my white grandmother. A woman who helped raise me. A woman who sacrificed again and again for me. A woman who loves me as much as she loves anything in this world. But a woman who once confessed her fear of black men who passed her by on the street. And who on more than one occasion has uttered racial or ethnic stereotypes that made me cringe.

These people are part of me. And they are part of America, this country that I love.

Now, some will see this as an attempt to justify or excuse comments that are simply inexcusable. And I can assure you it is not. And I suppose the politically safe thing to do would be to move on from this episode and just hope that it fades into the woodwork. We can dismiss Reverend Wright as a crank or a demagogue, just as some have dismissed Geraldine Ferraro, in the aftermath of her recent statements, as harboring some deep-seated bias.

But race is an issue that I believe this nation cannot afford to ignore right now. We would be making the same mistake that Reverend Wright made in his offending sermons about America, to simplify and stereotype and amplify the negative to the point that it distorts reality.

The fact is that the comments that have been made and the issues that have surfaced over the last few weeks reflect the complexities of race in this country that we've never really worked through—a part of our union that we have not yet made perfect. And if we walk away now, if we simply retreat into our respective corners, we will never be able to come together and solve challenges like health care, or education, or the need to find good jobs for every American. [applause]

Understanding this reality requires a reminder of how we arrived at this point. As William Faulkner once wrote, "The past isn't dead and buried. In fact, it isn't even past." We do not need to recite here the history of racial injustice in this country. But we do need to remind ourselves that so many of the disparities that exist between the African American community and the larger American community today can be directly traced to inequalities passed on from an earlier generation that suffered under the brutal legacy of slavery and Jim Crow.

Segregated schools were, and are, inferior schools; we still haven't fixed them, fifty years after *Brown v. Board of Education*. [applause] And the inferior education they provided, then and now, helps explain the pervasive achievement gap between today's black and white students.

Legalized discrimination—where blacks were prevented, often through violence, from owning property, or loans were not granted to African American business owners, or black home owners could not access FHA mortgages, or blacks were excluded from unions, or the police force, or the fire department—meant that black families could not amass any meaningful wealth to bequeath to future generations. That history helps explain the wealth and income gap between blacks and whites, and the concentrated pockets of poverty that persist in so many of today's urban and rural communities.

A lack of economic opportunity among black men, and the shame and frustration that came from not being able to provide for one's family, contributed to the erosion of black families. A problem that welfare policies, for many years, may have worsened. And the lack of basic services in so many urban black neighborhoods—parks for kids to play in, police walking the beat, regular garbage pickup, building code enforcement—all helped create a cycle of violence, blight, and neglect that continues to haunt us.

This is the reality in which Reverend Wright and other African Americans of his generation grew up. They came of age in the late fifties and early sixties—a time when segregation was still the law of the land and opportunity was systematically constricted. What's remarkable is not how many failed in the face of discrimination, but how many men and women overcame the odds, how many were able to make a way out of no-way, for those like me who would come after them.

But for all those who scratched and clawed their way to get a piece of the American dream, there were many who didn't make it. Those who were ultimately defeated, in one way or another, by discrimination. That legacy of defeat was passed on to future generations. Those young men, and, increasingly, young women who we see standing on street corners or languishing in our prisons, without hope or prospects for the future. Even for those blacks who did make it, questions of race, and racism, continue to define their worldview in fundamental ways. For the men and women of Reverend Wright's generation, the memories of humiliation and doubt and fear have not gone away. Nor has the anger and the bitterness of those years. That anger may not get expressed in public, in front of white co-workers or white friends. But it does find voice in the barbershop, or the beauty shop, around the kitchen table.

At times, that anger is exploited by politicians, to gin up votes along racial lines, or to make up for a politician's own failings. And occasionally it finds voice in the church on Sunday morning, in the pulpit and in the pews. The fact that so many people are surprised to hear that anger in some of Reverend Wright's sermons simply reminds us of the old truism that the most segregated hour of American life occurs on Sunday morning. [applause] That anger is not always productive. Indeed, all too often, it distracts attention from solving real problems. It keeps us from squarely facing our own complicity, within the African American community, in our condition. It prevents the African American community from forging the alliances it needs to bring about real change. But the anger is real. It is powerful. And to simply wish it away, to condemn it without understanding its roots, only serves to widen the chasm of misunderstanding that exists between the races.

In fact, a similar anger exists within segments of the white community. Most working- and middle-class white Americans don't feel that they've been particularly privileged by their race. Their experience is the immigrant experience. As far as they're concerned, no one handed them anything. They built it from scratch. They've worked hard all their lives, many times only to see their job shipped overseas, or their pension dumped, after a lifetime of labor. They are anxious about their futures, and they feel their dreams slipping away. And in an era of stagnant wages and global competition, opportunity comes to be seen as a zero-sum game, in which your dreams come at my expense. So when they are told to bus their children to a school across town, when they hear an African American is getting an advantage and is landing a good job or a spot in a good college because of an injustice that they themselves never committed, when they're told that their fears about crime in urban neighborhoods are somehow prejudiced, resentment builds over time.

Like the anger within the black community, these resentments aren't always expressed in polite company. But they have helped shape the political landscape for at least a generation. Anger over welfare and affirmative action helped forge the Reagan coalition. Politicians routinely exploited fears of crime for their own electoral ends. Talk show hosts and conservative commentators built entire careers unmasking bogus claims of racism, while dismissing legitimate discussions of racial injustice and inequality as mere political correctness or reverse racism. [applause]

And just as black anger often pr
white resentments distracted attentio
class squeeze: a corporate culture rife
accounting practices and short-term
lobbyists and special interests. Econom
many. And yet, to wish away the resent
them as misguided or even racist, withou
legitimate concerns, this, too, widens the
to understanding.

This is where we are right now. It's a rac
for years. And contrary to the claims of son   ...ite,
I have never been so naive as to believe tha   ...t beyond our racial
divisions in a single election cycle. Or with a single candidate. [applause]
Particularly a candidacy as imperfect as my own.

But I have asserted a firm conviction, a conviction rooted in my faith in
God and my faith in the American people, that working together, we can
move beyond some of our old racial wounds. And that in fact we have no
choice—we have no choice if we are to continue on the path of a more perfect union.

For the African American community, that path means embracing the
burdens of our past without becoming victims of our past. It means continuing to insist on a full measure of justice in every aspect of American life. But
it also means binding our particular grievances—for better health care, and
better schools, and better jobs—to the larger aspirations of all Americans,
the white woman struggling to break the glass ceiling, the white man who's
been laid off, the immigrant trying to feed his family. And it means, also,
taking full responsibility for our own lives. By demanding more from our
fathers, and spending more time with our children, and reading to them,
and teaching them that while they may face challenges and discrimination in
their own lives, they must never succumb to despair or cynicism. [applause]
They must always believe that they can write their own destiny.

Ironically, this quintessentially American—and, yes, conservative—notion of self-help found frequent expression in Reverend Wright's sermons.
But what my former pastor too often failed to understand is that embarking
on a program of self-help also requires a belief that society can change.

The profound mistake of Reverend Wright's sermons is not that he spoke
about racism in our society. It's that he spoke as if our society was static. As
if no progress has been made. As if this country—a country that has made

wn members to run for the highest office in the
ion of white and black, Latino, Asian, rich and poor,
still irrevocably bound to a tragic past. [applause] What
we have seen, is that America can change. That is the true
this nation. What we have already achieved gives us hope—the
ty to hope—for what we can, and must, achieve tomorrow.

Now, in the white community, the path to a more perfect union means acknowledging that what ails the African American community does not just exist in the minds of black people. That the legacy of discrimination, and current incidents of discrimination, while less overt than in the past—that these things are real and must be addressed. Not just with words, but with deeds. By investing in our schools and our communities. By enforcing our civil rights laws and ensuring fairness in our criminal justice system. By providing this generation with ladders of opportunity that were unavailable for previous generations. It requires all Americans to realize that *your* dreams do not have to come at the expense of *my* dreams. That investing in the health, welfare, and education of black and brown and white children will ultimately help all of America prosper. [applause]

In the end, then, what is called for is nothing more and nothing less than what all the world's great religions demand: that we do unto others as we would have them do unto us. Let us be our brother's keeper, scripture tells us. Let us be our sister's keeper. Let us find that common stake we all have in one another, and let our politics reflect that spirit as well.

For we have a choice in this country. We can accept a politics that breeds division and conflict and cynicism. We can tackle race only as spectacle, as we did in the O.J. trial. Or in the wake of tragedy, as we did in the aftermath of Katrina. Or as fodder for the nightly news. We can play Reverend Wright's sermons on every channel, every day, and talk about them from now until the election. And make the only question in this campaign whether or not the American people think that I, somehow, believe or sympathize with his most offensive words. We can pounce on some gaffe by a Hillary supporter as evidence that she's playing the race card. Or we can speculate on whether white men will all flock to John McCain in the general election, regardless of his policies. We can do that.

But if we do, I can tell you that in the next election, we'll be talking about some other distraction. And then another one. And then another one. And nothing will change. [applause]

That is one option. Or, at this moment, in this election, we can come together and say, "Not this time." This time, we want to talk about the crumbling schools that are stealing the future of black children and white children and Asian children and Hispanic children and Native American children. [applause] This time, we want to reject the cynicism that tells us that these kids can't learn, that those kids who don't look like us are somebody else's problem. The children of America are not those kids; they are our kids, and we will not let them fall behind in the twenty-first-century economy. Not this time.

This time, we want to talk about how the lines in the emergency room are filled with whites and blacks and Hispanics who do not have health care, who don't have the power, on their own, to overcome the special interests in Washington, but who can take them on if we do it together.

This time, we want to talk about the shuttered mills that once provided a decent life for men and women of every race. And the homes for sale that once belonged to Americans from every religion, every region, every walk of life. This time, we want to talk about the fact that the real problem is not that someone who doesn't look like you might take your job, it's that the corporation you work for will ship it overseas for nothing more than a profit. [applause]

This time, we want to talk about the men and women, of every color and creed, who serve together and fight together and bleed together under the same proud flag. We want to talk about how to bring them home from a war that should have never been authorized and should've never been waged. [applause] And we want to talk about how we'll show our patriotism by caring for them and their families and giving them the benefits they have earned. [applause]

I would not be running for president if I didn't believe with all my heart that this is what the vast majority of Americans want for this country. This union may never be perfect, but generation after generation has shown that it can always be perfected. And today, whenever I find myself feeling doubtful or cynical about this possibility, what gives me the most hope is the next generation. The young people, whose attitudes and beliefs and openness to change have already made history in this election. [applause]

There is one story, in particular, that I'd like to leave you with today. A story I told when I had the great honor of speaking on Dr. King's birthday at his home church, Ebenezer Baptist, in Atlanta. There is a young, twenty-three-year-old woman—a white woman—named Ashley Baia, who organized for our campaign in Florence, South Carolina. She had been working to organize a mostly African American community since the beginning of this campaign. And one day she was at a roundtable discussion where everyone went around telling their story and why they were there. And Ashley said that when she was nine years old, her mother got cancer. And because she had to miss days of work, she was let go and lost her health care. They had to file for bankruptcy, and that's when Ashley decided that she had to do something to help her mom.

She knew that food was one of their most expensive costs. And so Ashley convinced her mother that what she really liked, and really wanted to eat more than anything else, was mustard and relish sandwiches. Because that was the cheapest way to eat. That's the mind of a nine-year-old. She did this for a year, until her mom got better. And so Ashley told everyone at the roundtable that the reason she joined our campaign was so that she could help the millions of other children in the country who want and need to help their parents, too.

Now, Ashley might have made a different choice. Perhaps somebody told her along the way that the source of her mother's problems were blacks who were on welfare and too lazy to work, or Hispanics who were coming into the country illegally. But she didn't. She sought out allies in her fight against injustice. Anyway, Ashley finishes her story, and then goes around the room and asks everyone else why they're supporting the campaign. They all have different stories and different reasons. Many bring up a specific issue. And finally they come to this elderly black man who's been sitting there quietly the entire time. And Ashley asks him why he's there. And he doesn't bring up a specific issue. He does not say health care or the economy. He does not say education or the war. He does not say that he was there because of Barack Obama. He simply says to everyone in the room, "I am here because of Ashley."

"I'm here because of Ashley." Now, by itself, that single moment of recognition between that young white girl and that old black man is not enough. It is not enough to give health care to the sick, or jobs to the jobless, or education to our children. But it is where we start. It is where our union grows stronger. And as so many generations have come to realize over the course of the 221 years since a band of patriots signed that document, right here in Philadelphia, that is where perfection begins.

PERMISSIONS

Kathleen Cleaver, Speech delivered at Memorial Service for Bobby Hutton, 1968. Courtesy Kathleen Cleaver.

Bobby Seale, Speech delivered at the Kaleidoscope Theater, 1968. Courtesy Bobby Seale.

Ella Baker, Speech to Southern Conference Education Fund, 1968. Courtesy Carolyn D. Brockington.

Shirley Chisholm, Speech at Howard University, 1969. Courtesy Estate of Shirley Chisholm.

Angela Y. Davis, Speech delivered at the Embassy Auditorium, 1972. Courtesy Angela Y. Davis.

Vernon E. Jordan Jr., Speech delivered at the National Press Club, 1978. Courtesy Vernon E. Jordan Jr.

Dorothy I. Height, Speech delivered at the first Scholarly Conference on Black Women, 1979. Courtesy National Park Service, Mary McLeod Bethune Council House NHS, National Archives for Black Women's History.

James H. Cone, "The Relationship of the Christian Faith to Political Praxis," 1980. Courtesy James H. Cone. Full-length recording may be obtained at Educational Media at Princeton Theological Seminary.

Toni Morrison, Nobel Prize Lecture, 1993. Courtesy the Nobel Foundation.

Colin Powell, Commencement Address at Howard University, 1994. Courtesy General Colin L. Powell, USA (Retired).

Mary Frances Berry, "One Hundredth Anniversary of Plessy v. Ferguson," 1996. Courtesy Mary Frances Berry.

Ward Connerly, "America: A Nation of Equals," 1998. Courtesy American Civil Rights Institute.

Condoleezza Rice, Speech to National Council of Negro Women, 2001. Courtesy Condoleezza Rice.

Maxine Waters, "Youth and the Political Process," 2003. Courtesy Representative Maxine Waters.

Henry Louis Gates Jr., "America Beyond the Color Line," 2004. Courtesy of the Commonwealth Club, www.commonwealthclub.org.

Michael Eric Dyson, "Has the Black Middle Class Lost its Mind?" 2005. Courtesy of the Commonwealth Club, www.commonwealthclub.org.

Barack Obama, "A More Perfect Union," 2008. Public domain.

NOTES

1. MALCOLM X

1. Malcolm X, *By Any Means Necessary: Malcolm X Speeches and Writings* (Atlanta, GA: Pathfinder Press, 1992), 59.
2. Malcolm X and Alex Haley, *The Autobiography of Malcolm X* (New York: One World Books, 1992), 43.
3. Henry Hampton, Steve Fayer, and Sarah Flynn, "Malcolm X, Our Shining Black Prince," in *Voices of Freedom* (New York: Bantam Books, 1990), 243.
4. "Malcolm X Scores U.S. and Kennedy," *New York Times*, December 2, 1963, 21.
5. Peniel E. Joseph, *Dark Days, Bright Nights: From Black Power to Barack Obama* (New York: Basic Books, 2010), 36; Peniel E. Joseph, *Waiting 'Til the Midnight Hour: A Narrative History of Black Power in America* (New York: Henry Holt, 2006), n. 322.
6. "Malcolm X's Detroit Date Sparks Battle of Ministers," *Afro-American*, Baltimore, MD, April 11, 1964.
7. Joseph, *Dark Days, Bright Nights*, 83.
8. "Malcolm X," *New York Times*, February 22, 1965, 20.
9. Ossie Davis, *Life Lit by Some Large Vision: Selected Speeches and Writings* (New York: Atria Books, 2006), 153.

10. James Cone, "Malcolm X: The Impact of a Cultural Revolutionary," *Christian Century* 109:38 (December 1992), 1189–94.

2. LORRAINE HANSBERRY

1. James Baldwin, "Sweet Lorraine" (1969), in *Lorraine Hansberry in Her Own Words: To Be Young, Gifted and Black*, adapted by Robert Nemiroff (New York: Vintage Books, 1995), xviii.
2. Nemiroff, *Lorraine Hansberry in Her Own Words*, 21.
3. Patricia C. McKissack and Fredrick L. McKissack, *Young, Black, and Determined: A Biography of Lorraine Hansberry* (New York: Holiday House, 1998), 18.
4. Ibid., 53.
5. *Guide to the Jefferson School of Social Science* (New York, NY), Records and Indexes 1931–1958, Tamiment Library/Robert F. Wagner Labor Archives, Elmer Holmes Bobst Library, New York University Libraries, 70 Washington Square South, New York, NY 10012.
6. Milton Esterow, "New Role of Negroes in Theater Reflects Ferment of Integration," *New York Times*, June 15, 1964.
7. Excerpt featured in *Black Protest: History, Documents, and Analyses, 1619 to the Present*, ed. Joanne Grant (New York: Fawcett Premier, 1968), 440.
8. Nemiroff, *Lorraine Hansberry in Her Own Words*, 237.
9. Harold Cruse, *The Crisis of the Negro Intellectual* (New York: New York Review of Books, 1967), 206.
10. Nat Hentoff, "The Town Hall 'Mugging,' " *Village Voice*, July 9, 1964.
11. Robert Nemiroff, *Lorraine Hansberry Speaks Out: Art and the Black Revolution* (New York: Caedmon Records, 1972), liner notes.
12. Nemiroff, *Lorraine Hansberry in Her Own Words*, 249–50.
13. Ibid., 250.

3. OSSIE DAVIS

1. Wil Haygood, "Ruby Dee and Ossie Davis: Their Activism Is No Act," *Washington Post*, December 5, 2004, N1.
2. Ossie Davis and Ruby Dee, *With Ossie and Ruby: In This Life Together* (New York: William Morrow, 1998), 2.
3. Davis and Dee, *With Ossie and Ruby*, 9.
4. Haygood, "Ruby Dee and Ossie Davis."

5. Peniel E. Joseph, *Waiting 'Til the Midnight Hour: A Narrative History of Black Power in America* (New York: Henry Holt, 2006), 15.

6. Henry Hampton and Steve Frayer with Sarah Flynn, *Voices of Freedom: An Oral History of the Civil Rights Movement from the 1950s Through the 1980s* (New York: Bantam, 1991), 250.

7. Ossie Davis, "Why I Eulogized Malcolm X," *Negro Digest*, February 1966, 65.

8. Davis and Dee, *With Ossie and Ruby*, 310.

9. Ibid., 310–11.

10. Hampton et al., *Voices of Freedom*, 261.

11. Ossie Davis, *Life Lit by Some Large Vision: Selected Speeches and Writings* (New York: Atria Books, 2006), 151–53.

4. MARTIN LUTHER KING JR.

1. Speech delivered at Victory Baptist Church in Los Angeles, June 25, 1967.

2. Ibid.

3. Interview with authors, January 23, 2008.

4. Don McKee, "King Says America Moving Toward Critical Crossroads," *Telegraph*, August 17, 1967.

5. Angela Davis, *Angela Davis: An Autobiography* (1974; New York: Random House, 1988), 176.

5. ROY WILKINS

1. "A Master of Power, Roy Wilkins," *New York Times*, July 17, 1967, 21.

2. Warren Brown, "U.S. Civil Rights Leader Roy Wilkins Dies at Age of 80," *Washington Post*, September 9, 1981.

3. Patricia Sullivan, *Lift Every Voice: The NAACP and the Making of the Civil Rights Movement* (New York: The New Press, 2009), 374.

4. Roy Wilkins with Tom Mathews, *Standing Fast: the Autobiography of Roy Wilkins* (New York: Penguin, 1982), 39.

5. Ibid., 41.

6. "He Overcame," *Time*, September 21, 1981, 21.

7. Ibid.

8. Simon Hall, "The NAACP, Black Power and the African American Freedom Struggle, 1966–69," *Historian* 69:1 (2007), 57.

9. Wilkins, *Standing Fast*, 299.

10. Brown, *Washington Post* obituary.

11. "Threat to Civil Rights Progress," *Los Angeles Times*, July 4, 1966, A4.

12. M.S. Handler, "Wilkins Says Black Power Leads Only to Black Death," *New York Times*, July 6, 1966, 1.

13. Roger Wilkins, *A Man's Life: An Autobiography* (New York: Simon & Schuster, 1982), 185.

14. Martin Arnold, "There Is No Rest for Roy Wilkins," *New York Times Magazine*, September 28, 1969, 45.

15. Ibid., 53.

16. Wilkins, *A Man's Life*, 328.

17. *Report of the National Advisory Commission on Civil Disorders* (New York: Bantam Books, 1968), 1.

18. Ibid., 203.

19. Wilkins, *A Man's Life*, 328.

6. BENJAMIN E. MAYS

1. *Newsweek*, April 9, 1984, 92.

2. Benjamin E. Mays, *Born to Rebel* (Athens, GA: University of Georgia Press, 1971), 1.

3. Frank J. Prial, "Benjamin Mays, Educator, Dies," *New York Times*, March 29, 1984, 23.

4. Richard Lischer, *The Preacher King: Martin Luther King Jr. and the Word That Moved America* (New York: Oxford University Press, 1997), 44.

5. Associated Press, March 28, 1984.

7. KATHLEEN CLEAVER

1. Ward Churchill, " 'To Disrupt, Discredit and Destroy': The FBI's Secret War against the Black Panther Party," in *Liberation, Imagination, and the Black Panther Party: A New Look at the Panthers and Their Legacy*, eds. Kathleen Cleaver and George Katsiaficas (New York: Routledge, 2001).

2. Kathleen Neal Cleaver, "Women, Power, and Revolution," in *Liberation, Imagination, and the Black Panther Party*, 123.

3. Kathleen Cleaver, *Target Zero: A Life in Writing—Eldridge Cleaver* (New York: Palgrave Macmillan), xiv.

4. Henry Louis Gates Jr. interviews Kathleen Cleaver for *The Two Nations of Black America*, spring 1997, WGBH Educational Foundation, transcript: http://www.pbs.org/wgbh/pages/frontline/shows/race/interviews/kcleaver.html.

5. Cleaver, "Women, Power, and Revolution," 124.

6. Ibid., 123.

7. Ibid., 125.

8. Ibid., 124.

9. Peniel E. Joseph, *Waiting 'Til the Midnight Hour: A Narrative History of Black Power in America* (New York: Henry Holt, 2006), 229.

10. Churchill, " 'To Disrupt, Discredit and Destroy,' " 81.

11. Vincent Harding, Robin D.G. Kelley, and Earl Lewis, "We Changed the World, 1945–1970," in *To Make Our World Anew: A History of African Americans*, eds. Kelley and Lewis (Oxford: Oxford University Press, 2000), 535.

12. Churchill, " 'To Disrupt, Discredit and Destroy,' " 78.

13. Harding et al., "We Changed the World," 535.

14. Ibid.

15. Churchill, " 'To Disrupt, Discredit and Destroy,' " 113.

16. Henry Louis Gates Jr. interviews Kathleen Cleaver for *The Two Nations of Black America*.

8. BOBBY SEALE

1. Vincent Harding, Robin D.G. Kelley, and Earl Lewis, "We Changed the World, 1945–1970," in *To Make Our World Anew: A History of African Americans*, eds. Kelley and Lewis (Oxford: Oxford University Press, 2000), p. 535.

2. Peniel E. Joseph, *Dark Days, Bright Nights: From Black Power to Barack Obama* (New York: Basic Books, 2010), 28.

3. Bobby Seale, *Seize the Time: The Story of the Black Panther Party and Huey P. Newton* (New York: Random House, 1968), 5.

4. Ibid., 34.

5. Sol Stern, "The Call of the Black Panthers," *New York Times Magazine*, August 6, 1967, repr. in *Reporting Civil Rights, Part Two: American Journalism 1963–1973* (New York: Library of America, 2003), 632.

6. Seale, *Seize the Time*, 67.

7. Peniel E. Joseph, *Waiting 'Til the Midnight Hour: A Narrative History of Black Power in America* (New York: Henry Holt, 2006), 176.

8. Huey P. Newton, *Revolutionary Suicide* (New York: Harcourt Brace Jovanovich, 1973; New York: Writers and Readers, 1995), 120–21.

9. Stern, "The Call of the Panthers," 625.

10. "FBI Brands Black Panthers 'Most Dangerous' of Extremists," *New York Times*, July 13, 1969.

11. Harding et al., "We Changed the World," 535. See also Ward Churchill, " 'To Disrupt, Discredit and Destroy': The FBI's Secret War against the Black Panther Party," in *Liberation, Imagination, and the Black Panther Party: A New Look at the Panthers and their Legacy*, eds. Kathleen Cleaver and George Katsiaficas (New York: Routledge, 2001).

12. Joseph, *Waiting 'Til the Midnight Hour*, 247.

13. Jason Epstein, "A Special Supplement: The Trial of Bobby Seale," *New York Review of Books*, December 4, 1969.

14. Joseph, *Dark Days, Bright Nights*, 164.

15. "Table of Contents 2," *Los Angeles Times*, April 17, 1968.

9. ELLA BAKER

1. Barbara Ransby, *Ella Baker and the Black Freedom Movement: A Radical Democratic Vision* (Chapel Hill, NC: University of North Carolina Press, 2003), 373.

2. Ibid., 15.

3. Charles M. Payne, *I've Got the Light of Freedom: The Organizing Tradition and the Mississippi Freedom Struggle* (Berkeley: University of California Press, 1935), 85.

4. Ibid., 93.

5. Ransby, *Ella Baker*, 228.

6. Marilyn Bordwell Delaure, "Planting Seeds of Change: Ella Baker's Radical Rhetoric," *Women's Studies in Communication*, 2008, 1.

7. Ibid.

8. Benjamin F. Chavis Jr., "The Spirit of Ella Baker Lives On," *Washington Afro-American*, January 27, 1987.

9. Howard Zinn, introductory remarks, "Salute to Ella Baker," Pacifica Radio Archives, BB3142.

10. Shirley Chisholm

1. Shirley Chisholm, *Unbought and Unbossed* (New York: Houghton Mifflin, 1970), xi.
2. Ibid., 24.
3. Julie Gallagher, "Waging 'The Good Fight': The Political Career of Shirley Chisholm, 1953–82," *Journal of African American History* 92:3 (2007), 393.
4. Richard L. Maddens, "Mrs. Chisholm Gets off House Farm Committee," *New York Times*, January 30, 1969, 16.
5. Shirley Chisholm, *The Good Fight* (New York: Harper & Row, 1973), 162.
6. Gallagher, "Waging 'The Good Fight.'"
7. "Reflections on Some of the Icons We Lost This Year, from Those Who Knew Them Well," *Essence* 36.8 (December 2005), 88.
8. Laura W. Murphy, letter to the editor, *Washington Afro-American*, January 21, 2005.

11. Angela Y. Davis

1. Peniel E. Joseph, *Waiting 'Til the Midnight Hour: A Narrative History of Black Power in America* (New York: Henry Holt, 2006), 272.
2. Bettina Aptheker, *The Morning Breaks: The Trial of Angela Davis* (Ithaca, NY: Cornell University Press, 1999), 1.
3. Joseph, *Waiting 'Til the Midnight Hour*, 273.
4. Amy Alexander, *Fifty Black Women Who Changed America* (Seacaucus, NJ: Birch Lane Press, 1999), 260.
5. Angela Davis, *Angela Davis: An Autobiography* (New York: Random House, 1988), 161.
6. Joseph, *Waiting 'Til the Midnight Hour*, 273.
7. Robin D.G. Kelley and Earl Lewis, eds., *To Make Our Word Anew: A History of African Americans* (Oxford: Oxford University Press, 2000), 549.
8. Aptheker, *The Morning Breaks*, 8.
9. Ibid., 22.
10. Ibid., 28.
11. Kelley and Lewis, *To Make Our World Anew*, 550–51.
12. "The Tragedy of Angela Davis," *New York Times*, October 16, 1970.
13. Kelley and Lewis, *To Make Our World Anew*, 547.

14. Aptheker, *The Morning Breaks*, 29.
15. Earl Caldwell, "Angela Davis Acquitted on All Charges," *New York Times*, June 5, 1972.
16. "Angela Davis Launches U.S. Tour of Thanks," *Los Angeles Times*, June 10, 1972.
17. Aptheker, *The Morning Breaks*, 11.
18. Davis, *Angela Davis*, 318.
19. Ibid., 162.

12. VERNON E. JORDAN JR.

1. "Vernon E. Jordan, Jr." in *Contemporary Black Biography*, vol. 35, ed. Ashyia Henderson (Farmington Hills, MI: Gale Group, 2002).
2. Vernon E. Jordan Jr., with Annette Gordon-Reed, *Jordan Can Read! A Memoir* (New York: PublicAffairs, 2001), 15.
3. Vernon E. Jordan Jr., with Lee A. Daniels, *Make It Plain: Standing Up and Speaking Out* (New York: PublicAffairs, 2007), 175.
4. Jordan and Gordon-Reed, *Vernon Can Read!*, 61.
5. Ibid., 142.
6. "Nation: One of the Great Unifying Forces in the Country," *Time*, June 9, 1980.
7. Jordan and Daniels, *Make It Plain*, 8.
8. Jordan and Gordon-Reed, *Vernon Can Read!*, 234.
9. "Vernon E. Jordan, Jr." *Contemporary Black Biography*.
10. Jordan and Gordon-Reed, *Vernon Can Read!*, 253.
11. Ibid., 316.
12. Jim Mutugi, "Vernon Jordan: More than a 'First Friend,'" *Harbus*, December 3, 2001.

13. DOROTHY I. HEIGHT

1. Dorothy Height, *Open Wide the Freedom Gates: A Memoir* (New York: PublicAffairs, 2003), 7.
2. Henry Louis Gates Jr. and Cornel West, *The African American Century: How Black Americans Have Shaped Our Country* (New York: Free Press, 2000), 295.
3. Height, *Open Wide the Freedom Gates*, 8.
4. Ibid., 64

5. Ibid.

6. Ibid., 83.

7. Karen Anderson, "National Council of Negro Women," in *Organizing Black America: An Encyclopedia of African American Associations*, ed. Nina Mjagkij (New York: Garland, 2001), 448.

8. Dorothy Height, " 'We Wanted the Voice of a Woman to Be Heard': Black Women and the 1963 March on Washington," in *Sisters in the Struggle: African American Women in the Civil Rights–Black Power Movement*, ed. Bettye Collier-Thomas and V. P. Franklin (New York: New York University Press, 2001), 87–88.

9. Ibid., 89.

10. John Maynard, "Dorothy Height Gets Congress's Top Honor," *Washington Post*, March 25, 2004.

11. Height, *Open Wide the Freedom Gates*, 218.

14. JAMES H. CONE

1. Lewis V. Baldwin, "Risks of Faith: The Emergence of a Black Theology of Liberation, 1968–1998," review, *Christian Century* 117:29 (October 25, 2000), 1084.

2. James H. Cone, *A Black Theology of Liberation* (1970; Maryknoll, NY: Orbis Books, 1990), v.

3. *Chicago Tribune* staff report, "Rev. Jeremiah Wright's Words: Sound Bite vs. Sermon Excerpt," chicagotribune.com, March 29, 2008.

4. Kelefa Sanneh, "Project Trinity: The Perilous Mission of Obama's Church," *New Yorker*, April 7, 2008.

5. Interview with Valerie Linson for PBS series, *This Far by Faith*, 2003, http://www.pbs.org/thisfarbyfaith/people/james_cone.html.

6. Nessa Rapoport, "The Struggles of James H. Cone," *Publishers Weekly* (February 15, 1991), 30(2).

7. Ibid.

8. Interview with Terry Gross for National Public Radio's *Fresh Air*, broadcast March 31, 2008.

9. Sanneh, "Project Trinity."

10. Rapoport, "The Struggles of James H. Cone."

11. Interview with Terry Gross.

12. Robert A. Raines, "Closer Than We Knew," *New York Times*, March 17, 1991.

13. Cone, *Black Theology*, back cover.

14. George M. Anderson, "Theologians and White Supremacy: An Interview with James H. Cone," *America* 195:16 (November 20, 2006), 10.

15. Toni Morrison

1. Press release, "The Nobel Prize in Literature," Swedish Academy, October 7, 1993, www.nobelprize.org.

2. Dick Russell, *Black Genius and the American Experience* (New York: Carroll & Graf, 1998), 235.

3. Claudia Dreifus, "Chloe Wofford Talks About Toni Morrison," *New York Times*, September 11, 1994.

4. Ibid.

5. Elissa Schappell, "Toni Morrison: The Art of Fiction," in *Toni Morrison: Conversations*, ed. Carolyn C. Denard (Jackson, MS: University Press of Mississippi, 2008), 76.

6. Russell, *Black Genius*, 233.

7. Ibid., 230.

8. Bonnie Angelo, "The Pain of Being Black: An Interview with Toni Morrison," in *Conversations with Toni Morrison*, ed. Danille Taylor-Guthrie, (Jackson, MS: University Press of Mississippi, 1994), 255.

9. Dreifus, "Chloe Wofford Talks About Toni Morrison."

10. Russell, *Black Genius*, 231.

11. Ibid., 237.

12. Unitarian Universalist Association, "A Bench by the Road: *Beloved* by Toni Morrison," in *Toni Morrison: Conversations*, 46.

13. Ibid., 227.

14. Toni Morrison, *Burn This Book: PEN Writers Speak Out on the Power of the Word* (New York: Harper Collins, 2009), 4.

16. Colin Powell

1. Wendy Melillo and Hamil R. Harris, "Dissent Raised as Ex-Farrakhan Aide Returns to Howard U.," *Washington Post*, April 20, 1994.

2. Clarence Page, " 'Free Speech' Gives School a Black Eye," *Chicago Tribune*, May 1, 1994.

3. Colin Powell with Joseph E. Persico, *My American Journey* (New York: Random House, 1995), 10.

4. Ibid., 21.

5. Ibid., 28.

6. David S. Broder, "For Colin Powell, Only the Beginning," *Washington Post*, September 29, 1993.

7. Henry Louis Gates Jr. and Cornel West, *The African American Century: How Black Americans Have Shaped Our Country* (New York: The Free Press, 2000), 372.

8. Karen DeYoung, *Soldier: The Life of Colin Powell* (New York: Knopf, 2006), 275.

9. Karen DeYoung, "Obama Endorsed by Powell," *Washington Post*, October 20, 2008, A01.

10. Maureen Dowd, "Moved by a Crescent," *New York Times*, October 22, 2008.

17. MARY FRANCES BERRY

1. Steven A. Holmes, "A Civil Rights Crusader Unafraid to Challenge Anyone," *New York Times*, May 1, 2000, 14.

2. Ibid.

3. Darlene Clark Hine, "From the Margins to the Center: Callie House and the Ex-Slave Pension Movement," *Journal of African American History* 91, no. 3 (2006), p. 311.

4. James Wright, "Berry Reflects on Civil Rights Commission Years," *Washington Afro-American*, February 18, 2005, HighBeam Research (accessed January 18, 2010), http://www.highbeam.com/doc/1P1=106717580.html.

5. Darryl Fears, "Civil Rights Commissioner Marches in Different Time," *Washington Post*, January 17, 2005, A15.

6. Wright, "Berry Reflects on Civil Rights Commission Years."

7. Charles A. Lofgren, *The Plessy Case: A Legal-Historical Interpretation* (New York: Oxford University Press, 1987), 193.

8. Richard Kluger, *Simple Justice: The History of Brown v. Board of Education* (New York: Vintage, 1977), 782.

18. WARD CONNERLY

1. Michelle Locke, "After 12 Turbulent Years, Ward Connerly's Term as UC Regent Ends," Associated Press, January 15, 2005.

2. Lyndon B. Johnson, "To Fulfill These Rights," commencement address at

Howard University, June 4, 1965, http://www.lbjlib.utexas.edu/johnson/archives.hom/speeches.hom/650604.asp (accessed January 19, 2010).

3. Eric Pooley, "Race in America: Fairness or Folly?" *Time*, June 23, 1997, p. 36.

4. Ward Connerly, *Creating Equal: My Fight Against Race Preferences* (San Francisco: Encounter Books, 2000), 19.

5. Barry Bearak, "Questions of Race Run Deep for Foe of Preferences," *New York Times*, July 27, 1997, 1.

6. William F. Buckley Jr., "The Texan Dreadnought," *National Review*, (August 30, 1999).

7. Pooley, "Race in America."

8. Connerly, *Creating Equal*, 265.

9. Mark J. Ambinder, "California Regent Defends Prop. 209," *Harvard Crimson*, April 7, 1998, http://www.thecrimson.com/article/1998/4/7/california-regent-defends-prop-209-pcalifornia (accessed January 17, 2010).

19. CONDOLEEZZA RICE

1. Marcus Mabry, *Twice as Good—Condoleezza Rice and Her Path to Power* (New York: Modern Times, 2007), xxxvii.

2. Adam Fairclough, *Better Day Coming: Blacks and Equality, 1890–2000* (New York: Penguin, 2002), 273.

3. David J. Garrow, *Bearing the Cross: Martin Luther King Jr. and the Southern Christian Leadership Conference* (New York: Perrenial Classics, 2004), 232.

4. Mabry, *Twice as Good*, 25.

5. Elisabeth Bumiller, *Condoleezza Rice: An American Life* (New York: Random House, 2007), 44–45.

6. Nicholas Lemann, "Without a Doubt," *New Yorker*, October 14, 2002, 171.

7. Stuart Silverstein, "Rice Considered a Centrist on Affirmative Action at Stanford," *Los Angeles Times*, January 25, 2003; Michael Eric Dyson, "Bush's Black Faces," *Nation*, January 29, 2001, 5.

8. Neil A. Lewis, "Bush Adviser Backs Use of Race in College Admissions," *New York Times*, January 18, 2003.

9. Silverstein, "Rice Considered a Centrist."

10. Bumiller, *Condoleezza Rice*, 131.

11. Linda Kramer Jenning and Norman Jean Roy, "The Champion for Women, Condoleezza Rice," *Glamour*, December 2008, 228.

12. Bumiller, *Condoleezza Rice*, 54.

13. Jay Nordlinger, "Star-in-Waiting: Meet George W.'s Foreign-Policy Czarina," *National Review*, August 30, 1999, 35.

20. MAXINE WATERS

1. Aldore Collier, "Maxine Waters: Telling It Like It Is in L.A.," *Ebony*, October, 1992, 35.

2. Chris Warren, "Running Water: Congresswoman Maxine Waters' Politics," *Los Angeles*, November 1, 1998, 64.

3. Maria Newman, "After the Riots: Washington at Work; Lawmaker from Riot Zone Insists on New Role for Black Politicians," *New York Times*, May 19, 1992, A18.

4. Kay Mills, "Maxine Waters: I Don't Pretend to Be Nice No Matter What," *Progressive*, December 1993, 32.

21. HENRY LOUIS GATES JR.

1. Henry Louis Gates Jr., *Colored People* (New York: Vintage, 1995), 25–27.

2. Ibid., 150.

3. Ibid., 83.

4. Ibid., 186.

5. Jack E. White, Sharon Epperson, and James L. Graff, "The Black Brain Trust," *Time*, February 26, 1996, 59.

6. Marcella Bombardiere, "Harvard's Gates to Step Down as Department Head," *Boston Globe*, April 16, 2005, 1.

7. "Time's 25 Most Influential Americans," *Time*, April 21, 1997, 46.

8. "Mary Poppins Is a Black Man," *Economist*, August 7, 1999, 72.

22. MICHAEL ERIC DYSON

1. Michael Eric Dyson, *The Michael Eric Dyson Reader* (New York: Basic Civitas Books, 2004), 5.

2. Ibid., 4.

3. Michael Eric Dyson, *Reflecting Black: African-American Cultural Criticism* (Minneapolis: University of Minnesota Press, 1993), xxvi.

4. Ibid.

5. Erin Aubry Kaplan, " 'These People': Bill Cosby's Criticism of Poor and Uneducated African Americans Set Off a Yearlong Debate," *Los Angeles Times Magazine*, July 24, 2005, 12.

6. Dyson, *Dyson Reader*, 18.

7. Juan Williams, *Enough: The Phony Leaders, Dead-End Movements, and Culture of Failure That Are Undermining Black America—and What We Can Do About It* (New York: Crown, 2006), 7.

8. Transcript of speech from American Rhetoric, http://www.american rhetoric.com/speeches/billcosbypoundcakespeech.htm.

9. Williams, *Enough*, 10.

10. "JBHE Book Critic's Corner: 'Is Bill Cosby Right? Or Has the Black Middle Class Lost Its Mind?' " *Journal of Blacks in Higher Education*, October 31, 2005.

11. Ibid.

12. David Pluviose, "All Jokes Aside," *Diverse Issues in Higher Education*, 23:9 (June 15, 2006), 10.

13. Jesse L. Jackson Sr., "Criticism of Bill Cosby Too Harsh," *New Pittsburgh Courier*, August 9–15, 2006.

14. Dyson, *Dyson Reader*, back cover.

15. Ibid., xx.

16. Ibid., xxiii.

23. BARACK OBAMA

1. George Packer, "Native Son," *New Yorker*, March 31, 2008, 46.

2. Barack Obama, *Dreams from My Father: A Story of Race and Inheritance* (New York: Three Rivers Press, 2004), 286.

3. Garry Wills, "Two Speeches on Race," *New York Review of Books*, May 1, 2008, 3.

4. Obama, *Dreams from My Father*, 294.

5. Alex MacGillis and Eli Saslow, "Tackling a Sensitive Topic at a Sensitive Moment, for Disparate Audiences," *Washington Post*, March 19, 2008; Jodi Kantor, "Obama Denounces Statements of His Pastor as 'Inflammatory,' " *New York Times*, March 15, 2008.

6. Kantor, "Obama Denounces Statements."

7. Omar H. Ali, "Obama and the Generational Challenge," in *The Speech:*

Race and Barack Obama's "A More Perfect Union," ed. T. Denean Sharpley-Whiting (New York: Bloomsbury, 2009), 38.

8. Keli Goff, "Living the Dream," in *The Speech*, 42.
9. Orlando Patterson, "An Eternal Revolution," *New York Times*, November 7, 2008.

TRACK LIST

1. Malcolm X
   "The Ballot or the Bullet," 1964
   (5:05)
2. Lorraine Hansberry
   "The Black Revolution and the
   White Backlash," 1964 (5:45)
3. Martin Luther King Jr.
   "Where Do We Go from Here?"
   1967 (5:22)
4. Roy Wilkins
   Speech on the National Advisory
   Commission on Civil Disorders,
   1968 (7:00)
5. Benjamin E. Mays
   Eulogy for Martin Luther King Jr.,
   1968 (3:53)
6. Kathleen Cleaver
   Speech delivered at Memorial
   Service for Bobby Hutton, 1968
   (1:48)
7. Bobby Seale
   Speech delivered at the
   Kaleidoscope Theater, 1968 (1:40)
8. Ella Baker
   Speech to Southern Conference
   Education Fund, 1968 (1:28)
9. Shirley Chisholm
   Speech at Howard University, 1969
   (5:02)
10. Angela Y. Davis
    Speech delivered at the Embassy
    Auditorium, 1972 (1:45)
11. Vernon E. Jordan Jr.
    Speech delivered at the National
    Press Club, 1978 (6:53)
12. Dorothy I. Height
    Speech delivered at the first
    Scholarly Conference on Black
    Women, 1979 (5:57)
13. James H. Cone
    "The Relationship of the Christian
    Faith to Political Praxis," 1980
    (6:02)
14. Toni Morrison
    Nobel Prize Lecture, 1993 (8:02)
15. Colin Powell
    Commencement Address at Howard
    University, 1994 (6:42)
16. Mary Frances Berry
    "One Hundredth Anniversary of
    Plessy v. Ferguson," 1996 (4:30)
17. Ward Connerly
    "America: A Nation of Equals,"
    1998 (4:31)
18. Condoleezza Rice
    Speech to National Council of
    Negro Women, 2001 (7:20)
19. Maxine Waters
    "Youth and the Political
    Process," 2003 (5:04)
20. Henry Louis Gates Jr.
    "America Beyond the Color Line,"
    2004 (7:38)
21. Michael Eric Dyson
    "Has the Black Middle Class Lost
    Its Mind?" 2005 (6:12)
22. Barack Obama
    "A More Perfect Union," 2008
    (5:33)